MARIE MADELEINE JODIN 1741–1790
ACTRESS, *PHILOSOPHE* AND FEMINIST

Women and Gender in the Early Modern World

Series Editors: Allyson Poska and Abby Zanger

In the past decade, the study of women and gender has offered some of the most vital and innovative challenges to scholarship on the early modern period. Ashgate's new series of interdisciplinary and comparative studies, 'Women and Gender in the Early Modern World', takes up this challenge, reaching beyond geographical limitations to explore the experiences of early modern women and the nature of gender in Europe, the Americas, Asia and Africa. Submissions of single-author studies and edited collections will be considered.

Titles in the series include:

Maternal Measures
Figuring caregiving in the early modern period

Edited by Naomi J. Miller and Naomi Yavneh

Marie-Madeleine Jodin 1741–1790
Actress, philosophe *and feminist*

Felicia Gordon and P. N. Furbank

The Political Theory of Christine de Pizan

Kate L. Forhan

Marie Madeleine Jodin
1741–1790

Actress, *philosophe*
and feminist

Felicia Gordon and P. N. Furbank

Ashgate

Aldershot • Burlington USA • Singapore • Sydney

Published by
Ashgate Publishing Limited
Wey Court East
Union Road
Farnham
Surrey, GU9 7PT
England

Ashgate Publishing Company
110 Cherry Street
Suite 3-1
Burlington
VT 05401-3818
USA

Ashgate website: http://www.ashgate.com

British Library Cataloguing in Publication Data
Gordon, Felicia
    Marie Madeleine Jodin 1741–1790: Actress, *philosophe* and feminist. –
    (Women and Gender in the Early Modern World)
    1. Jodin, Marie Madeleine—Relations with men. 2. Diderot, Denis—Relation with women. 3. Feminists—France—Biography. 4. Women—France—Biography. 5. France—Social life and customs—18th century. I. Title. II. Furbank, P.N. (Philip Nicholas).
    944'.034'092

US Library of Congress Cataloging in Publication Data
Marie Madeleine Jodin 1741–1790: Actress, *philosophe* and feminist /
    Felicia Gordon and P.N. Furbank.
        p.   cm. – (Women and Gender in the Early Modern World)
    Includes English translation of Jodin's *Vues législatives pour les femmes adressées à l'Assemblée nationale*. Includes bibliographical references and index.
    1. Jodin, Marie Madeleine, 1741–1790. 2. Actors—France—Biography. 3. Intellectuals—France—Biography. I. Furbank, Philip Nicholas. II. Jodin, Marie Madeleine, 1741–1790. *Vues législatives pour les femmes adressées à l'Assemblée national.* English. III. Title. IV. Series.
    PN2638.J58G67 2001
    792'.028'092—dc21   2001022921

ISBN 978-0-7546-0224-8

Transferred to Digital Printing in 2009

MIX
Paper from
responsible sources
FSC
www.fsc.org   FSC® C004959

Printed and bound in Great Britain
by Printondemand-worldwide.com

Contents

List of Illustrations

Preface and Acknowledgements

We, as authors, wish to thank the History Department of Anglia Polytechnic University for the research funding they gave to Felica Gordon for the early stages of this work and especially the Leverhulme Trust who awarded her a two-year Emeritus Fellowship to pursue research in a variety of European archives.

Our thanks also go to the staff of the following archives and libraries: Archives Municipales de la Ville d'Angers; Archives Municipales de la Ville de Tonnerre; Archives Départementales Seine et Marne; Archives Municipales de la Ville de Bordeaux; Bibliothèque de l'Arsenal; Bibliothèque-Musée de la Comédie Française; Bibliothèque Nationale; Bibliothèque de la Pologne, Paris; Statens Arkiver, Rigsarkivet, Copenhagen; Landesarchiv Magedburg; Landeshauptarchiv, Aussenstelle, Wernigerode; Sächsisches Hauptstaatsarchiv, Dresden; Archiwum Glowne ak Dawnych, Warsaw; Czartoryski Museum, Cracow; the Brotherton Library, Leeds, the British Library and Cambridge University Library.

A preparatory study on aspects Jodin's life and work by Felicia Gordon has appeared previously in *History of Political Thought*, XX, 4 (1999) ('*Vues législatives pour les femmes* 1790: A Reformist-Feminist Vision'). We are grateful to the editors of *History of Political Thought* for permission to use material first appearing in article form. We also wish to thank Macmillan Publishers for permission to incorporate material from *New Dawns* (Cross and Williams, eds, 2000), in a chapter by Gordon entitled 'The Gendered Citizen: Marie Madeleine Jodin (1741–1790)' and to *Women's History Review*, X, 2 (2001) permission to use work appearing in an article by Gordon '"This Accursed Child": the early years of Marie Madeleine Jodin (1741–90)'.

A book of this nature, which crosses over a number of disciplinary boundaries, as well as over various national boundaries, has led us to seek advice from many friends and colleagues who have been generous in sharing their expertise. We wish to acknowledge the kind assistance of the following: Dr Mary Abbott, Professor Tim Blanning, Count Frantz Bernstorff-Gyldensteen, Dr Richard Butterick, Alex Cain, Dr Anne-Marie Chouillet, Dr Máire Cross, Professor Richard J. Evans, Dr Robert I. Frost, Professor Therese Kostkiewiczowa, Dr J. T. Lukowski, Bridget Morris, Tom Morris, Professor Karen Offen, Judy Bibbins, Dr Thomas Munch-Petersen, Count Fritz von der Schulenburg, Professor Jacek Staszewski, Dr Don Watts and Professor David Williams.

We are very much indebted to Dr Peter Eckstein, Klaus Eckstein, Dr Kazia Gaseltine and Dr Jan Maciejowski for their translations of German and Polish material and for their enthusiastic response to Jodin's story. We wish to thank particularly Eva Bjerregaard, who undertook archival research for us in Copenhagen and who photographed the Schulenburg memorial at Salzwedel.

We are also most grateful to Conrad Smith for his constructive comments and detailed corrections to the text.

Clarissa Campbell Orr has been a marvellously loyal supporter of this project, listening to problems raised and always generously willing to share her wide knowledge of eighteenth-century European history. Finally, while this is a joint work, Felicia Gordon wishes to underline the encouragement and advice she received from P. N. Furbank when researching and writing the book. Her greatest debt of gratitude is to Ian Gordon who has read and commented on the whole and has borne with Marie Madeleine Jodin's many vicissitudes. The book has benefited enormously from his perceptive advice and unfailing support.

Introduction

Briefly notorious in her own lifetime, Marie Madeleine Jodin has since been almost lost to history, save as a footnote to Diderot studies. However, her life story forms an arresting narrative, opening, as it does, new perspectives on the world of eighteenth-century women, on the feuds and politics of European court theatres, and, above all, entailing the discovery of an important, and previously almost unknown, French feminist. We find that in 1790, Jodin, a former actress and protégée of the philosopher and playwright Denis Diderot, published a treatise entitled *Vues législatives pour les femmes* (*Legislative Views for Women*), the first signed, female-authored, feminist treatise of the French Revolutionary period.

Central to Jodin's story is her relationship with Diderot, a remarkable friendship between the volatile younger actress and the ebullient Enlightenment philosopher, recorded in the series of letters written to her by Diderot between 1765 and 1769, when she was in her mid-twenties. They have long been a subject of interest to eighteenth-century scholars, and are included in full in this study.[1] Saint-Beuve enthused about them as an 'admirable little course in practical morality', though he fell into a slightly patronising strain, not uncharacteristic of many scholars' treatment of women stage performers, when discussing Jodin: 'a pretty actress, a good and frank person, but volatile, turbulent and amorous'.[2]

Even with nothing more than Diderot's letters as evidence, one is intrigued by Marie Madeleine. For all of what Diderot called her follies and the 'violence' of her character, he clearly felt she mattered and took infinite pains to advise her on her acting, her morals and her financial affairs. Her vitality, intelligence, warmth of heart and impulsiveness emerge strongly from his letters. Other sources reveal a career of the most dramatic contrasts: a devastating upbringing; an agonising relationship with her father and an intense love–hate relationship with her fond, but foolish, mother; an early adult life passed in the back streets of Paris and in its prisons; a brief, but successful, career in court theatres; a growing participation in the intellectual culture of the newly emerging Republic of Letters; and finally, authorship of *Legislative Views for Women*. In Marie Madeleine we perceive a rebellious adolescent who eventually, after a contentious career on the stage, was, partly through the influence of her mentor, to turn *philosophe* herself. It was her intellectual passion combined with a wide experience of life, involving love affairs, scandals, libels and lawsuits, that eventually qualified her to write her *Legislative Views*. A contemporary of those other great eighteenth-century feminists, Mary Wollstonecraft and Olympe de Gouges, Mary Madeleine Jodin attempted to make women's rights and duties as citizens central to the legislative concerns of the Revolution.

Jodin's life also offers valuable insights into what is termed 'history from below'. Whilst memoirs and biographies of aristocratic women and upwardly mobile *salonnières* like Mme Geoffrin and Mme Roland abound, the chronicles of women lower down the social scale are far fewer in number, their lives often undocumented in contemporary records.[3] The traces of Jodin's rebellious career have to a great extent been preserved not in memoirs of polite society, but in police and other official files. Jodin, we learn, was the daughter of a Genevan watchmaker working in Paris, who shared her father's impatience with the dominance of birth over talent in the society of her day. Her childhood and adolescence exemplify the terrible effects of forced religious conversion as well as the fate of those women who refused to accept the discipline of the family, the convent and the morals police. As an actress she experienced both celebrity and public obloquy. Though fond of employing the tropes of feminine weakness and vulnerability in her writing, she demonstrated a ferocious tenacity in pursuit of her rights. We shall see that she was far from fulfilling the passive, feminine ideal of the period.

Debates on women's exclusion from 'the Rights of Man' in the French Revolution have primarily focused on women's clubs, on women of the Paris crowd and on militant individuals. However a study of this actress/intellectual gives us an insight into the political and civil marginalisation of other socially excluded groups, such as Protestants, actors and prostitutes in *ancien régime* France. Jodin's citizen's manifesto for women, written at the close of her life, was not an anomalous document by an actress bizarrely turned philosopher, but the mature product of a turbulent life devoted both to drama and to learning. Her final project was to turn Enlightenment theory into practice, to educate her sex for citizenship. Largely self-educated, she had read widely and experienced the intellectual excitement of the culture of *les lumières*. By her independence of mind, and eventually of fortune, Jodin strikes one in many ways as a very modern woman. The language of rights pervades her discourse. That she should have found it possible to theorise the problem of women's position in eighteenth-century French society demonstrates that she understood her own experiences as emblematic of wider social and political issues.

As the Saint-Beuve appreciation quoted above indicates, Jodin has hitherto been considered almost entirely in relation to the letters which Diderot wrote to her during her periods as an actress in Warsaw, Dresden and Bordeaux. In these he expanded, with great brilliance, his theory of a 'fourth-wall' concept of the stage, advocating a naturalistic style of acting. His advice to Jodin turned upon the notion that acting was a school of ethics. Nor, as Diderot was aware, was the theatre at all tangential to evolving political culture. The relationship between aesthetic theory and theatrical practice, developed in these letters, lies at the heart of eighteenth-century debates about morality, political representation and the moulding of good citizens.

Jodin's *Vues législatives pour les femmes*, like Diderot's letters, has never been available in English, and neither is there, either in French or in English any extensive analysis of its arguments. Jodin has received only the briefest mention in the numerous studies of early French feminism of the Revolutionary period. Whilst her career in Warsaw (1765–66) has been sketched in histories of Polish theatre (see Chapter 3), none of this material has been available in English, and Polish scholars seem to have been unaware of her subsequent evolution as a *philosophe*/feminist. Jodin's stay in Dresden (1767–68) has never been chronicled, neither has her love affair with the Danish envoy to Dresden, Count Werner von der Schulenburg XXV, nor the brouhaha and diplomatic fall-out it eventually provoked. Paul Vernière has written a sympathetic study of Jodin in the context of Enlightenment thought, but did not have access to the extensive archival material recently discovered by the present authors.

It must be admitted that one of the enduring if frivolous pleasures of archival research is the feeling that one is engaged in unravelling a detective story. Clues emerge from one archive which may be explained by documents in another place many miles away. Some mysteries, of course, remain unsolved. Diplomatic discretion, or the destruction of archives by fire and war, have obliterated important evidence, including the loss of the one known painting of the actress. But enough remains to construct a coherent portrait of a distinctive, powerful and disruptive personality, as well as to experience the feelings of alarm, exasperation and admiration that she inspired in her contemporaries. Much of our archival material takes the form of letters: the Jodin/Dutertre family's letters of accusation against Mme Jodin and her daughter; Diderot's letters to Jodin; Jodin's emotionally charged letters to the Court Chamberlain in Warsaw, pleading for justice and financial assistance; and diplomatic letters between the Saxon and Danish courts concerning the scandal surrounding Jodin and her lover, Werner von der Schulenburg. Jodin's biography, one feels, could easily have taken the form of an eighteenth-century epistolary novel.

This book is a collaborative work. It began as a project by P. N. Furbank to publish an English edition of Diderot's letters to Jodin and a translation of the *Vues législatives*, with accompanying commentary and notes. Subsequent archival research by Felicia Gordon revealed the possibility of writing a greatly expanded contextual biography. We have corresponded continuously over points of interpretation and we have had, amicably, to agree to disagree regarding Diderot's theories about the theatre. In other respects, our text demonstrates the way seemingly straightforward events are sometimes coloured, sometimes doctored and sometimes suppressed, both when they occurred and subsequently. We have occasionally been obliged to adopt a stance of speculative uncertainty before the archival evidence, but fortunately for the historian and the reader, the voices of the actors in Jodin's drama call out clearly to us across the distance of nearly two and a half centuries. We begin with the *cri de coeur* of her unhappy father.

Notes

1. The letters, twenty-one in number and first published in 1821, are reprinted in Denis Diderot, *Correspondance*, ed. Georges Roth, V–IX (Paris: Editions de Minuit 1959–63). Roth has also written an analysis of the letters, 'Diderot et sa pupille Mademoiselle Jodin', *Lettres nouvelles* (December, 1956), pp. 699–714, as has Paul Vernière, 'Marie Madeleine Jodin, amie de Diderot et témoin des Lumières', *Studies on Voltaire*, 58 (1967), pp. 1765–75.
2. C.-A. Sainte-Beuve, *Portraits littéraires* (Paris: Didier, 1852).
3. For an analysis of *salonnières* in eighteenth-century France, see Roland Bonnel and Catherine Rubinger, eds, *Femmes savantes et femmes d'esprit: Women Intellectuals of the French Eighteenth Century* (New York: Peter Lang, 1994).

CHAPTER ONE

'This accursed child'

On 16 February 1757, Jean Jodin, a Genevan watchmaker domiciled near Paris, wrote a despairing letter to his sister, Marie Jodin, painting his domestic circumstances in the blackest terms:[1]

> My dear sister,
>   I do not know how to describe my situation to you. You will judge my state best by the cruel but indispensable course of action that I am taking, rather than by the best-expressed and most moving narrative.
>   That daughter [of mine], or rather that monster clothed in a human face whom you have protected, each day gives me new causes for alarm. Every day this accursed child breaks another link in the chain that ties fathers and mothers to their children and whenever I come home, I find myself wondering whether I will find my daughter battered to death by her mother, or her mother dying from her daughter's blows. Indeed, I do not know whether death would not be preferable to the harsh treatment that this best of all mothers suffers several times a day. Finally, I am threatened with seeing my good name publicly reviled. This prospect terrifies me. I could not survive it and it is to prevent this misfortune that I beg you, my dearest sister, in the name of everything sacred and respectable, to get rid of this object of iniquity and torment for me by placing her in a house of correction. Time presses, and I keep her here, fearing she may escape. She must not sleep in our lodging tonight, which thought leads me to suggest the following.
>   You must immediately beseech les Dames des Nouvelles Catholiques to take care of her for a few days and during this time we will together make the necessary arrangements to remove her as far away as possible, so that her pension can suffice for her board and lodging and if the ladies' answer to this request that you present to them is favourable, you will have the sisterly goodness to come and fetch her this evening at twilight with your servant and a carriage to take her to her destination. I will not be at home because I feel that I may be less of a Stoic than I thought and at the moment of finishing this letter, I am paying to Nature a tribute from which I had thought to have freed myself. I embrace you with all my heart and am with all the most sincere friendship.
>   My very dear sister,
>   Jean Jodin

Jean Jodin had moved to Paris around 1730, where he made a distinguished name for himself in watchmaking. He became a friend of Denis Diderot and a contributor to the *Encyclopédie*. In this remarkable letter, Jean Jodin describes scenes of acute domestic violence, engaged in by both mother and daughter, in which the daughter is described as a 'monster' and 'object of iniquity', the mother as 'the best of mothers'. Both, according to the father, threaten to kill the other. Jean Jodin gives no *reason* for these horrific scenes, but he does express the fear that his good name will be reviled. Did he not know of the charge laid at the mother's door by relatives and neighbours that she, his wife, prostituted their daughter for gain? Was it possible that he could be so ignorant of his family's circumstances? Does he not reveal his knowledge of the activities by admitting that he fears for his good name? Finally the rhetorical flourish with which he closes: 'I am paying to Nature a tribute from which I had thought to have freed myself', a circumlocution for giving way to tears, has a markedly controlled and literary flavour, as though Jean Jodin paused in the midst of his domestic crisis to convey an emotive effect. The entire letter, from its meticulous planning of how to surprise his daughter and carry her off to the convent, to the dramatic rendering of the domestic scene, reads like one of Diderot's *drames,* though one which lacked a happy ending.

That 'object of iniquity and torment', that 'monster clothed in a human face' was Marie Madeleine Jodin (1741–90), then aged sixteen.[2] Her father's cry of despair forms part of the dossier of letters of denunciation from Marie Madeleine's uncles, aunts, cousins and neighbours which led to the incarceration of the girl and her mother in la Salpêtrière Prison in 1761 for approximately two years.[3]

Marie Madeleine Jodin initially engaged the interest of historians thanks to a series of twenty-one letters written to her between 1765 and 1769 from Denis Diderot, the philosopher, art critic and dramatist.[4] From these we learn that 'the monster' had, by 1765, been metamorphosed into a successful actress, joined the Comédie-Française, and had been engaged in the troupe of the entrepreneur, Carol Tomatis, to play in Warsaw. Diderot's letters, which are of absorbing interest in themselves, offered Marie Madeleine Jodin professional and personal advice, showing him in his role of moral tutor and practical philanthropist at the same time as they developed his own aesthetic on acting and the theatrical illusion.

In 1790, twenty-one years after the close of Diderot's correspondence, Marie Madeleine Jodin published what is probably the first signed and female-authored feminist treatise of the revolutionary period, *Vues législatives pour les femmes, addressées à l'Assemblée Nationale, par Mlle Jodin, fille d'un citoyen de Genève.*[5] One of the questions that naturally arises in considering her career is how did the teenage hoyden, described in Jean Jodin's letter, become first a successful actress and subsequently a well-educated intellectual?

This study will construct a series of portraits of Marie Madeleine Jodin in the context of her work as an actress and her intellectual life drawing on archival sources and eighteenth-century social and intellectual history.[6] It will link the 'monster' of Jean Jodin's account with the daughter's turbulent stage career, culminating in an analysis of her feminist convictions. Yet the idea that she only became a feminist at the end of her life is implausible. If being a feminist meant demanding the same rights of citizenship and social recognition for women as for men, one can find evidence that Jodin's fiery personality was not one to accept her status as being one of inferiority, either as a woman or in any other capacity, even in her early youth. Though there are lacunae in the chronological account of Jodin's life, her ebullient if mercurial character, her energy, her tendency to sarcasm and her love of conflict emerge consistently, both from her own sparse writing and the possibly biased, but nevertheless convincing, accounts of others. One can construct an archaeology of a troubled but talented individual who at the end of her life transformed both her traumatic experience of prison and her dramatic talents into a closely reasoned and socially conservative plea for women's right to control their own lives, hence the *Legislative Views for Women*. Women were to become not only citizens, but to legislate for themselves and their particular social needs.

The Jodin family was of French Protestant descent originating from Blois. Jean Jodin's father, Louis Jodin emigrated to Geneva about 1704 and gained the right of domicile on 8 June 1711. His domestic life, like that of his descendants, does not appear to have been exemplary. He was called before the Consistory Court for gaming (1708) and reproached with maltreating his wife and cohabiting with a maidservant (1714). Two of Louis Jodin's sons, Jean (born 12 June 1713) and Pierre, re-emigrated to Paris where they successfully continued the family trade of watchmaking, working under the aegis of a maternal uncle, Jean Baptiste Dutertre, master watchmaker, who had a prosperous workshop on the Quai des Orfèvres.[7]

Jean Jodin came into the public eye in 1754 when he published a technical treatise on watchmaking, *Les Echappemens à repos*, which incorporated a critique of the patronage and training system for watchmakers and pointed to the need for state encouragement for technical branches of knowledge.[8] It is evident, both from Jean Jodin's letter of 1757 and his *Echappemens* that he was a man of some culture as well as possessing technical gifts. Jean Jodin's treatise brought him to the attention of Denis Diderot whose work on the *Encyclopédie* had led him to cultivate literate artisans.[9] He drew 'on the help of artists [i.e. Craftsmen], because there are many precious and knowledgeable men among them, though, for reasons of social status, the doors of academies are shut to them.'[10] The *Encyclopédie* entry for 'Artisan' (page 745) elevates the status of watchmakers in particular and may have been an indirect tribute to Jodin: 'ARTISAN, masculine noun by which is designated those workers who practise those mechanical arts which are presumed to require the least intelligence. One says of a good cobbler, that he is a good *artisan;* and of a skilled watchmaker, that he is a great artist'. Jodin's treatise formed part of a larger polemic waged in the pages of the *Mercure de France* on the technical merits or demerits of watch mechanisms (the ancients in this quarrel backed the *échappement à recul*, the moderns, the *échappement à repos)*, which brought him the honour of a letter in the *Mercure* (August 1754) from the academician and astronomer Lalande, attacking his work. In the second edition of his *Echappemens* (1756), Jodin retaliated with a broadside at Lalande.

In his letter Lalande had raised not only technical objections to Jodin's thesis but had argued that a mere artisan would not have the necessary scientific and mathematical knowledge to theorise about the best watchmaking mechanism, no matter how skilled he might be in his craft. Having suggested that Jodin was by his trade and station in life excluded from scholarly debate, Lalande concluded by praising those very 'mechanical skills' which though remarkable nevertheless entailed severe intellectual limitations: 'I believe that M. Jodin is one of those most able to do honour to a profession as distinguished as that of watchmaking, in which one can both shine at invention and cleverness of execution and in the depth of thought and of resourcefulness in carrying it out.'[11]

Jodin replied to this compliment, which he interpreted as condescending, with ill-advised gusto. He was drawn to wax satirical (a tendency passed on to his daughter) at Lalande's expense. He challenged the Academician's *de haut en bas* attitude. Lalande, Jodin claimed, would be incapable of actually *making* a watch, but was happy to tell others how to do it. Though watchmaking derived from mathematics, a mathematician could not make a good watch. Watchmaking required practical experience as well as theoretical knowledge. Jodin showed particular annoyance at what he saw as Lalande's tendency to patronise him because the former was a member of the Academy of Sciences:

> I shall break one more lance against this Champion [Jodin wrote] purely because of his title Academician with which he is decorated. The manner in which he attacks me and the arguments he puts forward would not merit a response without this sublime quality [of Academician] which might impress people. In any case, a Worker, in combat with an Academician of the Royal Academy of Sciences, would be a struggle where even defeat would be honourable. What would it be like to be lucky enough to win?[12]

Jodin's polemical tone and the threat of further debate so alarmed Lalande that he complained to the official censor, Malherbes, in November 1755, alleging harassment by a mere watchmaker and asking that Malherbes exert his authority to prohibit publication of any further attacks from Jodin:[13]

> You will be only too well aware of how the impudence of a watchmaker has caused me annoyance some three months ago, not to wish to spare me any recurrence. Today, Sir, I have learned that when M. Lepaute's book in which I have published some observations appears, Jodin, along with the son of M. le Roy, prepares for my benefit some writings as tasteful as their first efforts.

Lalande's alarm seems to have won a sympathetic hearing from Malherbes. No more was heard from Jean Jodin in print. His despairing letter to his sister dates from two years after the Lalande affair and by the time of his death in 1761 the family appears to have been destitute. One wonders whether Lalande's enmity and influence had been sufficiently powerful to deprive Jodin of his livelihood.

This quarrel can be read in the broader context of the eighteenth-century debate on the importance of the practical arts and technologies. Jean Jodin defended experience or experiment over mere theory while admitting that for the artisan practitioner who must develop his expertise over many years of committed application, the leisure for speculation was difficult to obtain. 'One ceases necessarily to study when one works; one ceases to work when one studies … One is reduced to consecrate those short intervals available in handicraft labour to the study of principles that it is essential to know thoroughly …'.[14]

Though clockmaking in the eighteenth century was at the cutting edge of both pure and applied science, the artisan theorist was caught between the desire to innovate and the necessity of maintaining the traditional skills of his craft by constant application. The practical difficulties Jodin faced in innovation were, he claimed, compounded by the closed nature of the profession. Only those who had done their apprenticeship in Paris were eligible for the title of *Maître Horloger*. Foreigners were not admitted, even though Swiss clockmakers formed the backbone of the profession in France. Jodin's exclusion from the ranks of *Maîtres Horloger* could help to explain his precarious financial position. He was obliged to function as a workman, though as Lalande himself remarked; he was among the most skilled of his profession. Nor was the *Echappemens* without its political dimension; it included a patriotic paean to the 'industrious subjects of my Republic [Geneva] who have contributed so much to the advancement and excellence of watchmaking in France over the past thirty years'. In an age when rank and deference still were taken for granted, Jean Jodin displayed a republican impatience with both. This spirit of independence and a wider culture than that of the artisan's workbench was the principal inheritance he left to his daughter.

What is known of Madeleine Dumas Jodin, Marie Madeleine's mother and her role in her daughter's upbringing?[15] She was born in 1705 at Lunel, in Provence, the daughter of a French Calvinist refugee in Geneva. Married young to a M. Lafauzes, she was already widowed by the age of twenty-five when the impressionable Jean Jodin met her in Lyons. After her first husband's death, she had been imprisoned in Geneva for two years in a house of correction for 'libertinage', presumably prostitution. According to the unflattering and probably unreliable account of her brother-in-law, Pierre Jodin, she was a sexually experienced and designing young woman who, meeting Jean Jodin, then aged about fifteen, 'captivated and debauched him' and persuaded him to take her to Paris where he joined the workshop of his maternal uncle, Dutertre. The Dutertre family strongly disapproving of Jean Jodin's irregular union, insisted that he must leave the woman, or marry her, or quit his uncle's employ.

Jean Jodin chose marriage. As we see from his letter of 1757, he considered, or claimed to consider his wife 'the best of mothers' although Diderot later suggested to Marie Madeleine that the watchmaker had a poor opinion of his wife's character: 'She is, I think, the most unfortunate creature that I know. Your father thought that she had no capacity to feel anything; he did not know her well enough.'[16] Diderot and his wife showed great kindness towards Mme Jodin and evidently were fond of her. Mme Diderot, who was intensely respectable, would have been unlikely to include her in the family circle had she believed Mme Jodin had prostituted her daughter. In addition, as the same and subsequent letters testify, her daughter remained desperately committed to her mother. On the other hand we have the family depositions denoting terrible arguments between the two. Did Mme Jodin sell her daughter into prostitution and profit from her earnings as the family alleges? Certainly the inability to manage her finances seems to have been a source of anxiety for her family. Diderot charged her with extravagance and with being gullible in money matters. This could help explain the alleged exploitation of Marie Madeleine as a young girl and Jean Jodin's financial ruin.

From her letters, it is clear that Mme Jodin was less well educated than her husband. Although she could read and write, her spelling was almost entirely phonetic. However, in an age when literacy among women was very limited and spelling was not well taught to girls, it is perhaps more surprising that she was literate at all. Thanks to her husband's friendship with Diderot, Mme Jodin benefited from his protection, from 1765, when Marie Madeleine went to Poland, until her return to France in 1768. As indicated above, Diderot's views on Mme Jodin did not remain entirely positive. He came to appreciate the fact that she was a hopeless spendthrift and advised her daughter to be strict in apportioning an allowance. One may suppose that Jean Jodin was, as his brother alleges, captivated by the young widow in Lyons, who may have possessed considerable beauty, a legacy which was passed on to her daughter. Nevertheless, the central charge alleged against her by the family (and vigorously denied by Marie Madeleine and her mother) was that she prostituted her daughter and lived off her immoral earnings.

Jean Jodin's analysis of the economic disabilities suffered by Swiss nationals in France pointed to another key trauma in his daughter's childhood – her early abjuration of the Protestant faith. In 1750 at the age of nine, Marie Madeleine Jodin converted, or was converted, to Catholicism, which gained her a yearly pension of 200 *livres*, not a fortune but a respectable addition to the family's modest income. We can suppose that consent was not seen as an issue initially but that it became an issue because the child rebelled dramatically against the religious teaching and regime of the convents in which she was placed. While her parents settled at Saint-Germain en Laye, outside Paris, Marie Madeleine was put under the guardianship of her aunt, Marie Jodin and sent to the first of many convents, la Congrégation de Vernon, for instruction.[17] In the course of the next seven years, apparently resisting violently the disciplines of convent life and her conversion, she was expelled from one institution after another. By

1751 she was the subject of an *Ordre du Roi*, the equivalent of, or substitute for, a *lettre de cachet* and forcibly removed to the Maison des Nouvelles Catholiques in Paris, the same convent to which her father wished to send her in 1757.[18] Subsequent moves took her further and further away from Paris, ultimately to Auxerre in Burgundy. Marie Madeleine was returned to her parents in 1756, the despair of the convents and of her aunt, but the home environment did not, as we have seen from her father's letter, provide a happier solution.

Marie Madeleine Jodin's disruptive and rebellious youth is both personally and socially revealing. Her experiences as the daughter of a Protestant in eighteenth-century France reflect some of the major religious tensions of the period, which in their political impact formed an important strand in undermining royal authority.[19] This ferocious Protestant child, offering an instinctive rebellion against the disciplines of religion and the family, illuminates on an individual level the status of Protestants in eighteenth-century France. Though subjects of the King, they were not citizens. To convert to Catholicism was to make as much a civil as a religious choice in favour of the capacity to enjoy full civil status. So in Marie Madeleine's conversion, aged nine, we see mirrored some of the practical consequences of the Revocation of the Edict of Nantes (18 October 1685), which meant that from now on all French subjects must be registered at birth, at marriage and at death, according to Catholic ritual. Protestants had no civil route by which they could attain legal status for their families. Non-Catholics were excluded from public office and various professions. In effect, Protestants, apart from being forbidden to practise their religion formally, lacked a legal identity and could not pass on property to their descendants. Protestant parents were under great pressure to allow their children to convert: 'The authorities ... sometimes sequestered Protestant children in Catholic schools to preserve them from the errors of their parents, in spite of protests that this practice violated the principle of paternal authority upon which the crown itself rested.'[20] It was even alleged that the police kidnapped Protestant children, a belief that provoked riots in Paris in May 1750, the year Marie Madeleine was 'converted'.[21] It is therefore entirely possible that her conversion was not even willed by her parents, though clearly the pension of 200 *livres* would act as an emollient form of persuasion.

We may assume a clear link between the child's rejection of religious indoctrination as evidenced by her expulsion from six convents and the terrible rages which her father records in his letter of 1757. Jodin's tendency to outbursts of anger continued as a feature of her adult life, attested to by contemporaries in Poland and Diderot's remonstrances in his letters. Yet in spite of the humiliations of her arrest and imprisonment, she exhibited a strong sense of her own worth in terms of her intellect and pride in her birth. She made much of her status as the daughter of a citizen of Geneva which, like Rousseau, she felt conferred dignity on its bearer. She included this designation 'fille d'un citoyen de Genève' on the title page of her published work, the *Vues législatives*.[22] As Diderot said to Jodin in his first letter to her in Warsaw: 'you are an unhappy child, but a well-born one'. It would seem that Jodin identified with her father's republican and intellectual heritage and must never have known of his letter of denunciation included in the Bastille file. Ironically, as an adult, she fulfilled, with Diderot's encouragement, the role of dutiful daughter which her youth had done so much to disrupt.

Parental and royal authority: the legal context

Marie Madeleine and her mother were arrested at their flat on the rue Mazarine and imprisoned in la Salpêtrière on 16 November 1761.[23] What were the legal procedures employed and what were the crimes charged against them? At the core of their situation must be seen the idea of familial authority and the role of the *police des moeurs* (morals police or vice squad) in enforcing that authority.[24] Under the *ancien régime* it was not necessary that they should be tried in court or even formally accused. We find, however, that their case was carefully investigated, according to legal requirements, and records were kept of depositions against them as well as their own pleas of innocence. The question of the authority of the family lay at the centre of this domestic tragedy. To read the Jodin/Dutertre family's letters of denunciation of 1761 is to be confronted with what appears to be an almost complete breakdown of family loyalties, in the name of preserving the family reputation. Aunts', uncles' and cousins' depositions and the father's earlier letter of 1757 form a dossier of hostility and despair.[25]

When in October 1761, the Jodin/Dutertre family applied to the Comte de Saint Florentin, Minister of State, for the incarceration of Marie Madeleine and her mother, an application which had to be supported by signed written statements, the dossier of letters assembled by them as evidence revealed interesting confusions, both in what was being charged and who were the allegedly guilty parties. The Bastille dossier can be summarised as containing the following:

1. Letter, 27 November 1761 to le Comte de Saint Florentin from Madeleine Jodin, *mère*, and Madeleine Jodin, *fille*, pleading for clemency and claiming that the charges brought against them are false.
2. Letter from Jean Jodin to his sister, 16 February 1757, cited above and submitted as contributory evidence by his sister, Marie Jodin.
3. Three letters by Marie Madeleine Jodin, undated, to two male acquaintances, le Comte de Rochemore and M. Picard and presented to the authorities by her mother as evidence of her daughter's immoral life.

4. Joint letter of denunciation against Marie Madeleine Jodin, from Madeleine Jodin, mother, Pierre Jodin, uncle, Marie Jodin, aunt, Dutertre, uncle.
5. Six depositions against the mother and the daughter dated October 1761 from a neighbour, Mme Marbel and the Jodin and Dutertre family.
6. Summary of the case by the presiding police officer.
7. Account of the arrest of mother and daughter, 16 November 1761.
8. A largely illegible letter of four sides on poor paper from Mme Jodin to an unnamed relation or friend dated 2 March 1762, pleading for release into a religious community and out of the 'hospital' or prison. This letter reiterates the mother's and daughter's mutual devotion, as did their plea of 27 November 1761 to the Comte de Saint Florentin.

Though there was no public trial, as indeed was usual with most cases brought by the *police des moeurs*, it is tempting to describe it in terms of the case for the Prosecution and the case for the Defence. What were the safeguards for the accused, who did not appear before a tribunal and who could have no strategy for defence, against purely malicious accusations? Though secretive, the system was not entirely arbitrary. A law of 1708 required that the declarations of the accusers/denunciators be signed and could not be anonymous; that of 1713 required that the accusers swear their depositions on oath. There was also the possibility of appeal against conviction to the Parlement. However, no appeals have been recorded, and the vast majority of cases, like Jodin's own, were summarily judged.[26] Nevertheless, the fact that we have the letters of the Bastille Archive duly signed and dated and that the police officer in charge interviewed neighbours and assembled a dossier at least points to a methodical investigation of the charge. Yet the outlook for the Defence in any such case cannot have been hopeful.

The case for the Prosecution is the easiest to mount. The police summary of the Jodin affair offers a version of the shifts of familial strategy towards this troublesome daughter. Initially, the Jodin/Dutertre family, in a letter also signed by her mother, accused Marie Madeleine of refusing conversion, of being a libertine, of having been expelled from six convents due to bad behaviour and of having exhibited murderous violence towards her mother. The mother, Madeleine Jodin, subsequently retracted these accusations whereupon her in-laws, the Jodin/Dutertre families, united in denouncing her, bringing the following charges against mother and daughter:

> That her mother conducts herself in as reprehensible a manner as her daughter, that she was a debauchee before her marriage, that she prostitutes her daughter and divides with her her earnings from *libertinage*, that this division gives rise to differences between them which lead them to threaten reciprocally to kill each other, that the profit which she (the mother) gains from her daughter is the only motive which led her to retract her accusations

which she had formerly brought against her, and that finally both equally merit being locked up.[27]

It is alleged that, as a child, Marie Madeleine refused conversion and indulged in 'libertinage'. This was an elastic term whose meaning ranged from freethinking to insubordination to indulgence in sexual licence. At the core of the concept was the refusal to accept authority, hence the pivotal example of the Don Juan myth in the seventeenth and eighteenth centuries, as depicted by Molière and Da Ponte/Mozart, of someone whose sexual profligacy is based on the rejection of familial and godly authority. For women the idea of libertinage included that of disobedience to one's family: 'A girl is a libertine when she does not wish to obey her mother, or a wife her husband'.[28] 'Libertine' suggested lack of order, even unreason, in women, and, almost inevitably, loose morals. Though often used as a synonym for prostitution the two were by no means synonymous. A libertine girl might be one who had a lover or lovers before marriage, though not necessarily for gain. The deposition of Marie Madeleine's uncle, Pierre Jodin, who signs himself 'Privilegié du Roi', illustrates this point. Alleging that the evils of the mother's 'libertinage' before marriage were passed on to the children (of whom apart from Marie Madeleine no other mention is made), he described the mother and daughter as: 'an unnatural mother and a perverted daughter. An unnatural mother who while her husband was alive and without his knowing it, had already on numerous occasions prostituted her daughter … of which fact I learned from the very lips of this daughter with as much sorrow as surprise.' He then goes on to speak of the mother's attempt to oppose her daughter's '*fantasy and libertinage which did not bring in the same advantages*' (my italics).[29] This 'fantaisie et libertinage' must refer to Marie Madeleine's attempts to follow her own fancy and to engage in a love affair, but not for monetary gain. The semantics of 'libertinage', then, are central to Jodin's case. The idea of a young woman leading an independent life and perhaps taking lovers was to be distinguished from prostitution and, from the point of view of both familial and state authority, could be considered as a worse threat to the social order.

The Jodin Bastille file illustrates the adage that under the *ancien régime* society was composed of families rather than individuals. This was particularly true for women who did not have rights over their own person, but were under parental guardianship until married.[30] In Marie Madeleine's case, not only was she accused of refusing religious authority but also of rebelling against her mother. Yet if the Jodin and Dutertre relations were telling the truth, the mother had undermined her own maternal authority by prostituting her daughter. There was, however, no disposition by the family, or the authorities, to treat Marie Madeleine as a victim.

Apart from the family's allegations, what evidence is there for the charge of prostitution? The mother, Mme Jodin, submitted three letters written by her daughter as proof of the latter's immoral conduct. The first, addressed to the

Comte de Rochemore, asked for a rendezvous and referred to an unnamed 'project' upon which they were jointly engaged:[31]

> I waited for you Sir, the whole day, as you asked me to do. This lack of consideration alarms me for I know that there is little stability in those projects which drag on. Nevertheless, since the work is so advanced, I flatter myself that you will certainly wish to instruct me whether I should continue it. I have not yet planned to show it to anyone and if you repeat your promise to me, I would be pleased to keep it for you, no matter what difficulties that would cause me. Remember that I told you the other day that I was concerned. I will try to satisfy him by the time you have finished since apparently you cannot do it sooner. [This comment is obscure.] I beg you to answer me in person to see where we are at this juncture.
>
> Sir, Your very humble and obedient servant, Jodin. If your business permitted you to call this afternoon, I would be very much obliged.[32]

This missive does not sound like a letter of romantic assignation unless it is a highly coded one. Jodin addresses the Count with some formality but speaks as though they were fellow scholars engaged on a joint project. Though one might think that this letter had little that was sinister about it, from a prosecution standpoint a young woman of respectable family did not enter into a clandestine correspondence. It would not have been the content of this letter as much as the fact of having written it that would have seemed suspicious to her family and the police. It is especially tantalising that we do not know the nature of the 'project' to which she refers.

The next two letters (ff. 167 and 170) are addressed to a M. Picard, a merchant draper living opposite the market, rue Saint Honoré. These do appear to reveal a liaison of some kind, since Jodin was giving Picard his marching orders, in a mocking and scornful style. The two former lovers had apparently quarrelled and were threatening each other with exposure. In her letter, Jodin rejects Picard's apparent accusation that, because she fell in love with him, she was a loose woman. Although undated, these letters would seem to be written after her father's death in March 1761:

> I am not at all pleased by your treatment. Dare if you like to do me all the harm that you have imagined. I defy you to frighten me. The faults that I may have committed were learned from you. I am not at all concerned as to what all the scum that surround you might say. By their behaviour they are not fit to kiss the tips of my shoes. You advise me to be ruled by others. I have only ever taken advice from my own brain and if I were to follow yours, you would need to act differently. Goodbye, Sir. Don't bother to reply for I will return your letter unopened.
>
> As to the threat I made against you, this is also a police matter. We have the same rights as you.

Though parts of this letter are illegible, Jodin's defiant tone is clear. The remark: 'We have the same rights as you' is particularly striking.

The second letter continues the quarrel but on a lighter note:

You are wrong, Sir, to claim that I am a *femme en monde* [prostitute]. If I were to force you to provide proofs, you would find yourself in grave difficulties. I have kept your letters which will show, when the time comes, that you made every effort to attract me, and if I made public my letters to you, they would prove that I gave way to love and not to [monetary] interest. Love is a feeling for which I would never blush (of which I should never feel ashamed). You are certainly made to inspire it in any case. My aunt Dutertre has no rights over me, however I behave, as long as my mother is alive. One doesn't despise those people who are in one's thoughts. This proves that I am not entirely indifferent to you. Joking aside, I will reject you because of this *louis* [was money offered?] or other insult. I will complain to your father. I will show him your letter and all the copies of mine [revealing] the details of your conduct and mine. I will inform (show) him what I am and even without the letters I will find means to converse with him. So, believe me, keep quiet and do me the favour of forgetting me. In order to avoid all temptation when you see me again, I am returning my letter so that you may do with it whatever you wish.

These three letters reveal aspects of Marie Madeleine's character that one could categorise as enduring. Sheer bravado shines out in the last two. In the first, to the Count de Rochemore, in spite of what must have been a disastrous educational experience in her vertiginous passage through six different convents from the age of ten, and in spite of stormy domestic relations, she appears to have attained a good level of education and writes to the Count with intellectual and social confidence. This view of Jodin as an aspiring intellectual receives some confirmation from another letter in the Bastille file from a neighbour, Marie Anne Marbel Sousignon (f. 174). She attested that it was well known that Jodin's parents had 'often sent her to the convent to procure for her a good education and to make her abjure the Protestant religion into which she had been born'. Most of Marbel's evidence against Jodin was pure hearsay (for example, she had heard that the girl had been treated for venereal disease). However, she claimed to have been present when Marie Madeleine returned home at ten in the morning saying that she had slept in the house of a wig-maker, rue Saint Jacques, lodging in a furnished room *where she kept her books* (my italics).

Though Mme Marbel and later the authorities clearly thought that the idea of a girl sleeping away from home in order to be with her books fell into the category of 'a likely story', it may have been true. The glimpses we have of Jodin throughout her life show two consistent traits: firstly, temperamental violence and secondly, – often equally seen as a cause of reproach – intellectual aspirations. To own books and to cherish them in the context of an artisan's household may have seemed an anomaly to her relations. Did she perhaps inherit her father's books? Certainly Diderot writes of her as 'an educated young woman',[33] and his letters continually advise her to study (admittedly to study his theories of acting in particular) and to withdraw for this purpose for a time from the frenetic life of the stage. She was thought by her actor colleagues to be the author of the 'public letter' lampooning the French actors and showing considerable critical sophistication.[34] An anonymous libel attacking Jodin in Poland mocked her intellectual pretensions, pointing to the fact that she was known to have scholarly interests, and an anonymous poem written in her honour in 1775 emphasised her talent, genius and learning.[35] In 1770 we know that she was reading d'Holbach's *Système de la nature*.[36] The cumulative effect of these scraps of evidence suggests that Jodin's emergence as the feminist intellectual of the *Vues législatives* was the product of a gradual evolution and not a sudden transformation. Mme Marbel's damning evidence about Jodin's implausible story of leaving home to read books is not necessarily the moral indictment it may have seemed at the time and may even have been the literal truth.

Parental authority

Why did Jodin threaten Picard with his father and the police? The assumption must be that Picard senior would not have sanctioned an affair out of wedlock. Young men, as well as young women, could be incarcerated by their parents if they disobeyed them by entering into irregular unions.[37] Diderot, who was to become Jodin's adviser and friend, had also been locked up by his father in a monastery, by means of the *lettre de cachet*, in 1743, because he wished to marry Anne-Toinette Champion, a Parisian linen and lace seller. Diderot only spent a few days in his prison before escaping but his experience was not unusual for children under the *ancien régime*.[38] As Jean Louis Flandrin argues: 'The authority of the father of the family and the authority of God not only legitimised one another; they served to legitimise all other authorities. As late as the age of Louis XIV, to say that an authority was "paternal" was to proclaim its legitimacy and the absolute duty of obedience on the part of those subject to it.'[39] To claim, like Jodin, that one accepted only the authority of one's own mind was, therefore, hubris of a high order, as well as smacking of 'Protestant' tendencies.

Familial authority in eighteenth-century France was powerfully reinforced by the *police des moeurs*. Artisan families had recourse to the state to assist them in controlling their daughters and to save the family reputation. In this respect the Jodin/Dutertre family grouping seems to have been fairly typical of families with unruly daughters of this period. A wayward daughter, or a sexually profligate one, would by definition become unmarriageable (though as we have seen this was not the case with Mme Jodin herself). While there was widespread official tolerance of prostitution, public morality was more concerned with the issue of notoriety than of the mercenary sale of sex. Any young woman who left home to live independently without parental permission or who frequented a public house was assumed to be living immorally and was likely to be the subject of police surveillance.[40] Thus Jean Jodin, Mme Marbel and the Jodin/ Dutertre relations attest that Marie Madeleine's conduct was *public* (for example, she came home at ten in the morning, she *was known* to lead an irregular life, her father felt his good name would be vilified and so on). Her relatives were primarily exercised about the family's reputation, especially as they represented a respectable branch of commerce.

La Salpêtrière

Jodin's period of imprisonment in la Salpêtrière Hospital was to have a profound effect on her life. Its echoes are heard in the bitterness she demonstrated towards prostitutes, expressed in her *Vues législatives*. The hospital/prison, though housing ordinary criminals, had by the mid-eighteenth century become synonymous with the containment and punishment of prostitutes. The founding of la Salpêtrière in 1656 had coincided with attempts to halt or contain the spread of syphilis and reflected the fears inspired by the disease beginning in the fifteenth century. Internment, either permanent or temporary, became the classic treatment for prostitutes.[41] Throughout most of the eighteenth century, including the period of the Jodins' residence, la Salpêtrière housed between 7000 and 8000 women in four wards or sections. The first, the Commune, was designated for the *debauchées*. The second, the Correction, was for young women locked up by their families who were willing to pay their board and lodging. Jodin would probably have fitted into this category. The third, *la Prison* was for those imprisoned by *ordre du Roi* and the fourth, *la Grande Force* held women sentenced to life imprisonment. The period of imprisonment for 'libertines' incarcerated by *lettre de cachet de famille* was generally longer than that of women locked up as simple prostitutes thanks to the payment of a pension by the family.[42]

While in theory these categories of prisoners were separated, in practice there was very little segregation. Artisan parents who had paid, they believed, to send their daughters out of harm's way complained of the conditions imposed and the company their daughters were forced to keep. The prison was a place of promiscuity and extreme hardship. Six women shared a room with four beds. Blankets were only provided in winter. The women worked at carding wool and were frequently and severely punished if their productivity slackened. The shaving of heads and beatings were common.

Two glimpses of Jodin's Salpêtrière experience emerge. The first is her mother's almost illegible letter dated 2 March 1762. The intended recipients are not known, though they could have been Denis Diderot and his wife, Antoinette. Since the letter remains in the Bastille file, it almost certainly never reached its intended recipients:

My very dear and good friends,
I don't know if you have heard of my detention for the past seven months
in the hospital. My daughter loves me very much although she often causes
me great pain. Our aunt had us locked up by Monsieur le Comte Saint
Florentain. There are cowards plotting against us. I would like very much
to be sent to a [religious] community not a hospital.[43]

It was possible to enter a religious establishment for repentant women such as
the Bon Pasteur, where women underwent a rigorous regime of prayer,
repentance and work.[44] Evidently Mme Jodin felt that even this Spartan regime
would be preferable to 'the hospital'. One also notes from this letter that Mme
Jodin stresses her devotion to her daughter, which had also been the main theme
of their joint letter of appeal to the Comte de Saint Florentin in November.

This mother [Madame Jodin] wishes to testify to your Highness the contrary
of those infamies which are included in the Memoire and to assure you that
far from having a daughter capable of violence and lacking any education,
she loves her so much that if she is deprived of her, she will be deprived of
her only consolation.[45]

The second unreliable but potentially revealing reference to Jodin's period in
la Salpêtrière emerges in the anonymous libel targeted against Jodin during her
residence in Warsaw (1765–67).[46] The author or authors mocked Jodin for,
among other things, her two-year period of imprisonment, alleging that the
beatings she received in prison were marks of shame that could still be seen on
her shoulders. We know that women prisoners in la Salpêtrière were regularly
beaten, either for disobedience or for falling below productivity standards in
their wool-carding work. 'You display', the writer of the libel asserts, 'shoulders
on which one can still see traces of the whip lashes that you received in la
Salpêtrière.'[47]

It is often not possible to disentangle gossip, malice and rumour from fact
in Jodin's life. But we do know that this period in la Salpêtrière was a reality.
At every point in Marie Madeleine Jodin's youth one is confronted with accounts
of her power to disrupt her surroundings and her family circle. If one takes as
true the detailed accounts of her youthful misdemeanours, one is even more
astonished by the fact that she emerged from the horrors of prison capable of
taking up an acting career and shining in it and, even more remarkably, gaining
the respect and affection of the *philosophe* who was to become her mentor,
Denis Diderot. Though Diderot was happy to scold her in his letters, he never
wavered, even at his most censorious, from affectionate regard and from his
efforts to encourage her to recover her own self-respect through the manner in
which she lived her life as well as through her profession.

Jodin's early youth presents a portrait of a disturbed, angry and problematic
individual, whose beauty, talents, sense of pride and self-assertiveness made
her an instinctive rebel against authority. As we will see, she clearly did come

to respect Diderot, whose advice she seems, on the whole, to have taken. But Diderot also noted the violence of her character, which drove her father to despair. Seven years of early, adolescent revolt led her assembled family to imprison her, alleging that nothing could control her, neither convents nor her parents. Pierre Jodin, her uncle and Marie Jodin, her aunt, having to account for their failure as guardians, painted her as the scourge of the family:

> From this time [her return to her parents in 1756], this young person has not ceased to render us desperate by her unexampled *libertinage* and the impossibility of controlling her. Her father who has just died, insolvent and from grief, has also made us fear for the life of the mother.[48] Our family, which has made it its duty to be (morally) irreproachable, begs your Highness to give orders to lock her up ... We will pay all necessary expenses.[49]

One should note that the family's generosity in this regard was only apparent. Marie Madeleine's board and lodging in la Salpêtrière would have been paid for by her state pension.

Marie Madeleine Jodin's youthful trajectory, though exceptional on one level, can be seen as characteristic of those many girls, particularly the daughters of artisan families hoping to maintain a respectable rank in society, who escaped parental control. What is astonishing is that a year after her release, Jodin was licensed as an actress with the Comédie Française, had left for Poland to act in Tomatis's troupe, and was accepted as an experienced actress. But like Protestants, actresses too were proscribed persons. Jodin, leaving behind her two categories of outsiders, Protestants, who could not be full citizens, and libertine women who were continually under police surveillance, joined a glamorous but also marginalised group. Nevertheless, the theatre was a recognised avenue out of poverty and prostitution. Until November 1774, 'it was enough for a woman to be listed, to be on the rolls of the Opera ... to enjoy 'common inviolability' and entered into the absolute possession of her person.'[50] Such women were, in effect, emancipated from the arbitrary authority of family and police. For them, the theatre became the site of personal liberty. Warsaw was to be the stage upon which Jodin enacted the drama of her new-found freedom.

Notes

1. Bibliothèque de l'Arsenal, Archives de la Bastille 12, 124 (1761), f. 163. All translations from archival material are by the authors.
2. Marie Madeleine Jodin was born in Paris on 27 June 1741. Denis Diderot, *Correspondance,* V, ed. Georges Roth (Paris: Editions de Minuit, 1959), p. 97.
3. Archives de la Bastille 12, 124 (1761), ff. 160–210. The Archive 12695, showing lists of the Salpêtrière prisoners and the releases effected for 1750–65, omits the years 1763–64, the probable date of Jodin's and her mother's release. They do not

appear on the lists of freed prisoners for 1762. We know Jodin went to Warsaw in 1765 (August). It seems likely, therefore, that she and her mother spent between eighteen months and two years in the Salpêtrière.

4. Diderot, *Correspondance* V, VII, IX, ed. Georges Roth (Paris: Editions de Minuit, 1959–63).

5. Marie Madeleine Jodin, *Vues législatives pour les femmes, addressées à l'Assemblée Nationale* par Mlle Jodin, fille d'un citoyen de Genève (Angers: Chez Mame, 1790). Mary Wollstonecraft's *Vindication of the Rights of Women* and Olympe de Gouges', *Declaration of the Rights of Woman and Citizen* date from 1792 and 1791 respectively.

6. The most detailed study of Marie Madeleine Jodin to date is that of Paul Vernière, 'Marie Madeleine Jodin, amie de Diderot et témoin des Lumières', *Studies on Voltaire*, 58 (1967), pp. 1765–75. Vernière sees Jodin as a particularly interesting example of 'intellectual contagion' – a proof that Enlightenment thought reached beyond a narrow élite to an actress and daughter of an artisan watchmaker.

7. Eugène Ritter, 'Jean Jodin (1713–1761) et son frère, Pierre Jodin. Lettres de Diderot à Mlle Jodin (1765–1769)' *Mémoires et Documents de la Société de l'Archéologie de Genève*, XXII (1886), 2e série, 2, pp. 366–71.

8. Jean Jodin, *Les Echappemens à repos comparés aux échappemens à recul, avec un mémoire*, Horloger à Saint Germain en Laye (Paris: Ch. A. Jombert, 1754).

9. See the discussion of practical science and technology versus abstract mathematics in P. N. Furbank, *Diderot: A Critical Biography* (London: Secker and Warburg, 1992), pp. 109–11 and 129–30.

10. Furbank, *Diderot*, p. 129.

11. 'Lettre de M. de Lalande de l'Académie Royale des Sciences, à l'Abbé Raynal, au sujet du nouvel échappements', *Mercure de France* (August 1754), pp. 156–73.

12. Jean Jodin, *Examen des dernierès Observations de Monsieur de La Lande de l'Académie Royale des Sciences insérées dans le Mercure de Juillet dernier* (Paris, le 20 juillet, 1755), p. 5.

13. 'Affair de M. de Lalande avec Jodin horloger', Fonds Anisson-Dupéron 87, *Librairie Lettres et Mémoires sous M. de Malherbes*, FR22147 (103–4).

14. Jodin, *Les Echappemens*, p. 42.

15. Archives de la Bastille 12, 124 (1761), f. 186, 'Deposition du Pierre Jodin, oncle paternel contre Marie Madeleine Jodin', 5 October 1761, offers a very unflattering picture of the mother. Diderot in his letters to Jodin defends the mother, though agreeing that she is unable to manage her affairs.

16. Diderot, *Correspondance*, V, letter 346, 'A Mademoiselle Jodin, à Varsovie', 21 August 1765, p. 103.

17. Archives de la Bastille, 12, 124 (1761) and Vernière, 'Marie Madeleine Jodin, amie de Diderot et témoin des Lumières', who has offered the fullest account to date of Jodin's early youth.

18. For an explanation of the *Ordre du Roi* as a substitute for the *lettre de cachet* see Erica-Marie Benabou, *La Prostitution et la police des moeurs au XVIIIe siècle* (Paris: Perrin, 1987), p. 75.

19. See Jeffrey W. Merrick, *The Desacralisation of the French Monarchy in the Eighteenth Century* (London: Louisiana State University Press, 1990), pp. 134–64.

20. Ibid., p. 139.

21. Ibid., p. 139, n. 8; le Chevalier de Beaumont, *l'Accord parfait de la nature, de la raison, de la révélation et de la politique* (2 vols, Cologne: 1753), II, p. 97.

22. For a discussion of citizenship and its meaning in eighteenth-century Geneva see: Clarissa Campbell Orr, 'A republican answers back: Jean-Jacques Rousseau, Albertine Necker de Saussure, and forcing little girls to be free', in *Wollstonecraft's Daughters, Womanhood in England and France 1780–1920*, ed. Clarissa Campbell Orr (Manchester: Manchester University Press, 1996), pp. 61–78; Linda Kirk, 'Genevan Republicanism', in *Republicanism, Liberty and Commercial Society, 1649–1776*, ed. David Wootton (Stanford, California: Stanford University Press, 1994), Jean Jacques Rousseau, *The Confessions*, Book 1 (1781), trans. J. M.Cohen (London: Penguin Books, 1953).

23. Letter of Delavillegauden to M. Chaban informing the latter of the Jodins' arrest, Archives de la Bastille 12, 124 (1761), f. 198.

24. One notes that Paul Vernière, in his otherwise excellent analysis, cannot credit the father with this letter of 1757 and invents an uncle by the same name. There seems little doubt that Jean Jodin, *horloger*, it was who categorised his daughter as a monster, since the letter refers to the daughter as his.

25.

26. Benabou, *La Prostitution*, p. 24.

27. Archives de la Bastille, 12, 124 (1761), f. 196.

28. Furetière, *Dictionnaire*, quoted in Benabou, *La Prostitution*, p. 36.

29. Archives de la Bastille, 12, 124 (1761), f. 186.

30. See Benabou, *La Prostitution*, pp. 39–40; Jean Louis Flandrin, *Families in Former Times* (1976), trans. Richard Southern (Cambridge: Cambridge University Press, 1978), p. 118; Edmond and Jules de Goncourt, *The Woman of the Eighteenth Century*, trans. Jacques de Clercq and Ralph Roeder (London: Allen and Unwin, 1929), p. 189.

31. Rochemore was possibly Alexandre-Henri Pierre, marquis de Rochemore, born at Nîmes, who died in 1790. He was the author of some poetry and books on the antiquities of Nîmes. Biographical notes make no mention of a Parisian sojourn. *Nouvelle Biographie Générale depuis les temps les plus reculés*, Dr Hoefer (ed.) (Paris: Firmin, 1866).

32. Archives de la Bastille, 12, 124, (1761), f. 164.

33. Diderot, *Correspondance*, V, letter 361, 'A Mademoiselle Jodin, à Varsovie', November 1765, p. 202.

34. See Julian Lewanski, 'Teatr, Dramat I Muzyka za Stanislawa Augusta', *Pamietnik Teatralny*, Rok IX, Zeszyt 1 (33) (Warszawa 1960).

35. 'Vers à Mlle Jodin', *Journal de Politique et de Littérature*, 3 (Brussels, 1775).

36. Diderot, *Correspondance*, X, 3 July 1770.

37. See Benabou, *Prostitution*, pp. 21–4. However, Benabou argues that women were more likely to experience parental/police repression.

38. Furbank, *Diderot*, pp. 17–22.

39. Flandrin, *Families in Former Times*, p. 120.

40. Benabou, *La Prostitution*, pp. 30–37.

41. Ibid., pp. 20–21.

42. Ibid., pp. 77–82.

43. Bastille Archive 12, 124 (1761), f. 202. The translation is approximate, given the difficulties of orthography and legibility, but the sense is fairly exact.

44. Benabou, *La Prostitution*, p. 89.

45. Bastille Archive 12, 124 (1761), f. 162.

46. Bibliothèque de la Pologne: Manuscrit 58, Jean Heyne, Archiwum Ks. Ksawerego Saskiego t. III, no. 224, f. 987, dated 20 August 1765.

47. Ibid.
48. The family's concern for the mother's welfare must be questioned. From the moment that Madeleine Jodin sided with her daughter, the Dutertre/Jodin clan turned against the mother and included her in their indictment to the police.
49. Bastille Archive, 12 124, (1761), f. 173.
50. Edmond and Jules de Goncourt, *The Woman of the Eighteenth Century*, pp. 188–92.

Figure 1.1 *French Prostitutes taken to la Salpétrère Prison*, early eighteenth century. [Courtesy of the Mary Evans Picture Library]. The prison hospital where Jodin and her mother were incarcerated in 1761.

CHAPTER TWO

The débutante actress and her profession

In his *Paradoxe sur le comédien*, Diderot, describing the debased status of the acting profession in his own day, evoked the début of a young actress who might have been modelled on his protégée, Marie Madeleine Jodin, when she went for an audition with a leading *comédienne*:[1]

> An unhappy creature who has wallowed in the mire of debauchery; tired of this most abject of states, that of a lowly courtesan, learns a few roles off by heart; one fine day she goes to see Clairon as the slave in ancient times might have gone to the councillor or the priest.[2] The latter takes her by the hand, asks her to perform a pirouette, touches her with his wand and says: 'Go and make the vulgar [curious, gapers] laugh or cry.'

Diderot claimed that neither men nor women would willingly choose the acting profession except as a last resort: 'Why do they put on the sock and buskin? – failures of upbringing, of poverty and [a life of] debauchery. The theatre is a resource never a choice ... It makes me angry ... that an honourable man or woman should be so rare a phenomenon among actors.'[3] He then underscored the religious status of actors as underlining the paradox of their profession: 'They are excommunicated. Their audiences who cannot do without them, despise them. They are slaves constantly under the rule of other slaves.'[4] In a similar vein, Diderot had written to Jodin a decade earlier (May 1766):

> When one thinks of the reasons which have decided a man to become an actor, or a woman to become an actress – of the place where Providence found them and the bizarre circumstances which attracted them to the stage – one is no longer amazed that talent, good behaviour and probity are all equally rare among the acting fraternity.

Diderot's *Paradox* forms part of a corpus of his writing, in which one may include his twenty-one letters to Jodin, which discuss the intertwined aesthetic, ethical, religious and social issues in eighteenth-century French theatre summed up in what he aptly termed the 'Paradox of the Actor'. His letters to Jodin (1765–69) develop his theories of bourgeois tragedy and reflect the long-standing 'quarrel' over the status of actors and the theatre, brought to a head by Rousseau in 1758 with his *Lettre à d'Alembert sur les spectacles*.[5] Although acting was a profession which enjoyed a reputation for glamour and actors and actresses were often courted by the aristocracy, it was nevertheless the case that the status of actors was one of 'infamy' and exclusion from civil and religious life.[6] On 16 May 1765, when Marie Madeleine Jodin was licensed to act by the Dukes Richelieu and Duras, First Gentlemen of the King's Chamber, who held ultimate authority over the official theatres, she joined what was literally an infamous profession. Actors in France (but not in Italy) were excommunicated by the Church and refused the sacraments. The French tragedian, Lekain, writing to David Garrick (July 1765), expressed the frustration of his profession:

> You [English actors] are in the good graces of your clergy, whilst our archbishop has sent us all to the devil; you are your own masters, and we are slaves; you enjoy a glory [fame] that is genuine, and ours is always in dispute; you earn a brilliant fortune and we are poor; here are some terrible contrasts for you.[7]

Although in 1641 Louis XIII, under the influence of Cardinal Richelieu, had formally freed actors from the Roman legal proscription of 'infamy', in practice it still continued to be applied by Church and State.[8] Since there was no civil mode of legalising births, marriages and deaths outside the Church, actors were excluded simultaneously from both civil and religious protection. In court cases, for example, there was no obligation on the part of the courts to take their evidence; they had no legal status.[9] Contradictions abounded. Actors could, if they renounced their profession before their deaths, be accommodated by a religious burial. However as civil servants in the employ of the Crown, they needed the permission of the Gentlemen of the King's Chamber to retire, and where this was refused (as it often was) they remained outside the Church and its sacraments. If they refused to fulfil their contracts with the Crown, they were imprisoned.[10] Of the three officially sanctioned French theatres, the Comédie-Française, the Opéra and the Comédie-Italienne, all of whose performers came under the jurisdiction of the Gentlemen of the King's Chamber, only the actors of the Comédie Italienne were free of Church condemnation because the Italian Church, curiously, took a more liberal attitude towards theatrical performances.

Yet the evident injustices suffered by the profession did not rouse much sympathy either with their popular audiences or with the bourgeois reformers. In the first half of the century when the authority of Church and Crown began to be contested by the largely Jansenist parlements, the latter regarded actors in a like manner to the Church.[11] As with executioners, actors were declared, or re-declared 'infamous'. In an age where caste or status was a defining mode of identity, infamy was no laughing matter.[12] Even as liberal a commentator as Diderot agreed, as we see from the *Paradox*, in condemning actors' status. He told Jodin in his letters that by her birth she was something better than an actress, and whilst urging her to act well according to his precepts, he indicated more than once that she should not be acting at all. That Jodin developed a love for her profession became something of a dilemma for her mentor.

Diderot was surely right to imply that the decision to become an actor or actress was less likely to be the result of a star-struck love of the theatre than a last resort, preferable to the army for a man or to the streets for a woman.[13] In

Jodin's case we know that from her childhood she rebelled against authority, as evidenced in her rebellious behaviour in convents and against her family. Like many in her position, by joining the theatre she effected an escape from one system of largely arbitrary power, comprising her family, the morals police and the prison, to the seemingly less onerous but none the less absolute power of the Crown. The official theatre was a recognised route out of police control and family jurisdiction:

> The theatre in effect was a site of immunity ... Any unmarried girl, whatever her age, who succeeded in being licensed as an actress, found herself, by this fact alone, emancipated and would escape completely from paternal or maternal authority. The same was true of the married woman; the rights of the husband broke down before that invisible asylum called the theatre.[14]

If such women were less harassed by the police than common prostitutes, they were nevertheless under police surveillance as the *Journal des Inspecteurs de M. de Sartines, 1761–1764* makes clear. The Chief of Police reported almost daily to the King the nocturnal goings-on of his courtiers, the vast majority of whom, according to Sartines, were carrying on affairs with actresses. He noted that freedom from parental control was a central advantage of the acting profession as was illustrated by the case of Marguerite Arivilleux, aged sixteen, who ran off with the appropriately named Comte de Joyeuse. The latter, fearing that Marguerite's mother would have her locked up (like Jodin), arranged for her to have dancing lessons so that she could be taken on at the Opera and be shielded from paternal authority. The dancing master, the inspector's report noted drily, was almost certainly giving her more than one kind of lesson.[15]

Site of infamy or site of freedom? The paradoxes did not end there. For this profession, reviled by the Church and the parlements was also the profession lauded and flattered by the nobility and gentry. From Marie Antoinette, who actually performed in the theatre of Versailles (to a restricted audience), to the noble lords and ladies who set up theatres in their châteaux and acted in them, the fever for dramatic representation and the admiration in which the professional theatrical stars were held can hardly be exaggerated.[16] One of the most notorious examples of this ambivalence can be found in the career of Mlle Clairon on whom Jodin modelled herself and whose retirement from the stage coincided fortuitously with Jodin's accession to it.[17]

In Diderot's *Paradox*, Mlle Clairon figures as shorthand for a great actress, as la Berma figures in Proust's *A la recherche du temps perdu*. 'Quel jeu plus parfait que celui de la Clairon ?' (Whose acting is more perfect than Clairon's?) Diderot's spokesman enthuses. For Diderot, Clairon represents the model of a controlled and deliberate artist, working not by inspiration but giving the illusion of spontaneity, through artifice, the very paradox that Diderot admired. On a more practical level, Mlle Clairon embroiled herself in theatre politics and headed a short-lived but significant movement by actors to be accorded their civil rights. Her career, though more illustrious, parallels that of Jodin and is further evidence of the blighted lives from which many actors and actresses attempted to escape to the stage. Clairon was born illegitimate, a designation implying that she could never aspire to honourable status. She was brought up by her mother in great poverty and had no formal education, being still unable to read or write by the age of eleven. Clairon describes herself as having an overwhelming vocation for the stage, joining the Comédie-Italienne in Rouen at the age of thirteen. Though her considerable success won her acclaim, she also became the target of an anonymous libel, which went into ten editions, detailing her alleged amorous affairs. It is probable that as well as being the work of a disgruntled former lover, this libel marked her success as an actress, as a mediocre actress would have been unlikely to attract this degree of venom. The libel that Jodin inspired in Warsaw can be interpreted in a similar light.

Temperamentally Clairon had the qualities associated in our own day with divas and movie stars. Her biographer remarks that:

> although her conduct was irregular [she had a number of long-lasting but well-publicised liaisons], she possessed an elevated soul, a certain natural pride … She admitted herself that she was naturally and unfortunately violent [temperamental] and proud; these faults which she did not strive to repress, made her many enemies, not only among her comrades but even among her audiences who wished to find modesty and simplicity allied to talent.[18]

We find here an echo of Diderot's strictures to Jodin: 'Moderate', he admonishes her, 'the violence of your character.' Clairon, in her 'Moral Reflections', appended to her *Mémoires*, saw her pride as her principal failing, not for Christian reasons, but because as someone of illegitimate birth and an infamous profession, who, as she put it, 'was nothing', she had no right to pride.

In the mid-eighteenth century, the debate on the purpose of the theatre and the status of actors generated an enormous number of pamphlets and sermons.[19] Contributors to the *Encyclopédie* like Marmontel and de Jaucourt argued that theatre was a legitimate activity because it taught morality. Diderot wrote two plays, *Le Fils naturel* (1757) and *Le Père de famille* (1758), which debated moral questions (illegitimacy and parental authority) from a serious point of view. In his *Discours de la poésie dramatique* he offered a powerful defence of the moral utility of the theatre to teach audiences to love virtue, to hate vice and to cultivate the social virtues. For Diderot, the chief purpose of his theatre was to dramatise his moral philanthropy.[20] Yet the liberal reformers faced an intractable problem. In the public's perception, actors were debased characters leading unruly and scandal-ridden lives, while on stage they spoke the language of heroism and morality. In short actors were regarded with the suspicion and disdain afforded to politicians today. Reformers believed that restoring actors to their civil status would lead to an eventual improvement in their moral behaviour, whereas conservatives argued that only incorrigibly immoral people became actors in the first place and that as a consequence they attracted the infamy they deserved.

Into this highly charged debate, Rousseau in 1758 dropped his explosive *Lettre à d'Alembert sur les spectacles*. A playwright himself and formerly a lover of the theatre, his *philosophe* friends were shocked to find him defending the right of Calvinist Geneva to ban theatrical representations. Worse, in a spirit reminiscent of Plato banning poets from his republic, Rousseau had used the Genevan issue as an opportunity to condemn theatrical representation generally. Rousseau attacked both the theatre's moral and aesthetic aspects. Firstly, actors were immoral: 'I see in general that the state of being an actor is a state of licence and bad morals in which the men are given over to disorder and the women lead scandalous lives.'[21] Secondly, it followed that to act or represent was by definition immoral because one was not representing oneself truthfully: 'What is the actor's talent?' Rousseau asked rhetorically, and answered, 'The art of counterfeiting oneself, of putting on a character other than one's own, to appear differently than one is, to throw oneself coldly into a passion, to say things other than one thinks as naturally as though one really thought them and to forget one's proper place [or status] by dint of taking on another's.'[22] In accordance with Rousseau's cult of sincerity, it was axiomatic that any representation of something or someone other than oneself was false and therefore wrong. Finally actresses in particular came in for censure since for a woman to display herself in public and for money was equivalent to prostitution: 'I wonder how a state whose sole object is to display oneself in public, and what is worse, to display oneself for money, is suitable for honest women and can be compatible with modesty and good morals?'[23]

In 1760, however, Clairon began a notable campaign on behalf of the rights of actors. She engaged a lawyer and parliamentarian, Huerne de la Mothe, to draw up a legal brief or '*mémoire*' arguing against the Church's writ of excommunication of actors, since as legally excluded persons, actors could not put a case before the parlement or King on their own behalf. La Mothe published a lengthy pamphlet entitled *Liberté de la France contre le pouvoir arbitraire de l'excommunication*, arguing that the Church did not have the rights of excommunication over French citizens, who were subjects of the Crown.[24] It says a great deal about a period which so prized wit that both Voltaire and Grimm, though partisans of reform, attacked this legal *mémoire* for its 'detestable style'. In addition, the Jansenist and Gallican parliamentarians, normally zealous defenders of lay privilege, found la Mothe's anti-clerical position too extreme and expelled him from the bar. By her courageous initiative, the unfortunate Clairon was blamed for having set back the actors' cause.

Clairon's attempt to lift the condemnation of infamy from actors formed part of a larger campaign to legitimise the moral role of the theatre in national life and had a considerable history. It was argued by Voltaire, Diderot and others that because actors were relegated to the margins of society, they would naturally tend to have few moral inhibitions. Furthermore, the discrimination affecting even the most gifted and morally virtuous actors was notorious. Voltaire had raged against the more shocking abuses of Church power to excommunicate actors ever since the death in 1730 of Adrienne Lecouvreur, a much-admired actress, whose body was refused burial in consecrated ground. Lecouvreur's case dramatised the contradictions of a society where actors were fêted and loaded with honours during their lifetimes but demeaned and defiled at their deaths.

Finally in 1765 a spectacular theatrical quarrel in which Clairon took a leading part broke out in the Comédie-Française epitomising the paradoxes of social attitudes towards actors by their audiences. The Dubois scandal, though well known, is instructive.[25] An actor named Dubois was taken to court by his doctor for failing to pay his bill for the treatment of venereal disease. At the trial, the court refused to accept Dubois's sworn testimony on the grounds that he belonged to an infamous profession. The actors of the Comédie-Française as a group demanded an apology from the court for this insult to their profession. However it was then discovered, to their dismay, that Dubois had, in fact, given false evidence. The troupe felt itself betrayed and decided to ostracise him. Mlle Clairon, on behalf of the troupe, appealed to the Duc de Richelieu that Dubois should be excluded. Richelieu dismissed the actors' complaint and ordered them to perform the hugely popular play, *The Siege of Calais*, with Dubois in a leading role. In a remarkable gesture of solidarity, the chief stars of the troupe, Lekain, Molé and Mlle Clairon refused to perform. The management substituted a comedy, but the audience, who had come expecting to see the *Siege of Calais*, threatened to riot. Richelieu asserted his authority and had the actors sent to prison for failing to fulfil their contracts.

Far from admiring the actors' principled stand against a dishonest colleague, the public, or groundlings, showed (according to Grimm) an almost total hostility to their position, threatening them with the traditional cry: 'à l'hôpital, au cabanon' (to prison [la Salpêtrière], to the dungeon). In contrast, the theatre's aristocratic patrons publicly supported Mlle Clairon and her fellow thespians. The prison where the troupe was lodged, Fors l'Evêque, received a flood of enthusiastic, noble visitors. Mlle Clairon's cell was elegantly furnished by her well-wishers; the surrounding streets were thronged with aristocratic carriages, as the nobility came to pay homage. Bachaumont in his *Mémoires secrètes* claimed that Mlle Clairon gave sumptuous dinners. The contrasting attitudes of the ordinary public with those of the theatre's aristocratic patrons starkly reveal the contradictory perception of the acting profession in eighteenth-century France.[26]

Although Voltaire (from the safe distance of the Swiss border) urged the actors to continue their strike, the company, unable to support the inevitable loss of income, permitted a grovelling apology to be uttered in its name and returned to work. Dubois was allowed to retire with an increased pension. Mlle Clairon, at her request, was released from her contract on the plea of ill-health and joined Voltaire for a time in Switzerland. In November 1765, however, she returned to Paris to pursue her campaign for actors' rights, submitting a *mémoire* to the effect that the Comédie-Française, rather than being an offshoot of the King's Chamber, should be turned into a professional academy. This would have given the actors both status and independence. M. de Saint-Florentin (who had been the official to whom Jodin and her mother addressed their pleas for clemency) read Clairon's *mémoire* to the council of ministers on 6 April 1766. It asked King Louis XV, to confirm the edict of 1641, which had, in principle, lifted the actors' infamy. Louis, however, replied: 'Actors will never be under my reign anything other than they have been under that of my predecessor. Speak to me no more of this matter.'[27] Following this definitive royal snub, Mlle Clairon formally retired from the theatre (25 April 1766) at the height of her powers.

Whilst the evidence of petty rivalries and scandals is not hard to find in the theatrical histories of this period, the 'Dubois quarrel' stands out as conflating virtually all the aspects of civil exclusion under which the acting profession laboured. When applauded by the public and courted by the aristocracy, their lack of seemingly abstract rights may not have seemed important. But in the Dubois case, actors' evidence under oath was refused by the court; actors were defined as persons without honour. Dubois's own perfidy did not contravene the insulting implication of this rule. And when the combined voices of the Comédie-Française troupe protested to the Duc de Richelieu in an effort to uphold their honour by ostracising Dubois, they were simply ignored, a privilege the Duke exercised by virtue of his rank. The troupe's solidarity was impressive but could not survive the financial losses soon accruing to the company, between 30,000 and 40,000 livres.[28]

Mlle Clairon's powerful role in these theatrical debates points to another radicalizing side of the actress's profession, the fact that at least in the Parisian Comédie-Française, male and female actors shared an equal role in governing the institution. 'The actresses at the Théâtre Français present the rare case of women sitting side by side on essentially equal terms with males in an important deliberative body.'[29] Though Jodin never performed on the Paris stage, most European theatrical troupes followed the custom of the Comédie-Française in making collective decisions on the repetoire, allocation of parts and so on. There was thus a *de facto* form of sexual equality within the troupes though, as will become evident throughout Jodin's career, this culture of equality was to be frequently contested by male actors and directors. The fact that Jodin modelled herself on the great Clairon may have represented more than the imitation of acting technique; she may also have admired the latter's powerful articulation of a woman's possibilities in the public sphere.

If we now return to the issue of the dishonourable status of actors and the ambition of *philosophes* like Diderot to turn the theatre into a forum for ethical debate, we can see that the letters he would write to Jodin can be read as a form of living experiment to reclaim the profession of acting, with Jodin at the centre of the experiment. In his twenty-one letters to Jodin, Diderot consistently developed the connections between the moral, the theatrical and the civic life. When Diderot reminded Jodin of the need for personal integrity and when he asserted his belief that Jodin could become a good and honest person, he was also engaged in refuting the broader principle of infamy. The arrogance of the Duc de Richelieu who as Lekain said: 'when he treated our most respectful representations with scorn, [revealed] his lack of delicacy and the excess of his pride' – this arrogance of power against the powerless and the notion that actors had no right to the concept of honour was contradicted on almost every page of Diderot's letters to the young actress.[30] Marie Madeleine Jodin, joining the Comédie-Française in 1765, joined a profession where actresses were stigmatised by the Church and perhaps, more woundingly, by the powerful voice of Rousseau as 'public women', 'women for sale'. The very concept of personal integrity for an actress would have seemed an oxymoron to many, but not to Diderot. His practical and moral encouragement to Jodin formed part of the *philosophes'* campaign to rehabilitate the theatre as a forum of ethical action.

An example of Diderot's ethical/aesthetic teaching arises in his first letter to Marie Madeleine in Warsaw, dated 21 August 1765. The young actress had just been launched in her career in the Polish capital, having signed her contract in April. Diderot clearly felt anxious about her professional success and what would occur in her personal life. The letter develops three main themes: firstly personal morality and integrity; secondly instruction on the art of acting; and thirdly, family concerns, especially the condition of Mme Jodin, left behind in Paris, three themes orchestrated throughout Diderot's correspondence with Jodin. This one-sided correspondence (all that remains to us) represents none the less a reciprocal process. Diderot needed Jodin as a sounding board for his theories about representation and Jodin needed Diderot's advice and moral support. One of the results of the correspondence and of Diderot and Jodin's continuing friendship after its close was to turn Marie Madeleine into a full-blown *philosophe*, perhaps not Diderot's intention but the effect of his adventurous teaching.

Diderot's first theme, the ethical dimension, begins with the premise that Jodin, having become an actress, has moved into a station of life to which she was not born and which is fraught with dangers. The honest soul with which she is endowed could, he warns her, be corrupted by theatre life. She risks such corruption, not so much by reason of any love affairs she may engage in, but by being led into affectation and gross behaviour. Any woman who thinks she can live free of convention is mistaken. The only way for a woman to free herself from the trammels of public opinion is by superior talents joined to high principles. It is also evident from his remarks that Jodin or an acquaintance of Diderot has revealed something about a new liaison into which she has entered. This too Diderot suggests should be a question not of abstract morality but whether she really cares for the man in question. The three paragraphs that make up this moral homily are therefore couched in the spirit of *Realpolitik*. For an actress, morality should be a matter of personal integrity and sincerity, not an unrealistic chastity:

[Paris, rue Taranne; 21 August 1765][31]
I have read, Mademoiselle, the letter you have written to Madame your mother. The feelings of tenderness, devotion and respect that fill it do not surprise me. You are an unfortunate child, but you are a well born one. Since Nature has given you a generous soul, value this gift at its true worth and do nothing to tarnish it.

I am not a prude or pedant; I have no intention of demanding of you a kind of virtue more or less incompatible with the profession you have chosen, and which women of the fashionable world – and I neither respect them nor despise them the more for belonging to this world – rarely manage to preserve, even in the midst of riches and free from the temptations which surround you on every side. Vice seeks you out; they seek out vice. But remember that a woman wins the right to defy the conventions of her sex only by superior talents and the most distinguished qualities of head and heart. A thousand real virtues are needed to cloak an imaginary vice. The more you prize your own inclinations, the more careful you must be over their objects.

People rarely reproach a woman for an attachment to a man of recognised merit. If you do not dare admit to your choice of a man, it will be because you despise yourself for it, and when one despises oneself it is rare not to be despised by others too. You will see that, for a man whom people call a philosopher, my principles are not austere: it would be absurd to ask a woman of the theatre to have the morals of a nun.

The subject of ethics leads Diderot on seamlessly to aesthetic questions. He reminds Jodin that as one not born to the stage but to better things, she would find failure or mediocre success even harder to bear than most. And he describes in a very telling way her gifts as an actress. Since in other moments (for example his letter of December 1766) Diderot was much more likely to chide Jodin for her failings or for unfortunate mannerisms, this passage is of particular interest. She gives the spectator, he says, the impression on the stage of a soul separated from itself, of someone who has become another person. When she leaves her role she seems to come back as from a long journey. This ability to immerse herself in a role was evidently one of the traits that attracted Diderot to her. Here, he must have felt, was an actress after his own heart who could incarnate his dramatic ideas. As a theorist of a new form of drama known variously as 'domestic' or 'bourgeois' tragedy and of a naturalistic style of acting which represented a complete break with the classical Comédie-Française tradition, he found in Jodin a pupil who, he hoped, could put his ideas into action.

She must forget the notion of performing before a mirror, or that there is an audience. The successful actor gives the illusion of naturalness, or rather suggests that there *is* no illusion. Again and again Diderot will tell her to try to achieve tranquil effects, to avoid the declamation and extravagance of contemporary style: 'The greatest sorrows are mute' he reminds her, describing a harrowing scene mimed by Garrick. The great tragedian when in Paris in the late 1750s had claimed to some friends that anything whatever could be conveyed by mime. When the company protested, he took up a cushion exclaiming: 'I am this child's father', and portrayed a father affectionately tossing his child into the air and by accident letting it slip out of his hands and fall through the window. His miming of the father's despair was so terrifying that some spectators had to leave the room:[32]

> Above all, perfect your talent; no one is more wretched, in my view, than a third-rate actress. I do not know whether the applause the public gives you is flattering and especially flattering to one whom birth and education destined to give praise rather than receive it, but I know that for such a person contempt would be all the more unbearable. I have not often heard you perform, but I gained the impression that you had great talent of a kind which it is possible cunningly to simulate, but which cannot be acquired at will: a soul able to *alienate* itself, to stir itself profoundly, to transport itself, to become *this* person or *that* and see and speak to this or that other personage. I was impressed to see how, after an excursion into passion, you seemed to return from far away, as if hardly recognising the place you had been in all the time and the objects which surrounded you.
>
> Acquire grace and freedom; make all your actions simple, natural and easy. One of the keenest satires on our theatre is the need the actor has for a mirror. Learn to do without show and without a mirror; find out the right decorum for your part and keep within it. As few gestures as possible; too many gestures squander energy and destroy nobility. It is the face, the eyes, the whole body which should move, not the arms. To know how to perform a scene of passion is to know very little; the poet has already done half the work. Concentrate on quiet scenes; they are the most difficult. It is here that an actress, if she possesses them, shows her taste, intelligence, finesse, judgement and delicacy. Study the accents of the passions; each passion has its own and they are so powerful that they reach my heart almost without the need for words. It is the primitive language of nature. The meaning of a fine line may escape some listeners, but all are affected by a long sigh drawn from the entrails. Uplifted arms, eyes turned towards heaven, inarticulate sounds, a weak and plaintive voice; they are what touch, move and trouble people's souls. I wish you had seen Garrick play the role of a father who has let his child fall down a well. There is no maxim so much forgotten by our poets than that great sorrows are mute. Remember it on their behalf and palliate the impertinence of their tirades by your acting. It is within your power to gain more effect by silence than by their fine speeches.

Turning next to the personal and familial we hear of the troubles of Madame

Jodin, also newly released we remember from the Salpêtrière, installed in a little apartment and who has just had the misfortune to be robbed of everything she possessed. What security did she have? None save her daughter. Diderot evidently feared Marie Madeleine might find it easy to forget her geographically distant and necessitous relative. His adjurations that she must succour her mother were characteristic of his charitable officiousness. Though extremely busy, for with Voltaire exiled in Ferney he was effectively the leader and organiser of the 'philosophic' fraternity, he was deep in writing art criticism, was advising Catherine the Great on her art purchases and had begun a vast correspondence on the subject of 'posterity' with the sculptor Falconet, he nevertheless saw it as part of his role as philosopher and man of feeling to intervene in his friends' moral lives. Appealing to Marie Madeleine on behalf of her mother constituted part of his programme to make the former responsible for her family and for her own destiny:

> So many things to say, and not a word about the true subject of my letter. It concerns your mother. I think she must be the most unfortunate person I know. Your father thought that nothing made any impression on her. He did not really know her. She was heartbroken at parting from you, and had by no means got over it when she had to bear another disaster. You know me, you know that no motive, however supposedly good, would make me say what was not the precise truth. So take what I tell you literally.
>
> She had gone out and during her absence someone picked her lock and robbed her. They left her her clothes, fortunately; but they took whatever money she had, her table-silver and her watch. She was desperately upset, in fact it has quite altered her. In her distress, she asked for help from all those she might expect to show her friendship and compassion. But you have discovered yourself how rare and meagre and short-lived these feelings are, apart from the fact that people are often embarrassed, especially ones with no experience of poverty, at offering charity, and only do so as the last resort.
>
> Your mother takes such things to heart as much as anyone. She cannot possibly live on her present tiny resources. We have asked her to take her meals with us every day, and we did it, I think, with good enough grace for her to accept without pain. But food, though the most pressing of her needs, is not the only one. It would be bad luck indeed if, her clothes having been spared, she had to part with them. She will fight on, but the fight is a bitter one; it is costing her her health, and you are too good not to warn her against this or prevent it. Now is the moment to prove the sincerity of all you said to her upon leaving.
>
> I have the feeling that you care for my good opinion. So bear in mind that I intend to judge you; and I do not think it is putting too high a price on my opinion to let it depend on how you deal with your mother, particularly in circumstances like the present. If you are going to help her, as you ought to, do not delay. What was mere humanity on our part is a duty on yours. Let it not be said that, on the boards as in the pulpit, the actor and the Sorbonne doctor are as eager as each other in preaching right conduct and as expert in not performing it.

Finally Diderot returns to the ethical questions that opened his dissertation. He invokes his friendship for Jodin's father as giving him certain quasi-parental rights over her. And he does not pull his punches: 'You are violent ... this is the fault most contrary to your sex ... which is to be obliging and kind.' Whereas dissimulation was one of the qualities which women were commonly encouraged to practise (we think of Rousseau's prescriptions for the education of Sophie in *Émile*), Diderot demands straightforward dealing and honesty of his pupil, what he might have thought of as a masculine trait. One of the most intriguing aspects of Diderot's friendship with Jodin is that whilst he sought to mould her into his idea of an acceptable 'feminine' woman as this was understood in the eighteenth century, he nevertheless must have admired the less compliant aspects of her personality. At the same time he lamented her lack of discretion, her quarrelsomeness and recklessness. Rousseau, one feels, would have run away from Jodin in a panic. Diderot, though wishing for her own self-preservation that she would conform to the mores of her sex and class, nevertheless seems to have found her beauty, her assertive character and her intelligence beguiling or he would not have persevered with his mentor role. The femininity he urges her to espouse is, like her theatrical roles, necessary for survival in the world. But he implies that within that role there is room for an honest human being: 'Deceive no one; the woman who deceives, first of all deceives herself.'

> I have the right, from my age, my experience, my friendship with your late father, and the interest I have always taken in you, to hope that the advice I give you on your conduct and your character will not be taken in the wrong spirit. You are violent; people are alienated by violence, it is the fault most contrary to your sex, which is complaisant, tender and gentle. You are vain. If vanity has no good basis, it makes people laugh; and even if one's self-esteem is deserved, it humiliates other people and offends them. I only approve of feeling one's own worth and showing it, when people forget it to an unpardonable degree. Only the short of stature are *always* standing on tiptoe.
>
> I am afraid you may not respect truth enough in what you say. Mademoiselle, be true, make a habit of it. I only permit lying to the wicked and the foolish – to the one, as a disguise; to the other as compensation for the intelligence he lacks. Go in for no tricks, no ruses, no devious strategies. Deceive no one; the woman who deceives, first of all deceives herself. If you have a petty character, you will be petty as an actress. The *philosophe,* who has no religion, cannot have too much morality [*moeurs*]. The actress, whose profession engenders so much prejudice against her morals, cannot be too careful of herself and of the figure she cuts. You are careless and spendthrift; a moment of carelessness can cost dear, and time always revenges itself on the spendthrift.
>
> Pardon these severe strictures and put them down to friendship. You would listen all too easily to the voice of flattery. I wish you every success.
>
> I salute you and am, without insipid and vain compliments,
>
> DIDEROT

There followed a tearful postscript from Mme Jodin and a warm-hearted and more reassuring one from Mme Diderot. With Marie Madeleine in Warsaw, Mme Diderot and Mme Jodin saw the opportunity of buying Polish or Russian fur. Sartorial notes crop up intriguingly throughout the correspondence. Though she largely appears in Diderot's other correspondence as a harrassed and jealous wife, Mme Diderot's affectionate kindness to Marie Madeleine and her mother shows a happier side to her character. Both the Diderots had taken the Jodin family under their wing.

Postscript from Mme Jodin.
My dear child how long it is since I heard from you. Only a letter from you will console me in the trouble I am in which the Lord preserve you from. For I think only of you and what you will write to me and you will send me something out of your goodness. Send it to Mr. Diderot. For it is only they I trust. Meanwhile I embrace you with all my heart and am your affectionate mother Jodin. Adieus my dear child.

Postscript from Mme Diderot
Mademoiselle, I finish your letter begging you not to forget me as regards the fur and if it is cheap you could send it to your Mama letting us know the real price and she might make something out of it. But if it is dear only send me enough for a fringe for a pelisse. We do what we can to console your dear mother who is greatly changed. Look after yourself for her sake and write to her as soon as possible. Adieu I embrace you and am your very humble servant.

wife DIDEROT

This 21 August 1765

When Jodin, barely launched on her new career in a strange country, read Diderot's letter in Warsaw, she must have found more than enough to ponder and worry about in this home news. She had received, in effect, the first chapter of a narrative to be constructed by Diderot of the person he hoped she would become, self-controlled, well-mannered, skilful in her profession, honest in her relationships. All this was predicated on his belief in her good heart, shown in particular towards her mother, whom in spite of the terrible scenes of her adolescence, she continued to support and care for. The other side to this narrative lay in the letters Jodin wrote to Diderot, which we do not possess, reassuring him as to her warmth of heart, care for her mother, success on the stage, but not on the score of her volatile temperament. Against Diderot's construction of a more or less ideal Marie Madeleine Jodin, seeking a semblance of order and self-control in her life, there runs the counter-narrative of her Warsaw adventures.

Notes

1. Denis Diderot, *Paradoxe sur le comédien*, (1777), *Oeuvres Complètes*, ed. Roger Lewinter, X (Paris: Club Français du Livre, 1971), p. 415.

2. Clairon, Mlle Claire-Josèphe Hippolyte Léris (1723–1803), one of the leading actresses in the Comédie-Française, much admired by Voltaire and Diderot for her dramatic powers, she also reformed conventions of costume toward a greater degree of realism. See Henry Lyonnet, *Dictionnaire des comédiens français*, I (Paris: E. Joul, n.d.), pp. 342–51.

3. Diderot, *Paradoxe sur le comédien*, p. 462.

4. Ibid., p. 468.

5. J.-J. Rousseau, *Lettre à Mr. D'Alembert sur les spectacles*, ed. M. Fuchs (Genève: Droz, 1948). For a discussion of the status of actors and Rousseau's contribution to the debate see: Frantz Funck-Brentano, *La Bastille des comédiens: le For l'Evêque* (Paris: Fontemoing, 1903); John McManners, *Abbés and Actresses: the Church and the Theatrical Profession in Eighteenth-Century France* (Oxford: Oxford University Press, 1986); Gaston Maugras, *Les Comédiens hors la loi* (Paris: Calmann Lévy, 1887), Barbara G. Mittman, 'Women and the Theater Arts', *French Women and the Age of Enlightenment*, ed. Samia I. Spencer (Bloomington: Indiana University Press, 1984); Mary Maxwell Moffat, *Rousseau et la querelle du Théâtre au XVIIIe siècle* (Paris: Broccard, 1930); André Tissier, 'La Comédie-Française au XVIIIe siècle ou les contradictions d'un privilège', *Revue d'histoire du théâtre*, 32, II (1980), pp. 127–41.

6. See Diderot, *Correspondance*, XVI, p. 73 for Jodin's 'Ordre de Début'.

7. *Some Unpublished Correspondence of David Garrick*, ed. George Pierce Baker (Boston: Houghton Mifflin and Co, 1907), p. 81.

8. Moffat, *Rousseau et la querelle du théâtre*, pp. 5–15.

9. Maugras, *Les Comédiens hors la loi*, p. 214.

10. Ibid., pp. 203–9.

11. Ibid., pp. 214–19.

12. See Richard J. Evans, *Tales from the German Underworld* (New Haven and London: Yale University Press, 1998), pp. 97–8 for a discussion of the implications of the shift from a status- to a class-defined society.

13. Leonard R. Berlanstein, 'Women and Power in Eighteenth-Century France: Actresses at the Comédie-Française', in Christine Adams, Jack B. Censer and Lisa Jane Graham, eds, *Visions and Revisions of Eighteenth-Century France* (University Park: Pennsylvania State University Press, 1997), p. 162 notes that 'Those who came from outside the profession almost always had very humble origins.' Marie Madeleine Jodin, though evidently reduced to poverty by 1761, was considered by reason of her birth and her father's honourable artisanal status, as well as her education, to be of superior status to the ordinary run of actors and actresses, a point Diderot frequently stresses in his letters.

14. Maugras, *Les Comédiens hors la loi*, p. 217.

15. *Journal des inspecteurs de M. de Sartines*, Première série, 1761–1764 (Paris: Denteu, 1863), p. 83.

16. See Mittman, 'Women and the Theatre Arts', pp. 156–9.

17. Clairon's life is chronicled in *Mémoires de Mlle Clairon* (Paris: Ponthieu, 1822), in Lyonnet, *Dictionnaire des comédiens français*, pp. 342–51, and in Edmond de Goncourt, *Mademoiselle Clairon, d'après ses correspondances et les rapports de police du temps* (Paris: 1889). For a more recent assessment of her political as

well as her theatrical importance see Jeffrey S. Ravel 'Actress to Activist: Mlle Clairon in the Public Sphere of the 1760s', *Theater Survey, The Journal of the American Society for Theater Research*, 35, 1 (May 1994), pp. 73–88.

18. Clairon, *Mémoires*, p. xliii.
19. Moffat, *Rousseau et la querelle du théâtre* lists at least fifty-five works between 1755 and 1767 concerning this theatrical polemic, pp. 403–10.
20. Ibid., pp. 50–54; Denis Diderot, *Discours de la Poésie dramatique*, *Oeuvres Complètes*, pp. 312–13 and P. N. Furbank, *Diderot*, p. 141.
21. Rousseau, *Lettre à Mr. d'Alembert sur les Spectacles*, p. 101.
22. Ibid., p. 106.
23. Ibid., p. 120.
24. Moffat, *Rousseau et la querelle du théâtre*, p. 191; Maugras, *Les Comédiens hors la loi*, p. 266.
25. The Dubois affair has been well chronicled in Grimm's *Correspondance littéraire, philosophique et critique*, ed. Maurice Tourneux, VI (Paris: Garnier Frères, 1877), pp. 258–9; Bachaumont, *Mémoires secrètes*, 3 (7 April 1766), (London: Adamson, 1784), p. 18; Moffat, *Rousseau et la querelle du théâtre*, pp. 224–9; Maugras, *Les Comédiens hors la loi*, Chapter XVII; Mittman, 'Women and the Theatre Arts', pp. 159–60; Funck-Brentano, *La Bastille des comédiens*, pp. 207–18. The last remarks intriguingly that the official documents relative to this affair which were lodged in the Archives de la Bastille have disappeared.
26. Funck-Brentano, *La Bastille des comédiens*, p. 263.
27. Bachaumont, *Mémoires secrètes*, vol. 3, (7 April 1766), p. 18.
28. Funck-Brentano, *La Bastille des comédiens*, p. 217.
29. Lenard R. Berlanstein, 'Women and Power in Eighteenth-Century France: Actresses at the Comédie-Française', p. 156.
30. Ibid., p. 215.
31. Denis Diderot, *Correspondance*, V, p. 346. 'A Mademoiselle Jodin à Varsovie', 21 August 1765, pp. 100–106.
32. Diderot returned to this theme two years later. See Diderot's letter to Mme Riccoboni (27 November 1768). Garrick, who rather unnervingly seems to have performed this grief-stricken mime as a party piece, based it on a real incident. A neighbour of the actor had accidentally dropped his child out of the window and gone mad with grief, thereafter endlessly replaying the scene of the accident. Garrick visited him and observed him with care: 'There it was', said Garrick, 'that I learned to imitate madness; I copied nature, and to that owed my success in King Lear.' *The Works of Arthur Murphy, Esq.* (London: 1786), pp. 28–30, quoted in Ian McIntyre, *Garrick* (London: Allen Lane, 1999), p. 49.

CHAPTER THREE

The view from Warsaw – the Polish adventure

To Marie Madeleine Jodin, recently released from prison and having performed in a few private theatricals at most, the opportunity to travel to Warsaw and to feature as a leading lady in a troupe engaged to play before the Polish court must have been an extraordinary transition. This young woman who had just emerged from the most degrading of prisons was not only to perform before the Polish king, she was to attend court balls and find herself the object of royal admiration. The warnings Diderot would repeatedly send her about not letting fame or admiration go to her head may have been a necessary corrective, but not to have felt a little excitement and even not to have revelled in a certain amount of vanity would have been inhuman.

Jodin probably owed her appointment in the French troupe to the *salonnière,* Mme Geoffrin, a good friend of Diderot and of the new Polish King, Stanislas Poniatowski.[1] Poland had an elected king, a post that passed in 1763 to Stanislas and out of the control of the Electors of Saxony, who had formerly held it. Having travelled in France and England and mixed in philosophical circles, Stanislas sought to turn Warsaw into a Western capital replete with theatres, palaces and cosmopolitan culture. Like other European monarchs, notably Catherine of Russia and Frederick II of Prussia, he had caught the contagion of French Enlightened thought. A fulsome letter from Jean François Noverre, a famous ballet master anxious to gain a commission from Stanislas, gives one some idea of the reputation the King had acquired, or hoped to acquire, as the philosopher king of *les lumières.* Comparing the King to the Emperor Titus and to Saint Louis for his virtues, to Augustus Caesar and Louis XIV for his taste, Noverre praised Stanislas, illuminated as he was by 'the torches of Philosophy and Humanity', for his enlightened patronage of the sciences and the arts.[2]

Noverre's flattery was not entirely unjustified. In 1765 Stanislas founded a Polish literary society to publish Polish literature and a new periodical, *The Monitor*, imitative of *The Spectator*. Three theatre companies, Italian, French and German, were subsidised by the King as well as a native Polish theatre. For the first time the Warsaw public had the opportunity to see the plays of Corneille, Molière, Racine, Voltaire, Diderot and Goldoni. However, these theatrical troupes funded by Stanislas, as well as the ballets and other festivals organised for the court, entailed enormous expense. For example, in the summer of 1765, shortly after Jodin's arrival in Warsaw, the *Gazette de France* reported on a typically lavish fête of the period:

On the 27th of this month, the anniversary of the King's election to the throne, His Majesty, accompanied by all the nobles of the Court as well as the foreign dignitaries gathered on the plain between Mlodum and Tarchomin. Count Moszynski, the High Chamberlain of the Crown, gave there, under a number of marquees, a sumptuous repast, followed by displays of fireworks, which were set off from an island in the middle of the Vistula. Among other spectacles of rejoicing there took place two village weddings. This fête lasted until three o'clock in the morning, after which the King returned to his Palace.[3]

In the following autumn and winter, the *Gazette de France* reported further theatrical performances in Warsaw, 'performed by persons of the greatest distinction', followed by balls and additional sumptuous repasts. At a time of political unrest, with the Polish nobles at loggerheads with the King and with Russia and Prussia preparing the eventual dismemberment of Poland, such cultural projects, reminiscent to his critics of fiddling while Rome burned, became the subject of mockery. Already by 1767 the King was under fire for extravagance and felt himself unable to invite Mlle Clairon to perform in Poland, as he had wished, saying to Mme Geoffrin that he could not afford or justify her fees.[4] 'That same public which amuses itself in my theatre nevertheless blames me for the care and the money that I consecrate to it, especially in this moment of crisis' (letter of 20 March 1767 to Madame Geoffrin).[5]

But when Marie Madeleine Jodin arrived, probably in April 1765, Stanislas Poniatowski was only beginning his cultural experiment, and hopes were high.[6] Jodin was recruited along with the other actors gathered together by the Polish trader, Czempinski, whom the King had charged with forming a suitable troupe under the direction of Carlos Tomatis. They were assisted by Mme Geoffrin, who recommended Louis François Villiers, an actor-cum-entrepreneur, as theatre manager, under Tomatis. Villiers was given a free hand in the choice of actors, provided that he kept to an agreed budget. The actors' contract gave them the exalted title of 'artists to the Polish King'. However, the reality was that the majority of this troupe had never acted before.[7] Indeed, Jodin's own apprenticeship cannot have been more than a few months, yet she passed as an experienced actress, which no doubt reflected her native talent but also the still greater inexperience of her colleagues. Even before leaving Paris, Czempinski warned the King of the theatrical débâcle that was likely to result: 'I cannot claim, despite my best efforts, that I have succeeded in forming a good company this year.'[8] Stanislas and his chancellor, Count Moszynski, who had overall responsibility for the regulation of the theatres, soon recognised that in this Comédie-Française they had commissioned a group of amateurs. Even worse, by mid-summer, the French troupe found itself competing with an Italian company, which boasted far better singers and dancers, and for whom the Warsaw audiences deserted the Comédie-Française in droves.[9]

Our knowledge of the French troupe in Stanislas's court is partly indebted to a series of twice-weekly reports by a Saxon agent in the Polish capital, Johann Heyne (or Heine). He was employed as an informer on all aspects of the Polish court and political life by a pretender to the Polish throne, Prince Xavier of Saxony (1730–1806), the younger son of Augustus III, the previous king of Poland and Elector of Saxony. After the election of Stanislas Augustus in 1763, Xavier still continued to nourish hopes of gaining the Polish throne. At this period Xavier was living in Dresden, acting as co-regent during the minority of the hereditary elector. Heyne, on his patron Xavier's behalf, would have been hostile to Stanislas. His reports, therefore, stressed the extravagance of court life, quarrels with the nobility and, as he saw it, the failure or futility of the King's ambitious cultural projects, such as the theatre.[10] Heyne also criticised Stanislas' chamberlain, Count Moszynski, who he said: 'plays the role of a handy helper, to the astonishment of rational people as to why he has this lowly obsession. Perhaps he is motivated in his chasing after this un-newsworthy retinue by the vanity of appearing experienced or capable or possessing flair.'[11]

Unlike the enthusiastic spin-doctoring of the *Gazette de France*, noted above, Heyne's reviews of court festivities and the French troupe's performances were damning. On the occasion of the King's birthday, 8 May 1765, the Comédie-Française performed two operas by Egid Romoald Duni.[12] Whereas other accounts described this fete as a delightful occasion, Heyne reported that the production 'inclined one to vomit'. 'This gang of actors', he went on, 'is completely incompetent … First, these hooligans perform a pastoral play, accompanied by the loud and exaggerated applause of the King. Then the music diddled on for an hour while they got dressed for the proper play.' While it is likely that the level of incompetence reported by Heyne may have been as bad as he suggested, it is also clear from this and subsequent reports to Xavier, that the King's patronage of the French troupe, part of his larger project to bring Western European culture to what Diderot unkindly called 'gloomy Poles and barbarians', was being reported in its most negative light.[13] All this was intended to reflect badly both on the actors and, of course, on Stanislas himself.

It was not at all unusual for totally inexperienced actors to launch themselves on the stage, hoping to find indulgent audiences. At the same period, Casanova recounts the case of a French actress he met in St Petersburg who had been recruited to the *Comédie Italienne* by an actor whom she met by chance. She had had absolutely no previous experience, but he convinced her that she had a wonderful theatrical future. The girl told Casanova:

> I thought that just as in Paris, a young person joins the chorus of the Opera or the ballets without having learned to sing or dance, so one joins an acting troupe. How could I think otherwise when an actor like Clerval (the man who engaged her) told me that I was born to shine on the stage? Two weeks after our arrival here I made my debut, and I was given a terrible reception.[14]

In the eighteenth century, actors learned from their errors and from watching other actors, but there was little formal instruction, a point Diderot made to Jodin in his letter of December 1766, when he warned her against expecting to receive coaching from colleagues in the profession. One recalls Mlle Clairon's enlightened proposal to found an acting academy which would have had as one of its functions the training of actors. As far as the Warsaw theatre was concerned, it seems clear that whatever native skills the actors possessed, the majority of Villiers's newly organised French troupe were in the position of Casanova's St Petersburg débutante.

To imagine the responses of Marie Madeleine Jodin to life on the Warsaw stage requires a glimpse of the city life in which she found herself. Warsaw when Jodin arrived in the April or May of 1765, was a remarkable mixture of the primitive and the sophisticated, as recounted in the memoirs of a contemporary English visitor:

> This metropolis itself seems to me, like the Republic of which it is the head, to unite the extremes of civilization and of barbarism, of magnificence and wretchedness, of splendour and misery; but unlike all other great cities of Europe, these extremes are not softened, approximated and blended by any intermediate gradations ... Palaces and sheds, the mansions of the great, and the cottages of the poor, compose exclusively the larger portion of Warsaw. It is like an assemblage of nobles and slaves, of lords and vassals, such as the darkness of the middle ages when feudal tyranny prevailed universally might have exhibited, but which happily for mankind, is now nowhere to be seen except in Poland ... At the close of the late reign, in 1763, Warsaw was almost wholly unpaved. Even at present, and in this season of the year, after violent rain, many of the streets are totally impassable on foot and nearly so on horseback ... In front of Stanislas' palace, so indecently neglected are the sewers that the smell is pestilential ... Yet, by a singular contradiction, Warsaw presents under other aspects all the refinement of Paris, the arts of Florence and the splendour of Petersburgh.[15]

Jodin's experience in Warsaw, like the city itself, would combine the grand and the base, the elevated and the farcical.

As might have been predicted, the French actors who had been gathered to play in Poland proved something less than an unalloyed success. In July 1765, Heyne reported that the Comédie-Française could not attract an audience of more than eighty; the actors were incapable of singing (a skill demanded of all actors, not just operatic singers), nor was their spoken delivery much better. Given the lack of success of Villiers' direction, Count Moszynski found an opportunity to make a clean sweep of the French troupe. In October 1765, the actor-manager Josse Rousselois, who had just left Vienna as a consequence of the court being in mourning, came to Warsaw and was appointed to replace Villiers. He reconstituted the Comédie-Française as a troupe of seventeen actors, eleven from the former Viennese company and six from the original Villiers

company who were thought worthy to be retained. Among these were Mlle
Jodin and de Marsan (the protégé of Mlle Clairon and Mme Geoffrin).[16]

By August 1766, Jodin, although she had no singing voice and was not
suitable for the operatic interludes accompanying most dramatic performances,
had been judged to be capable of performing leading roles of queens, noble
mothers and so on. Her contract, signed by Auguste Moszynski, 'Stolink', ran
for two years from 1 April 1766 to 1 April 1768. Jodin's salary was four hundred
and seventy-six ducats and seven florins per year.[17] She wrote to Diderot and
her mother, announcing her success and exulting in her feelings of excitement
and triumph.

The troubles of the French troupe did not end with Moszynski's efforts at
reorganisation. When the French actors in Warsaw had found themselves
confronted with declining audiences, they had written to the King in August
1765 accusing Tomatis of favouring the Comédie-Italienne and neglecting their
fortunes. Tomatis seems to have possessed a gift for intrigue and passed off his
troupe's failures on others. He retained Stanislas's favour long after it was clear
that he was unable or unwilling to carry out his contractual obligations. He
succeeded in securing large, and it would seem, unjustified sums for himself
from the King, as well as a title because he had been willing to marry one of the
King's mistresses, Catherine Gattai, a dancer. As reported in the *Gazette de
France* of 12 October 1765:

> His Majesty, wishing to show M. Tomatis how satisfied he was with the
> success of the commissions which he fulfilled in his trip to Italy, has re-
> established him as the Director General of Entertainments, and, at the same
> time, has given him the title of Count with a pension of 1500 ducats, in
> addition to his travel expenses.[18]

A major scandal, erupting in the spring of 1766, illustrates the hothouse
atmosphere in which the court and the acting fraternity lived. Tomatis had entered
into a feud with Mme Binetti, an Italian dancer much admired by the King and
therefore a rival to Mlle Gattai (now Mme Tomatis) for his favour. After a
period of complex intrigue and rivalry, Count Branicki, a champion of the Binetti
faction, fought a duel with the adventurer Casanova, then visiting Warsaw,
who had taken the part of Mlle Gattai. Both duellists survived, but Casanova
was forced to leave Warsaw hurriedly.[19] The feud did not end there. Following
the duel with Casanova, Branicki's life was thought to be in danger. As the
Gazette de France reported: 'The King often goes to the Palace of Prince
Poniatowski, his brother, to see Count Branicki whose wound does not yet give
any hope of a cure.'[20] A friend of the wounded man, named Biszewski, Colonel
of Light Infantry in the King's Household, was so enraged at Branicki's state,
that blaming Tomatis as the instigator of the duel, he attacked him first with a
pistol, which missed, and then with a sword, which wounded him. Count
Moszynski, who witnessed the attack, must have despaired over his role as

Cultural Secretary to the Crown. Heyne, with his usual hyperbole, compared the life of the court and the theatre to Sodom.

Not only was Tomatis embroiled in personal vendettas, in his professional capacity he did not enjoy good relations with his French actors. They accused him of treating the French actresses with grossness and contempt.[21] Mlles Brabant, Thélis, Cohendet and Jodin all complained of 'terrible unpleasantness' and 'brutality' by the director. They also complained about their managers, first Villiers and then Rousselois. In an interesting argument over working conditions we find the actors attempting with some success to assert their customary rights to free theatre tickets and transport. These were not frivolous demands. To watch other actors perform was effectively the only formal training actors enjoyed. As for transport by carriages, since most actors paid for their own costumes and the streets of Warsaw were filthy even by eighteenth-century standards, to arrive at the theatre unbespattered required a carriage of some description. On this and other occasions, the actors campaigned with considerable solidarity.

Count Moszynski attempted to bring discipline to what Heyne called this 'rabble' by drawing up a new series of strict regulations, specifying what seats the actors were allowed to occupy in the theatre (there were attempts to segregate them from the paying patrons), limiting their use of a carriage to those days on which they performed (no gadding about), instituting fines for late arrival at rehearsal and decreeing that failure to perform on schedule or causing a disturbance could result in prosecution and imprisonment.[22] Any actor who engaged in a quarrel with his comrades would be put in prison and if the quarrel went so far as coming to blows, s/he would be submitted to the judgement of the Grand Marshal. Any actor who was dismissed as a punishment following a major offence would pay a penalty. The threat of imprisonment for relatively small infractions, particularly the refusal to perform when required, hung over the Warsaw actors, as over their French counterparts. These regulations, which stipulated the contractual relationship between the court and the actors, differed from the notions of contract of employment that we think of today in certain important respects. As in other European court theatres, the actors were employed by the king or prince and owed a duty of obedience to him. Disobedience became, effectively, *lèse-majesté*. While the employer, the Crown, contracted to pay the actors and to provide transport to the theatre, the emphasis was on their obedience to the sovereign's 'pleasure'. Enshrined in these contractual relations, therefore, was the notion of sovereign and very possibly arbitrary power on the part of the employer, and of obligation and obedience on the part of the employee.

By October 1766, when the company of Josse Rousselois had replaced that of Villiers (Moszynski and the King being utterly disillusioned with the latter's direction), Jodin, as one of six actors from the original troupe to be asked to join the already experienced players from Vienna, had achieved something like celebrity status in Warsaw. From Paris, Diderot watched Jodin's progress in Poland with a mixture of anxiety and admiration. His protégée was well launched as a leading lady and was apparently earning considerable sums. The dress ordered for her performances (actors wore elaborate contemporary costumes, regardless of the period of the play) consisted of taffeta, trimmed with green chenille and decorated with fifty rows of pearls. It cost 108 ducats, nearly a quarter of her yearly salary.

All did not go smoothly with Rousselois, the new actor-manager. An undated letter, in Jodin's handwriting, from the Comédie-Française to the King, probably written in the spring of 1766, complained about Rousselois's rudeness, his lack of consideration for his actors, and that he relayed injurious gossip concerning them, 'of the most indecent and offensive nature', particularly in relation to M. d'Hercourt and Mlle Jodin. This complaint helps to explain the major row that Jodin was soon to have with Rousselois, particularly as the letter notes that 'several of our ladies have been insulted by him', suggesting both grossness of language and unwelcome sexual overtures. Furthermore, the letter writers claimed that in answer to a complaint from Mlle Dorsainville, Rousselois remarked that he 'never bothered to reply to fools or sluts'.[23] This less than conciliatory behaviour to women would be replicated in his further dealings with Jodin.

Underlying these quarrels between managers and actors lay the question of sexual politics. Though the troupe functioned in a quasi-democratic and sexually egalitarian manner, it was clear that gender inequality persisted. Thus actresses could be routinely insulted in sexual terms while still prized for their professional acting skills. Jodin, who championed the concepts of honour and respect for her sister actresses, was soon to find herself pilloried for sexual profligacy, a judgement not likely to afflict her fellow actors. These tensions would re-emerge in subsequent engagements and were characteristic of the distrust of 'public women' both on the stage and in court circles.[24]

Sometime in early August 1766, a new wave of dissension and speculation hit the Comédie-Française. A 'public letter' was circulated in Warsaw (and copied by Heyne to Prince Xavier on 15 August) which analysed in meticulous and often witty detail the characters and acting skills of all members of the French and Italian troupes. Speculation raged about its authorship.[25] Though purporting to be written by 'a simple Pole from the country' to his more sophisticated and widely travelled friend, the author was someone, it was patently clear, with a detailed knowledge of the theatrical troupes then acting in Poland and familiar with the dramatic theories of Diderot and Riccoboni, as well as sympathetic to Polish nationalism.[26]

'My plan', the anonymous author wrote, 'was to study the genius of each actor, to understand the character appropriate to his part, to grasp the nuances by which he varied his roles, to see, in a word, if he had enough feeling to make others feel.' Polish theatre audiences were not genuinely critical, he implied; they were in the grip of cabals: 'Recently I applauded a speech rendered powerfully and truthfully; unfortunately I did not know that the actress [possibly Jodin?] was not a member of certain accepted cliques.' The theory of *good* acting which emerged from the generally negative comments about the individual actors closely paralleled the ideas about greater naturalness in acting put forward by Diderot.

Negative attributes enumerated by the 'simple Pole from the country' concerned artificiality, coldness, lack of variety, exaggerated movements and declamation, all the stock-in-trade of classical French acting. For example, the actor Clavareau was described as gauche, addicted to excessive gesturing and striving for sublime effects which only made him seem ridiculous. His daughter, Victorine, was dismissed as being without grace or bearing, although another daughter, Lucie, was praised as more graceful and lively. D'Hercourt's acting was an example of 'art which crushes nature, either too cold or too exaggerated'. Rousselois, the new director, came off no better, being characterised as a has-been, a mere shadow of himself, an actor who ought only to play peasant roles, but who unfortunately attempted heroic and kingly ones. The writer concluded, damning with faint praise, that though Rousselois was vulgar, he did not lack intelligence. The most favourable though still somewhat jaundiced mentions were of de Marsan and Jodin. The former, who exaggerated in tragic roles, was praised for his good looks and his graceful air. Marie Madeleine Jodin's chief flaw was to hold an inflated idea of her own powers, precisely what Diderot had warned her against: 'La Jodin has talent: she would have more if she thought less well of herself. Her claims to play in the style of Dumesnil and Clairon do not stand up.' Her worst fault, according to this critic, was a tendency to bend forward on the stage, what Diderot was to refer to as an ugly rocking of the body (December 1766). 'I gather from some young gentlemen who have heard you that you do not know how to hold yourself on the stage, that you sway about in a very unpleasant manner.' One notes that this sketch of the French troupe, first circulated in Warsaw in early as August, had travelled to Paris by December.

The effect of these no doubt accurate but devastating sketches on the Comédie-Française, already demoralised by the Tomatis affair, Rousselois's management style and Moszynski's stern if sensible new regulations over the company, seems to have been poisonous. Jodin, who had a reputation for arrogance and overweening social and intellectual pretentions, was accused of being the author. It was perhaps, the relatively favourable mention of de Marsan, with whom she may have had an affair, and of herself, with some criticism but more praise, which gave her colleagues this idea, as well as her known friendship with Diderot and her espousal of his dramatic theories. Rousselois, in particular, cannot have been pleased by his pen portrait as a superannuated clown. Nevertheless, Diderot evidently did not think the sketch was by Jodin and she vehemently denied it.

Suspicion has also focused on Mme Geoffrin, then visiting Stanislas Poniatowski, especially as she had been instrumental in forming the French troupe in the first place. However, the fact that her fellow actors accused Marie Madeleine Jodin of being the author of this clever, witty, but by no means laudatory account of their performance, reveals that they believed she was intellectually capable of doing so.[27] She already had the dubious reputation for a woman in the eighteenth-century of being an intellectual. But Jodin continued to deny authorship: 'Mademoiselle Jodin has written to my wife', wrote a court official, Karl Schmidt to a correspondent in August, 'telling her that the French actors attribute the anonymous piece to her, though she swears to have taken no part at all in it.' As was customary with such documents, the 'public letter' was widely circulated. It had reached Schmidt in Marienburg by 12 August when he reported: 'The portrait of the actors is admirable; it is so true to life that here people recognised each actor simply by my reading the sketch aloud, without my naming a single person. Count Fleming soon recognised little 'Lucie' [Clavareau].'[28] Diderot rapidly got wind of it too, as is clear from comments in his subsequent letters to Jodin. If neither Mme Geoffrin nor Jodin, was the author, it was certainly written by someone with inside knowledge of the theatre and it is entirely possible that Jodin contributed her opinions even if she had not actually written the letter.

There was thus covert warfare between Jodin and her fellow actors. A week or two later (on 19 or 20 August) a second anonymous letter was circulated, containing the most ferocious personal attack on her. One gathers from it that a bawdy play or improvisation, *The Pleasures of Daphne* – allegedly by Frosy or Frocy, one of the actors of the original Villiers troupe and a minor playwright – had recently been performed or perhaps merely circulated, satirising 'Daphne's' vain behaviour, her loose morals and implicating the King, Stanislas Poniatowski, in her scandalous activities. The text of the play has not survived, but the author of the 'second letter' exploited it with great venom as a weapon against Jodin. He or she wrote as follows:

> I learn, Mademoiselle, that ill-intentioned persons claim that M. Frosy meant to have sketched your adventures in his skit, 'The Amusements of Daphne'. I have read this work and if the testimony of a disinterested man can calm your alarms, I dare to assure you that if some traits resemble you, others completely destroy that illusion.
>
> All those who know you, on seeing this portrait, cried in one voice: Jodin is the model! The adventures in the *Palais Royale*, the name of Mlle Louis d'or [gold-digger, money-bags], the apple-green dress [possibly a reference to the grand dress made for Jodin in January 1766 which had a green chenille trim], the little dog Medor, the address cards and more than all that, your

little two-year period of retirement in la Salpêtrière, these traits only seem to fit you. But a closer examination has put me on the path of truth, for three reasons.

First Observation

The person that is being described in 'The Amusements of Daphne' is designated by the flattering title of 'Melpomène de la Pologne'. Since you are ignorant of more things than you might imagine, it is right to tell you that Melpomène is the Muse presiding over Tragedy and superior talents are sometimes designated by the names of the Muses who preside over these same talents. Thus with reason, Mademoiselle Dangeville is called the Thalée of France, Mademoiselle Sallé the Terpsichore, etc. But a Jodin Melpomène of Poland would be a prostitution of the title. If the author had you in view, the irony is too blatant. Do justice to yourself and admit with good grace that of the ten or dozen roles that you have played since coming to Warsaw, you have not grasped a single one; that you have often taken fervour for warmth, the trivial for the natural, the languorous for the tender, contortions and cries for the viscera of expression.

No one has been fooled by this and the general opinion is that conceit does not create talent. Why the sameness in all your roles? Are all these characters the same or do you not know the art of grasping their differences? What can people of taste say when they see you play Mademoiselle Argaut as though she were Madame la Resource, Agrippine as though she were Monime. And after all this you have the effrontery to say to the King himself that within a year you will not dread Mlle Clairon as a rival. In one year, in ten years you will acquire something: this will be a stronger dose of conceit and impertinence and perhaps a greater ease at mounting a horse, but as far as talent is concerned, nature has not given you a grain of it.

Second Observation

In 'The Amusements of Daphne' the latter is described as beautiful; take this letter in one hand and your mirror in the other and let us analyse your face. Two cold inanimate cats' eyes, incapable of expression, a twisted nose, a mouth interminably large, a hard skin, spotted, with more holes than a sieve, the throat of a [market woman], shoulders where one still sees traces of the whip-lashes that you received in la Salpêtrière, big flat feet, a walk like an inn servant's, add to this an air of dirtiness and filthiness which even the most brilliant hairdo cannot hide. Allow me on this occasion to give you some sound advice. Instead of renting country houses, you should buy some underclothes, some petticoats and some handkerchiefs.

Third Observation

The mere title of the play persuades one that it is not about you. 'The Amusements of Daphne' is about a young and tender shepherdess, beautiful and sweet, naïve and decent. You are not young. You are at least thirty years old; we are sure, in spite of the erasures on you baptismal certificate and your obstinate cry that you are only twenty-three. With all your pretensions to beauty, you are not beautiful. You have not yet seen at your feet even the dirtiest Polish moustache. You are not tender [compassionate]. Of voluptuousness, you only know its caprices and detours. It was said of you that it was not surprising that you had failed in the role of Zaïre, because in order to express tenderness well, one must first be capable of feeling it. You have no sense of decency, the motives for your break up with Marsan, which you have not been able to hide, your favourite expression of 'Sacré de J.F.' and the publicity given to your adventures, do not publicize a sense of decency. You are not naïve and truthful; a thousand similar faults point up your falsity and perfidy.

You are not sweet. The slightest contradiction to your own feelings, even proposed with politeness, make you exhale gross insults. You live without a servant because none can put up with the violence of your behaviour and of your language. If the author of 'The Amusements of Daphne' had had the intention of depicting you, he would have chosen another style, for example the fury of Messalina [legendary Roman prostitute], the festivals of Priapus [erotic festivals] or the pastimes of Laïs [a famous Greek courtesan].[29]
So here are a few slight observations on your talents, your face, your character; one could make them too about your wit, and your pride would gain nothing. You seem to think that wit consists of persiflage (or sarcasm). Liveliness of mind is agreeable but only when it is accompanied with fairness, sweetness, moderation, politeness, wit and reason. This is what makes a cultivated person according to Rousseau.

If you find any hard and humiliating truths in this letter, pardon the sincerity of a friend who would like to correct you and in order to succeed better will make his observations public.

This poisoned missive reads like a parody of Diderot's letters (see Chapters 2 and 4), a deformed echo of his sometimes hectoring, severe but always friendly advice. It is as though the author, an intimate of Jodin, had read her letters from Diderot and was adopting the most wounding possible version of the same style.[30] In Warsaw, ephemeral writings were all the rage:

fragments of quatrains, stitchings of flyleaves, replications and duplications, newspapers, pornography, whole theatrical works, odes; they passed from hand to hand: Polish, French, Latin; the word was a weapon; it appeared to determine or did determine the life of the country, the honour of patriots, the actor's fate.[31]

In the libel directed against Jodin, though the author of the letter poses as a critic, he or she indulges primarily in personal abuse, especially focused on Jodin's supposed sexual behaviour. One plausible interpretation of this second letter, apart from the obvious one that the actress has made enemies, is that she was the focus of bitter jealousy from her fellow actors. The anonymous writer alleges that: she is a bad actress; she is ugly; her character is violent, her language crude and her sexual habits perverse. Overall she violates accepted standards of femininity.

One of the accusations levelled against Jodin was that she had boasted to the King that she did not fear the great Mlle Clairon as a rival. In addition, she was suspected – and possibly with reason – of having had an affair with the King. Clues emerge from a number of sources. The second public letter refers to the *Palais Royal*, presumably the King's palace in Warsaw, but also the well-known *rendez-vous* for prostitutes in Paris, as 'Daphne's' place of assignation. Heyne also reported the existence of a lampoon about the French troupe and the King, indubitably *The Pleasures of Daphne*, and that the King had offered a reward for information about the author, suggesting that he was concerned to suppress gossip over his private life. The second public letter was sent to Stanislas, presumably with the intent of discrediting Jodin to him.[32] The idea that she may have been his mistress is strengthened by a letter which Jodin wrote to Stanislas Poniatowski in 1777, eleven years after her Polish sojourn. It was distinctly familiar, indeed flirtatious, in tone. She spoke of 'the pleasure that I had the happiness to give you, and [I am hopeful] that the desire will awaken in you to see me again. You will find me entirely disposed to satisfy you.'[33]

However, the aspect of the second 'public letter' which must have devastated the young actress the most was the revelation – destined to become public, the anonymous writer tells her with gloating – of her imprisonment in la Salpêtrière. Jodin's efforts to start a new life on the stage, to use her talents in a profession which, though as Diderot frequently reminded her, was beneath the status to which she had been born, yet a profession which permitted her to be financially independent and to win acclaim and admiration, all this would have seemed to her ruined by the letter's two damning asides: 'your little retreat of two years in la Salpêtrière' and 'the traces of whip-lashes that you received in la Salpêtrière'. In eighteenth-century Europe, part of the purpose of imprisonment and in particular of corporal punishment, often publicly inflicted, was to shame and humiliate the offender, in order to underline that crime entailed a fall in status. To be imprisoned with prostitutes, whatever the truth of the events surrounding one's incarceration, was in most people's understanding to be imprisoned as a prostitute. Marie Madeleine Jodin must have hidden her carceral past when she went to Poland, but servants or a lover could have read her letters and indeed seen the marks on her shoulders. It must have seemed to Jodin on that day in August that her project of self-reconstruction was in ruins.

It is doubtless no accident that on the very day (or at most the day after) of her receiving this shattering blow, Jodin was involved in a most spectacular fracas with Rousselois and her fellow actors. The sequence of events was as follows: Rousselois had posted the list of actors for a forthcoming play, placing the letter M. (Monsieur) before each. Jodin, arriving for rehearsal, then had added 'Mademoiselle' before the names of the women actors – in order, so she said when Rousselois upbraided her, to give him a lesson in politeness. By accident or deliberately (and one must suspect the latter) she added 'Mademoiselle' before d'Hercourt's name as well, clearly impugning his masculinity. Alas, this was to prove a joke too far. There are three accounts of what ensued, in the form of letters to Count Moszynski from Rousselois, Jodin and d'Hercourt. They agree broadly on facts but not on motives.

Rousselois stated that following shocking remarks from Jodin, he had attempted to return to his office, '*after having told her that I would not answer a word to a woman*' (our italics). According to Jodin, Rousselois began abusing her with epithets only suitable for prostitutes. Rousselois admitted that under stress, the expression 'salope' (whore) escaped him. This was almost certainly a reference to the second public letter that, as we know, conveyed the information that Jodin had spent two years in la Salpêtrière. D'Hercourt at this juncture entered the fray, 'annoyed at the poor joke Mademoiselle Jodin had played against his name', and remonstrated with her. Jodin then spat in his face, she claimed, inadvertently – they claimed, deliberately and, it was agreed by all three, that d'Hercourt kicked her. D'Hercourt said in his version:

> Mademoiselle Jodin having made me a laughing stock by writing the word *mademoiselle* above my name, on the poster that lists rehearsals, I reproached her with all possible moderation. Mademoiselle Jodin's reply, having been as full of hauteur as her tone was scornful, reminded me at that moment of the other aspects of her spitefulness with regard to me [this might have to do with her reputed authorship of his unfavourable review] and I said to her that she was a very wicked woman. At that, Mademoiselle Jodin spat in my face, an affront so humiliating that for an instant I was deprived of my reason, and I had the misfortune to allow a kick to escape me.[34]

As may be imagined, the repercussions were fearful. Rousselois wrote a letter, signed also by Clavareau, Duponchelle, Moulan, Duclos and Caron (but interestingly not by de Marsan) to Moszynski, complaining of these scandalous events, whilst d'Hercourt hastened to write him a letter of humble apology for having kicked a woman. Some of the willingness of Jodin's fellow actors to bear witness against her may go back to the first public letter. Clavareau, Duponchelle, Moulan and Duclos had all received very bad reviews, as of course had Rousselois and d'Hercourt.

Jodin, for her part, demanded a public apology from her tormentors, insisting to Count Moszynski, with whom she seems to have been on good terms, that her assailants should appear on the stage of the theatre and apologise to her on their knees. This dramatic representation, not surprisingly, never took place. Moszynski having received the letter of explanation and remorse from d'Hercourt, who may also have been fined, did not countenance Jodin's insistence on his and Rousselois's public humiliation. One fears that she was committing the very error that Diderot was to warn her against, of carrying her stage roles of queens and leading ladies into real life. On the other hand, she was clearly outraged at the imputation to her reputation. Writing to Moszynski, Jodin expressed her humiliation and anger:

> After having wiped off all the filth that his [Rousselois's] mouth had vomited over me, I said to him that his remarks were ill suited to a man who sold his honour. [The imputation, according to Rousselois, that she called him a pimp.] I finish, Sir, by asking you in justice that these two gentlemen ask pardon of me on their knees in the theatre ... I have been sufficiently insulted that I should not be condemned for saying that I will not perform again until I have obtained satisfaction.[35]

On receiving Rousselois's and d'Hercourt's letters, Moszynski wrote to Jodin saying that both men as well as the other signatories had given evidence that she was the aggressor. She was commanded to return to rehearsals and play her assigned parts:

> If I am obliged to judge this affair, I can only do so in light of so many witnesses worthy of belief and it seems to me that this affair will not do you credit. I can, therefore, give you no better counsel than to put off a final decision on the matter until tomorrow and to play your role without further rehearsals. It is not up to you whether I make my decision [about the affair] today or tomorrow but it is your obligation to submit to what I order you to do, without which I will be forced, in spite of myself, to constrain you to obey or to take such steps as would another time convince you to obey your superiors' orders.[36]

Moszynski, in asserting his authority, in accordance with the regulations he had drawn up, was acting no differently than had Richelieu in the Dubois affair by threatening Jodin with prison if she did not obey: 'I will be forced, in spite of myself to constrain you to obey or to take such steps as would another time convince you to obey your superior's orders.' He turned out, however, to have a softer heart than Richelieu's and seems not to have carried out his threat.

Jodin still adamantly refused to return to the stage, saying she could no longer work with the troupe. Commentators (Roth in his edition of the Diderot correspondence and Lewanski), have implicitly and explicitly put this down to her violent temperament, an idea encouraged, as will be clear in Chapter 4, by Diderot's admonitory letters. While there is little doubt that temperamental excess may have had a good deal to do with fuelling this row, the effect has been to characterise Jodin as a more or less irrational figure, confronting the reasonable Rousselois and d'Hercourt with her diva-like tantrums. This seems a very partial view of affairs. The initial inserting of 'Mademoiselle', in order, as she said, to teach Rousselois a lesson in politeness, stemmed from her attempt to assert actresses right to a title. They were normally referred to only with the pejorative or at least dismissive, definite article, 'la', as in 'la Clairon'.[37] Other evidence of her motives emerges, in two short notes to Count Moszynski. Here she pleaded that she was too upset, both by the betrayal of her comrades and *by re-reading a scurrilous letter that she had just received to perform in the scheduled play* (my italics). It is clear that she blamed the quarrel on her distress at discovering the two libels in circulation about her. She begged for an interview with the Count:

> I am just packing my things to go wherever it pleases you to take me. I have all possible respect for your orders, for your illustrious existence. But the fact that my comrades have made depositions against me is yet another injustice that adds to my distress and makes it impossible for me to perform on the stage without having gained satisfaction. When engaging myself for the services of this court, I had not imagined that one could be treated with so little consideration. This is the way travelling actors are treated when

they perform on the public squares. I await the soldiers to arrive [to arrest me], for I am not sufficiently calm to rehearse my role.

Jodin remained devastated by the satirical bombshell directed against her, as well as by the lack of support she received from her fellow actors. Her efforts to stand on her honour and demand an unconditional apology from Rousselois and d'Hercourt not only failed but would have seemed absurd to many, including the generally sympathetic Moszynski. Yet a man in her position might well have fought a duel, as Casanova did, and would have been seen as justified in defending his honour, even in an illegal manner. In the quarrel, Rousselois had almost certainly made reference to the wounding accusations in the second public letter. Why should Jodin not, like her male counterparts, have had recourse to the concept of honour when her reputation had been impugned? As she said to Moszynski, 'Your Excellency knows very well that every *état* [status] has its concept of honour. Mine at the present moment is not to perform with a company against which I have such grievances that I am rendered incapable of fulfilling my obligations.'[38] Moszynski, having written his stern letter, agreed to see Jodin; he was certainly not dismissive, but neither was he prepared to authorise the dramatic scene of apology and contrition that she had envisaged:

> I appeal to your Excellency to have Messieurs Rousselois and d'Hercourt brought to the theatre, to order them to make their complaint and to hear mine afterwards. He who is found to be in the wrong will undergo what I demand, namely to ask pardon on his knees and to wait until he is told to rise. The whole matter will take no more than half and hour. Then, my mind at rest, I will be in a fit state to act the play.[39]

Jodin recalled bitterly, in a reference to *The Pleasures of Daphne* and the second 'public letter', 'the damaging gossip which has been spread about concerning my morals, my heart and my character, which have made me lose, Monseigneur, both your esteem and that of other eminent people.' She expressed outrage at the way her reputation had been ruined and refused point-blank to perform again in Warsaw without having obtained satisfaction:

> I am resolved to suffer anything rather than to perform without having been granted satisfaction. I prefer death to hypocrisy. If I cannot find justice five hundred leagues from my parents, my friends and my protectors, and if the most sacred rights of society are treated with derision, then I do not wish to contribute to the pleasures of those who despise me and are the first to break the fundamental laws which make up the security of citizens.[40]

This letter represents a remarkably daring piece of self-assertion from a woman and an actress who knew she risked prison. It is couched in the language of rights, citizenship and natural law, the very Enlightenment discourse which would be so fully developed in her *Vues législatives pour les femmes*.

Fortunately for Jodin, her interview with Moszynski appears to have placated him, though in writing to the King he reported it with heavy irony:

La Jodin has just left my house; there were tears and eloquence. I answered as emolliently as I could, always bringing my moral homily to bear on the necessity of subordination [i.e. following orders] and on the merit of gentleness. What disturbed her the most was that 'Hospital' [prison]. I said that surely it was a misunderstanding, here, as it was in Paris, when they took her there – and 'pace, pace, pace' will be, I hope, the end of this memorable debate. The despairing Milady is insistent. You will have difficulties in keeping her from going public. Your financial discovery is a good one. I will use it.[41]

According to Moszynski, the actress's distress arose from the revelations concerning her Salpêtrière imprisonment as well as from the threat that, if she disobeyed orders, she could be imprisoned again. Though emollient in his approach, he noted her histrionics, referring to her somewhat patronisingly as 'la Jodin' and 'Milady' (implying that she put on airs). Finally, he insisted that she honour her contract and return to the theatre, whilst warning the King about the possibility of a continuing public scandal. It seems evident that the linkage of Jodin's name with the King and her threat to 'go public' (whatever that might have meant) was not a welcome prospect.

The upshot of the whole anguishing affair was that Jodin determined to leave Warsaw. She was obliged first, however, to obtain permission from Stanislas to break her contract which ran from April 1766 to April 1768.[42] Before leaving, probably in the late autumn of 1766, she was in almost constant correspondence with Count Moszynski, trying to arrange for her release from the troupe and to persuade him to settle her not inconsiderable debts. In contrast to the defiant tone of the earlier letters, those appealing for money employ the courtly language of flattery and submission to superior rank, a tone which appears more grovelling to twenty-first-century readers for whom conventions of a status-ordered world may seem foreign. For example in a long and detailed letter to Moszynski asking him to pay her debts amounting to 77 ducats, her preamble is one of pure flattery:

Penetrated by your goodness, do you imagine that after having been overwhelmed by it, I would appeal to you again? Why are you the only Seigneur worthy of that name? I will say it aloud. You, Sir, outweigh by the grandeur and beauty of your behaviour, all the vileness of certain others who would dishonour the Polish nobility, if it was not sustained by men like you, worthy to lift it up, and makes one forget their faults by covering them with your merits which only becomes more striking and places you head and shoulders above both foreigners and your fellow citizens ... Even if you were to refuse me the favour I am about to ask, I would broadcast all the same my justification of you with just as much warmth ... You know the price of honour and probity. I am putting both in your hands.[43]

Another intriguing clue to emerge from this letter concerns her comment about 'the vileness of certain Polish nobility'. It seems to suggest that the author of *Les amusements de Daphné'* could have been a nobleman at the Polish court.

Jodin's letters to Moszynski grew ever more desperate, praising him for his generosity but begging for more money:

> I beg of you, don't close your heart to me. The only resources I have flow from your goodness. I will never forget them. I will make such use of them that you will be praised for having granting them to me. Look at my situation. See how deplorable it is ... Do not let me leave with such a small advance [payment]. If the theatre management gives me sixty or eighty ducats and the King one hundred ducats, make it up to a round three hundred ... I am leaving on Thursday without fail. How little time remains! I will have the honour of calling on Your Excellency this morning to demand with my tears in the name of humanity the benefits that I would have hoped that you would grant me. You will never oblige anyone who would be more grateful. If my blood were required to prove my feelings for you, I swear from the bottom of my soul that I would shed it for you. It is not for me, *Monseigneur*, that I beg your kindness, but for a tender mother, overwhelmed with misery and whom I wish to make happy.[44]

We may think, contemplating the debts she had contracted that Marie Madeleine was in danger of following in her mother's spendthrift footsteps. Some seven letters to Moszynski asked for financial assistance, gave details of Jodin's debts and begged for his intercession with the King. But even more stressed than the money was her anxiety to obtain permission to leave. She pleaded with Moszynski to arrange for her departure before the winter set in (letter no. 117), expressing concern that the King was delaying her departure unduly and asked Moszynski to exert pressure on him:

> It is likely that the delay authorised by the King under the pretext of pressure of business will result in his refusing to accede to my request or that he will only accede to it after the Diet meets, which will put me in breach of contract, so that I cannot claim my salary and would make me the butt of insulting comments ... and many other difficulties. [45]

There is considerable ambiguity about Jodin's actual movements after the great quarrel of August 1766. Since Diderot continued to write to her in Warsaw, he seems not have known her whereabouts. Indeed a letter from Diderot of June or July 1767 was addressed to 'Mademoiselle Jodin, actrice au service de Sa Majesty le roi de Pologne, à Varsovie', but the address was crossed out, with Dresden substituted, then Leipzig, then Breslau.[46] Jodin's mother joined her briefly that year and Jodin may have returned to Paris in order to collect her mother. It is difficult to imagine Mme Jodin negotiating the complexities of travel across eighteenth-century Europe on her own. However it is now clear from the recent discovery of Jodin's theatre contract in Dresden that she had been engaged (16 March 1767), along with her Warsaw fellow actor de Marsan, to play in the Comédie-Française of the Saxon court to which she had been recommended by the French ambassador, Baron Zuchmantel, possibly through Moszynski's intervention.[48] By November 1767 she is mentioned in a letter from Dresden to a correspondent in Warsaw, having attracted a certain notoriety as the acknowledged mistress of Werner XXV von der Schulenburg, Danish Envoy to Saxony: 'You must have seen in Warsaw a theatre actress, Mlle Jodin, who is now here and plays leading roles in our theatre. She is the friend of Count Schulenburg.'[49] This affair was to prove a 'grand passion' in the grand manner. It would also have considerable diplomatic repercussions. The first stage of Jodin's theatrical career had ended in the bitterest acrimony. It remained to be seen what the second stage would bring.

Notes

1. Mme Geoffrin (Marie-Thérèse), 1699–1777. She visited Warsaw in 1766 and was treated royally by Stanislas Poniatowski, whom she had befriended in Paris. She may also have kept Diderot informed on Jodin's progress. See Marietta Martin, *Une Française à Varsovie en 1766: Madame Geoffin chez le roi de Pologne Stanislas Auguste* (Paris: Bibliothèque Polonaise, 1936). For King Stanislas Augustus see Adam Zamoyski, *The Last King of Poland* (London: Jonathan Cape, 1992).
2. Noverre à Louisbourg, 10 November 1766. Quoted from Ludwik Bernacki, *Theatr, Drama, Muzyka za Stanislawa Augusta*, II (Lwow: 1925), pp. 392–3, footnote 2.
3. *Gazette de France*, no. 76, 30 August 1765, p. 301.
4. Zamoyski, *The Last King of Poland*, pp. 134–7; *Correspondance inédite du roi Stanislas Auguste Poniatowski et de Madame Geoffrin, 1764 – 1777* (Paris: Plon, 1875).
5. André Morellet, Antoine Leonard Thomas, Jean le Rond d'Alembert, *Eloges de Madame Geoffrin, contemporaine de Madame du Deffand suivis de Lettres de Madame Geoffrin* (Paris: H. Nicolle, 1812).
6. Marie Madeleine Jodin was officially licensed as an actress with the Paris Comédie-Française on 16 May 1765, but she never performed on that stage. She probably journeyed to Warsaw with the French troupe, arriving with them in April of the same year. Her appointment, signed by the Duc de Richelieu and the Duc de Duras, nevertheless gave her an official status and the possibility of appearing on stage at the Paris Comédie-Française should she ever wish to avail herself of the opportunity. See Denis Diderot, *Correspondance*, XVI, pp. 73–4.
7. The company consisted of Mmes De Brabant, Cohendette, Dorsainville, Jodin and Thelis and MM. Caron, Duclos, Fouché, Du Frocy, de Marsan, Moulan, Louis de Montbrun, Paulin, de Villeclair and Vincent. Alina Zórawska-Witowska, *Muzyka na dworze I w Teatrze Stanislawa Augusta* (Warsaw: Zamek Królewski, 1995) pp. 135–40
8. Ibid.
9. For background on Polish theatre in the reign of Stanislas Poniatowski see: Jana Kotto, *Theatr Narodowy, 1765–1794* (Warsaw: PAN, 1967–68); Zórawska-Witkowska, *Muzyka na dworze I w Teatrze Stanislawa Augusta*; Bernacki, *Theatr, Drama Muzyka za Stanislawa Augusta*, II; Klimowicz, *Poczatki Teatru Stanislaswoskiego (1765–1773)* (Warsaw: Panstowowy Institut, 1966), pp. 32–4; Karyna Wierzbicka, *Zrodta Do Historii Teatru Warszawskiego: od roku 1762–do roku 1833* (Wroclaw: Wydawnictwo Zakladu Narodowego Imenia Ossolinskich, 1951); Karyna Wierzbicka-Michalska *Aktorzy Cudzoziemscy w Warszawie w XVIII*

Wieku (Warsaw: Akademii Nauk, 1975); Julian Lewanski, 'Teatr, Dramat I Muzyka za Stanislawa Augusta'.

10. Lewanski, *Teatr*, pp. 115–17.
11. Ibid., p. 117.
12. Zórawska-Witowska, *Muzyka*, p. 137, gives these as 'Les deux chasseurs et la laitière' and 'Le peintre amoureux de son modèle'.
13. Diderot, *Correspondance*, V, Lettre à Mlle Jodin, November 1765.
14. Casanova, *Mémoires*, ed. Robert Aberached, III (Paris: Bibliothèque de la Pleïade, 1960), pp. 475–6.
15. N. W. Wraxall, *Memoirs of the Court of Berlin, Dresden Warsaw and Vienna in the years 1777, 1778, 1779*, I (London: 1798), pp. 3–6.
16. The full list of the actors is as follows: Men: Josse Rousselois, Pierre Augustin Clavareau, Gabriel Soulé, Maulan, Louis de Montbrun, Joseph Etienne Clericourt, Duclos, Caron, d'Hercourt, de Marsan, Robert; Women: Mlles Jodin, Cohendette, Marie Rose Catherine Duponcelle, Saulaville, Victorine Clavareau, Lucie Clavareau.
17. Denis Diderot, *Correspondance*, V, p. 98.
18. *Gazette de France*, no. 88, 'de Warsovie', 12 October 1765, p. 349.
19. Casanova, *Mémoires*, III, pp. 480–89.
20. *Gazette de France*, no. 29, 'de Warsovie', 16 March 1766, p. 117.
21. Klimowicz, *Pozzatki Teatru Stanislawaskiego*, p. 32.
22. Ibid., p. 37; Wierzbicka, *Zrodta Do Historii Teatru Warszawskiego*, pp. 60–61.
23. Jodin Procès, 'Le Théâtre', Chapter XXII AGAD, 120/113.
24. Lenard R. Berlanstein, 'Women and Power in Eighteenth-Century France', pp. 186–8 for actors' backlash against the power of actresses in the Comédie-Française in 1789 and Lynn Hunt, 'The Many Bodies of Marie Antoinette' and Sarah Maza, 'The Diamond Necklace Affair', in Lynn Hunt, ed., *Eroticism and the Body Politic* (Baltimore and London: Johns Hopkins University Press, 1991) for accounts of resentment of femal power in court circles.
25. See Jean Heyne, Bibliothèque de la Pologne: Manuscrit 58, Jean Heyne, Archiwum Ks. Ksawerego Saskiego t. III. There is a helpful analysis of the authorship question in Julian Lewanski, 'Teatr, Dramat I Muzyka za Stanislawa Augusta'. Lewanski, however, seems strongly prejudiced against Jodin and accepts Rousselois' and d'Hercourt's version of events as well as pouring scorn on her as the alleged author of the public letter, as he assumes that because she was an actress, she would have been intellectually incapable of writing it.
26. François Riccoboni, *L'Art du Théâtre* (1750) (Genève: Slatkine Reprints, 1971).
27. K. Schmidt to Jacek Ogrodski, 18 August 1766, MSS 711, Czartorski Library, Museum Narodwe, Krakow.
28. Ibid.
29. See Ovid, *Amores* I, V, 12: 'multis Lais amata viris' for Thirnée (probably the Greek courtesan who was the lover of Praxiteles); Lewanski, 'Teatr, Dramat I Muzyka za Stanislawa Augusta', p. 136, notes 2 and 3.
30. The professional and sexual jealousy that the letter exudes and its vituperative tone would not have been unusual in the culture of scurrilous pamphlet satires. To take an English example, Alexander Pope was pilloried in over one hundred and thirty, usually anonymous, Grub Street pamphlets, quite apart from attacks by well-known literary figures. He was verbally flayed for his religion (Catholicism), his sexual prowess or lack of it and his physical deformity. For a discussion of the libels against Pope and the culture of personal abuse in pamphlet literature see J.

V. Guerinot, *Pamphlet Attacks on Alexander Pope 1711–1744* (London: Methuen, 1969), pp. xxi–xxviii.

31. Lewanski, 'Teatr, Dramat I Muzyka za Stanislawa Augusta', p. 122.
32. Klimowicz, *Poczatki Theatru,* p. 59.
33. Jodin Procès, N12, 281.
34. Jodin Procès, 128.
35. Jodin Procès, 118.
36. Jodin Procès, 134.
37. Diderot, however, always addressed Jodin as 'Mademoiselle', whereas as the abbé de Bouyon had noted in 1789 when he successfully campaigned for actors to be granted the full rights of citizens, actresses were commonly tainted by their usual mode of address, prefixing the definite article 'la' to their names, rather than a title such as Mademoiselle: 'One used to say: la Dumesnil, la Doligny; this word 'la' was only invented to imprint a wound on the name of an actress.' See Sylvie Chevalley, 'La Civilisation des comédiens', *Revue de la Société d'histoire du théâtre,* I, no. 161, 1989, p. 52.
38. Jodin Procès, 131.
39. Jodin Procès, 127.
40. Jodin Procès, 127.
41. Jodin Procès, Moszynski to Stanislas August, 115. The financial discovery to which Moszynski refers remains obscure, but may have related to the possibility of paying Jodin the remainder of her salary, even if she did not complete her contract, as well as a generous bonus from the King.
42. Wierzbicka, *Zrodta do Historii teatru Warszawskiego,* p. 118.
43. Jodin Procès, 121a.
44. Jodin Procès, 120.
45. Jodin Procès, 131.
46. Diderot, *Correspondance,* VII, p. 83, note 1.
47. Sachsen Landeshauptarchiv, Dresden, Acla Schauspiele und Redouten, Anno 1767 & 1768, Loc. no. l, 200, 25, Copy of Jodin's contract in German, dated 16 March 1767.
48. Letter from Mokrowskiego, Dresden, 11 November 1767, Krasinskich Library 4536, quoted in Ludwik Bernacki, *Theatr, Drama, Muzyka za Stanislawa Augusta,* II, p. 391, note 2.

Figure 3.1 *La Colonnade*, frontispiece illustration to Restif de la Bretonne's *Le Palais Royal*, vol 3 (Paris: au Palais Royal, 1790). [By permission of the Syndics of Cambridge University Library].

This illustration and Restif's verbal portraits of women soliciting around the Palais Royal offer a glamorised version of prostitutes' lives. The reference in the 'secondpublic letter' to Jodin and the Palais Royal intended to implicate her as having links with this notorious world of the demi-monde.

CHAPTER FOUR

The view from Paris –
Diderot's letters

The evidence of letters

The narrative of Jodin's adventures in Warsaw, Dresden and Bordeaux was initially revealed in the twenty-one surviving letters written to her by Diderot between 1765 and 1769. Additional evidence about her life emerges, as we have seen, in the two 'public letters' about the French troupe, as well as letters submitted by Jodin and others to Count Moszynski. Her further career in Dresden can be traced in diplomatic letters dealing with both public and private matters. It is striking, in relation to the archival material relating to Jodin's life and the theatrical world she inhabited, to note the extent to which historical evidence takes the form of letters, symptomatic in many respects of the public/private distinctions of eighteenth-century culture.[1] Secret letters (*lettres de cachet*), the means by which Jodin was imprisoned in la Salpêtrière, were simultaneously secret from the subject (Jodin) but public to the authorities, and revealed her private life to the police, a public authority. In addition, Jodin's private letters to Picard and Rochemore were made public, probably without her knowledge and certainly without her concurrence. In any case women had no 'rights' to privacy where transgressive behaviour was suspected.[2]

How public were Diderot's letters to Jodin? They were not published in his lifetime, but were preserved, presumably with a view to publication. They had a public role in view, given that Diderot's particular advice on acting was consistent with his public aesthetic and ethical programme. Diderot's letters to Jodin must also be read against the grain of the unknown series of letters from Jodin to which he was responding. How much did she tell him about theatre and court life and about her private and public imbroglios? How much did he glean from other sources?

Jodin, an actress, therefore a public woman with the inevitably pejorative meaning this phrase carried, maintained a private correspondence with a male public figure, Diderot. The masculine gender when attached to 'public' was not, of course, negative. Much of Diderot's advice to his protégée, both ethical and professional, represented an effort to marry artifice (acting) with integrity; public seeming with private being. It was legitimate to read the body and its manifestations as indexes of character. As John Brewer observes: 'There is a remarkable consciousness of how all aspects of the self – demeanour and body language, dress and material possessions, conduct and taste – are signs enabling the observer to understand the character and station of the observed.'[3] Diderot's letters attempted to educate Jodin in this language of signs, to train her bodily gestures on the stage to reflect, and indeed create, a moral persona.

The evidence of letters, the form letters took, and the audience for which they were intended, in Jodin's case, represent more than an archival curiosity. Letters illuminate the eighteenth-century public/private distinctions and confusions and indicate that for women, a private/public separation could not easily be maintained. A woman was either in the private realm of domesticity or, if she ventured into the public realm, she became a public and scandalous property. Yet through her correspondence with Diderot, Jodin participated in what Dena Goodman characterises as: 'the epistolary networks that embodied the ambiguity of a public sphere made up of private persons'.[4] Furthermore it was this tangential relationship with the public sphere as cultivated by the *philosophes* which encouraged Jodin ultimately to publish her *Vues législatives*, which made such a powerful case for admitting women to the public sphere as citizens.

In following Jodin's experiences in Warsaw and her broader educational progress as 'managed' by Diderot from Paris, one is confronted by two more or less parallel narratives, which interlock at various junctures. On the one hand as we saw in the previous chapter, there were the actual successes and disasters of Jodin's career there; on the other, and perhaps just as importantly, was the narrative already glimpsed in Chapter 2 of Diderot's wishes for her professional and personal welfare. These letters are among other things a monument to Diderot's concept of friendship. But though they of course concern Jodin, they are also essentially about Diderot himself and his theories which he was attempting to test on his promising if unreliable pupil. Unlike Rousseau's fictional Émile, Jodin was no passive recipient of advice, though she evidently valued Diderot's correspondence and must have been honoured to receive such detailed, brilliant, though often severe missives. She was after all a little-known actress; Diderot was the leading light of the Parisian *philosophes*. Yet Diderot evidently felt he was writing to someone of discrimination, who shared a similar outlook to himself. The letters reflect a creative partnership in which he developed his linkage between aesthetics and ethics, to be given mature expression in his *Paradoxe sur le comédien*.

Diderot's insistence on the moral dimension that Jodin should introduce into her life arose out of an atheist's conviction that morality was grounded in social behaviour, and was not a question of divine commandments. But if the divine sanctions had disappeared, they needed all the more to be re-introduced as a matter of individual conscience and responsibility. For Diderot in the 1760s, the correspondence which he carried out with Jodin allowed him to articulate in a practical context the interlinkage between morality in the theatre (his bourgeois *drames*) where the theatre becomes a site of ethical teaching and the leading of a moral if unconventional life. The five letters which he wrote from

November 1765 to December 1766 can be read in the light of the above preoccupations. Very often there is a considerable disjunction between what was happening to Jodin in Warsaw and what Diderot thought was happening, though he seems to have had considerable access to information from sources other than Jodin herself.

Jodin had evidently not been happy about some of the strictures from Diderot in his first letter of 21 August. In his following letter dated November 1765, he defends his harsh words on the grounds that they prove his concern for her. When she receives empty compliments from him, Diderot assures her, she will know that he is indifferent to her fate. By this time, rumour had reached him in Paris that Jodin has taken on a new lover, referred to here variously as an intelligent and sensible man and 'an intrepid man'. Diderot evidently felt that anyone who linked themselves to his protégée was tackling a whirlwind. Much of the letter concerns, for want of a better word, Jodin's deportment. Diderot does not wish her to imitate the loud and boisterous behaviour of other actors. Nor should she overly rejoice in her stage success; she is after all only performing to provincials. Showing himself a Parisian to his fingertips Diderot remarks loftily: 'It is not a question of pleasing your gloomy Poles and barbarians; it is the Athenians [Parisians] that you must seek to please.' Throughout the correspondence he will hold out for Jodin the goal of returning to Paris to perform at the Comédie-Française:

[Letter of November 1765][5]
You could not possibly have been offended by my letter, but perhaps your mother might have been. If you had considered more closely, you would have guessed that I only insisted so much on her need of your help in order to leave you in no doubt as to the truth about her mishap. The help arrived just when most needed, and I am very pleased to see that your soul has maintained its sensibility and good feeling, despite the toughness of your profession, which I would admire more if its members would have even half as much virtue as they need to have talent.

Mademoiselle, since you have the good fortune to interest a man of intelligence and good sense, as capable of advising you about your acting as about your conduct, pay attention to him, humour him, make up to him for the awkwardness of his role by all the consideration and docility you can.

I am sincerely delighted by your first successes; but remember that you owe them in part to the untutored taste of your audience. Do not be too carried away by applause of so little value. Your aim is not to impress gloomy Poles or barbarians; it is the Athenians that you must seek to please.

Moving from the theatre to private life, Diderot next reproves Jodin for her apparently ungovernable temper and counsels her to behave in public and in private in a manner that will gain her people's respect in spite of her profession. Emphasising the disadvantages attached to an actress's reputation, he reminds her that she was destined for better things. His reference to 'the unhappy reasons' that led her to the stage is a discreet reminder of her father's early death and her imprisonment in the Salpêtrière. Diderot's moral homily is not particularly consoling; if, he warns Jodin, she leads a disorderly life, she will have only herself to blame for any ensuing disasters:

> All the little repentances left by your fits of rage should be a lesson to you to control them. Do nothing that will earn you contempt. By decent, befitting and reserved manners and an educated style of conversation you can repress all those insulting familiarities which the common (alas, too well-founded) idea of an actress invites, especially from young idiots and the ill bred, who exist everywhere.
>
> Earn yourself the reputation of a good and well-conducted person. I hope very much you will be applauded, but I would like it even more if people sensed that you were destined for something other than a public stage and, without quite knowing the unhappy reasons that led you there, would pity you.
>
> Loud bursts of laughter, excessive gaiety, 'free' talk are signs of a bad upbringing and rarely fail to degrade. To be lacking towards oneself authorizes others to do the same. You cannot be too scrupulous in choosing the people you spend much time with. Judge of the general opinion about actresses from the few who succeed in consorting with them without scandal. Do not be content until mothers see their sons pay their respects to you without taking it amiss. Do not think that your conduct in society has no bearing on your success in the theatre. People grudge applauding those they hate or despise.
>
> Economize; always pay ready money. It will cost you less, and you will never let crying debt lead you into follies.
>
> You will tire your lungs on the stage all your life if, early on, you do not decide you were made for something else. I am not difficult to please; I will be content with you if you do nothing but what will bring real happiness. The caprice of the moment has its charms; who does not know it? But it brings bitter consequences, which one can avoid, if one is not a fool, by little sacrifices.
>
> My greetings to you, mademoiselle; behave well; be wise if you can; if you cannot, have at least the courage to bear the punishment disorder brings.

Diderot concludes with advice on acting. He was frequently to chide Jodin for the 'gulp' or *hoquet* that she affected when speaking her lines, a mannerism that was supposed to denote deep emotion, but was, according to her mentor, simply unpleasant and fatiguing. Someone, probably Mme Geoffrin, has kept him informed about her stage performances:

> Study perfection. Concentrate on quiet scenes; they are the only difficult ones. Give up those habitual gulps which people would have you believe were 'the voice of the entrails' and are really only bad technique – unpleasant, fatiguing, a tic as disagreeable on the stage as it would be in society. Have no fears about our feelings for your mother; we wish to serve her in every way we can.
>
> Give my respects to the intrepid man who has taken on the hard task of guiding you. May God reward his patience. I did not want to send you these letters that your mother gave me without a brief word to show the

interest I take in your fate. When I no longer care about you, I shall not take
the liberty of speaking harshly to you, and if I still write to you then, I will
end with all the usual polite nothings you could desire.

A major theme running through these letters is Diderot's insistence that as part
of the programme of moral responsibility on which he has enlisted her ('I will
judge you, Mademoiselle': letter of 21 August 1765), she must fulfil her
obligations towards her charming, flighty but generally helpless mother. The
issue of family loyalty (so flagrantly breached in Jodin's own childhood and
adolescence) becomes a way for Diderot to assert a humanistic moral standard.
He will stand in the place of her father whom he frequently evokes ('the
friendship which tied me to your father': 21 August 1765); ('By the interest I
take in you I am paying off the debts that I owe to your father: May 1766). We
can imagine Jodin, basking in her stage successes and the admiration of court
circles, being unwillingly reminded of her family obligations. Her prompt
response to Diderot's pleas to help her mother would please him enormously.

In his next letter (probably March 1766), the link that Diderot is making
between ethics and the theatre (introduced earlier), and also painting, begins to
become clear: 'If, when you are on the stage, you do not believe yourself to be
alone, all is lost.' This advice, from a theatrical point of view, expresses what
later came to be known as the 'fourth-wall' theory of the stage, a naturalistic
system directly contrary to the classical Comédie-Française tradition, according
to which the actors, assembled in a half-moon, addressed their speeches not to
one another but to the audience. It is also a theory he applied to painting, as an
antidote to the 'rococo' style. (He wrote to his mistress Sophie Volland, in July
1762, that: 'If, when one is painting a picture, one supposes the presence of a
spectator, all is lost.') But his remark to Jodin also epitomises his theory of
ethics as he would exemplify it in his novels and stories. No one, the theory
runs, is strong enough to content himself with his own good opinion, nor should
he do so. Virtue is a social matter; it is, anyway for an atheist, a matter of other
people's opinions. But for this very reason it is fatal, even a kind of madness, to
imagine one can directly manipulate public opinion. One has, rather, to act and
make moral choices as if one were alone and unseen ('learn to do without a
mirror') with the reward, if one is lucky, that one will be erecting a 'statue' of
oneself in other people's minds.

Diderot opens on his favourite theme of personal behaviour. He warns Jodin
not to carry the grandiloquent speeches and manners she must portray on the
stage into daily life. Nor should she make improper remarks. Knowing of the
fracas with Rousselois, we can appreciate that Diderot hoped for, but was to be
unsuccessful in moulding, an ideally feminine Jodin who would be capable of
curbing her temper, her tongue and her tendency to sarcasm. Certainly not a
sexual egalitarian, Diderot in a spirit of realism warns Jodin repeatedly of the
price she will pay in overstepping the decorum allotted to her sex. He was

acutely aware of the injustice of social prescriptions regarding women, but evidently felt that rebels like Jodin must learn to play the roles prescribed for their gender. Diderot's views on what he believed to be women's paradoxical character are developed in his essay, 'Sur les femmes'. Constrained by social convention, they have recourse to duplicity. They are both closer to nature than men (since they are ruled by their biology) and further from it by the rigours of their social training. We can see that his prescriptions for Jodin to act authentically on and off the stage were somewhat contradictory to his overall theory of women and might in his own terms have been called 'masculine' advice:[6]

> [Letter of March 1766][7]
> Mademoiselle, we have received all your letters, but it is difficult for us to guess if you have received all of ours.
> I am pleased with the way you are treating your mother. Continue to think and behave in the same way. You will have all the more merit for this in my eyes in that, being compelled to simulate all sorts of feelings on the stage, it is easy to retain none of them and for one's whole life to become a kind of mere play-acting, adapted to the circumstances one happens to be in.
> Be on your guard against a kind of absurdity that can grow on one imperceptibly and is difficult to shed later. I mean, when no longer on the stage, to go on speaking with the emphatic tones of the princess one has been playing. When taking off the costume of Merope, Alzire, Zaire or Zenobie, hang up everything connected with it on the same peg. Return to the natural tone of everyday society, the simple and decent deportment of a well-born woman.
> Never allow yourself to make improper remarks, and if anyone happens to make them in your presence, seem not to hear them. In any gathering of distinguished men, address yourself by preference to those of age, sound sense, reason and good morals.

However the greater part of Diderot's advice concerns acting. He reiterates his strictures on the tragic actor's 'gulp'. Depiction of passionate feeling should be approached by gradual stages, all part of his aesthetic of rendering an actor's stage presence more natural. He advises Jodin to study women in high society, 'le grand monde', in order to learn ease of movement, how to make an entrance and so forth. Indeed, the life of the court, to which she had recently been introduced (the actors frequented Stanislas's fêtes at the royal palace), gave her an opportunity for observation as opposed to mere dissipation. And though studying the manners of the great, she was to eschew 'mannerism': 'Mannerism is detestable in all the imitative arts ... nothing in this world is good but what is natural.' And then linking as ever the aesthetic and ethical: 'so be truthful on the stage and truthful off it.'

Diderot speaks continually of the need to 'perfectionner son talent'. This can be done, he suggests, by observing the way people actually behave – one must study real faces, real emotions. But there is also the cultural dimension; observe fine history paintings, he tells Jodin. In the hierarchy of genres, history painting was the equivalent of the epic in poetry, depicting sublime and universal human attributes:

> Next to the care you take of your personal reputation, devote yourself to perfecting your talent. Despise nobody's advice. It pleases Nature sometimes to bestow a feeling soul and a delicate tact on a man of the common rank.
>
> Make it your concern, above all, to have gentle, easy and graceful movements. Study women of the *grand monde*, those of the first rank, when you have the good fortune to be in their company. It is important, when one makes an entrance on the stage, to have this first moment all to oneself; and you will always achieve this if you have entered fully into your role. Don't allow yourself to be distracted backstage. It is there, above all, that one should distance oneself from flirtations and amorous speeches. Moderate your voice; be economical with feeling; approach passion by gradual stages. The general system of declamation of a play must correspond to the general system of the poet who wrote it. Without that, one may play part of a scene well, perhaps a whole scene, but will be playing the role as a whole badly. One will be passionate at the wrong moments; one will carry the audience along with oneself only at intervals. At other moments, one will leave it cold, with no blame to the author.
>
> You know very well what I mean by the tragic actor's 'gulp'. Remember that this is the most insupportable vice in acting, and the commonest. Examine men in their most violent accesses of fury, and you will witness nothing of the kind. Regardless of the poet's emphasis, stay as close to nature as you can; forget harmony, cadence and the 'hemistich';[8] have a clear, precise and distinct articulation, and for the rest, consult only feeling and sense. If you have a feeling for real dignity, you will never be basely familiar or absurdly bombastic, remembering moreover that every poet has his own different style and note.
>
> Have no mannerism. Mannerism is detestable in all the imitative arts.[9] Do you know why no one has ever been able to make a good painting of a stage-scene? It is because the actor's action has something affected and false about it. If, when you are on the stage, you do not believe yourself to be alone, all is lost. Mademoiselle, nothing in this world is good but what is true; so be truthful on the stage, truthful off it.
>
> Whenever you have the chance, go to see fine history-paintings in cities, in palaces and in private homes. Be an attentive spectator of human scenes in the streets and in ordinary households. It is there that you will see the real faces, movements and actions of love, jealousy, anger and despair. Let your head become a portfolio of these images and you can be sure that when you reproduce them on the stage, everyone will recognize them and applaud you.
>
> An actor possessing only good sense and judgement is frigid; one who only has verve and sensibility is mad. It is a certain combination of good sense and fire that makes a man sublime; and on the stage, as in the world, he who exhibits more than he feels makes people laugh instead of moving them. Therefore seek never to go beyond your actual feeling; try to make it true.

As a coda, probably because Diderot was worried that Jodin was having her head turned by mixing in court circles, he warns:

> I wanted to say a word to you about relations with the great. One always has a pretext, or reason, in the respect one owes them, to keep one's distance from them and to keep them at a distance and thus not to be exposed to their familiarities. It is a matter of behaving in such a way that they treat you the hundredth time as they did on the first.
> Keep well; you will be happy if you are well behaved.

This was perhaps a reference which we have also seen in *The Pleasures of Daphne* and the 'second public letter' to links between Jodin and the King. Keeping one's distance was, he suggested, a guise of deference but in reality a mode of self-preservation.

Whether or not Diderot's advice was having any effect on Jodin, it was certainly having none on her mother. Somewhere about this time, she made the experiment of setting up house with one of her brothers-in-law, Pierre Jodin, one of the Jodin relations responsible for her own and Marie Madeleine's imprisonment, though she could not have known this. Home-sharing turned out to be an ill-judged move, for Pierre Jodin sponged upon her shamelessly. Diderot marvelled and despaired at Mme Jodin's unquenchable optimism, based on a rather terrifying simplicity:

> [Letter of End of May 1766][10]
> We are always just as willing, Mademoiselle, to serve your mother, and we have not changed in our feelings for you. Your mother is a good creature, born to be the dupe of all those she confides in, since she confides in the first comer and is perpetually amazed if he does not prove the most honourable man in the world. We exhaust ourselves in good advice to her, which she receives with a gratitude that I suppose might be very proper if she made the slightest use of it. Fortunately, disasters which would drive anyone else out of their mind have no effect on her good humour or her health. She enjoys the most beautiful *embonpoint* and will die at the age of a hundred with all the experience of the world she had when she was eight. But those who deceive her are more to be pitied than she is.

However, if Mme Jodin could not be held accountable for her actions, her daughter could. Diderot was not happy at the rumour that she had formed an attachment with another actor, possibly de Marsan. Whereas Diderot had been pleased to hear about the 'intrepid man', a person whom he knew either actually or by reputation, he could not approve her newest attachment, convinced as he was that she would not find honourable friends among the acting profession. Finally, the news Diderot passes on that Mlle Clairon has definitely retired was a signal to Jodin that she might hope to return to play the roles abandoned by the great tragedienne. He evidently believed she had the requisite talent to shine on the Parisian stage:

But as for you: will you never learn whom you should place confidence in? Do not hope to find friends among the men of your profession. Treat your companions with decency and goodwill; but do not form attachments.

When one thinks of the reasons which have decided a man to become an actor, or a woman to become an actress – of the place where Providence found them and the bizarre circumstances which attracted them to the stage – one is no longer amazed that talent, good behaviour and probity are all equally rare among the acting fraternity.

Here is something definite; Mlle Clairon will not return to the stage. The public has been compensated a little for her loss by a young woman, who is excessively hideous, has a sepulchral voice and makes grimaces, but who from time to time lets herself be so taken over by her role that her faults are forgotten and she wins all applause.[11]

Since I go the theatre very rarely, I have not seen her yet. I would not be surprised if she owed part of her success to the hatred felt for Mlle Clairon. It is less justice to the one than a desire to mortify the other. But this is only conjecture.

Practise continually, and perfect yourself. It looks as if on your return to Paris you will find the public disposed to welcome you, and the stage without any rival you need fear.

Good day, Mademoiselle. Be good, and remember that morals, decency and elevation of feeling cannot be lost without dangerous consequences for all the arts of imitation. There is a great difference between acting and feeling. It is the difference between the courtesan who seduces and the tender woman who loves and both enraptures and is enraptured.

Your mother did not want to close her letter[12] without a brief word from me, and I have taken rather a time over it. By the interest I take in you I am acquitting my debt to your father.

In Diderot's next letter worries about Mme Jodin and her spendthrift habits are joined with advice about behaviour towards 'les grands'. Jodin has evidently written about her social success at court:

[Letter of July or August 1766][13]
I shall not let this letter from your mother[14] go without adding a little pinch of friendship, advice and reason.

First of all, do not leave that good woman [Mme Jodin] here. She has not the faintest notion of economy; she will run you into endless expense and will be none the better for it. Persuade her to come to you. She will cost you less, and will be happier. She will not restrict your liberty and will even give you a certain respectability, especially if you behave properly.

If you meet great people, redouble your regard for their birth, their rank and all their other advantages. It is the only decent and sure way of holding them at a proper distance. No princess-like airs, which would make you laughed at there as here, for the ridiculous is the ridiculous everywhere, but always an air of politeness, decency, and self-respect. Respect for oneself teaches others the same respect. When men fail in respect to a woman, it is very often because she was the first to forget it. The more your situation invites insolence, the more you must be on your guard.

Diderot continues to expound the convention, according to which, as against the traditional Comédie-Française style, the actor should not display any consciousness of the audience. The attack on mannerisms continues: 'no gulps, no outcries' and, revealingly, 'a masculine style'. These calls for restraint and sobriety conclude in a transfer of such qualities to the private sphere. If the theatre can do away with falsity, so can her personal life:

> Study continually; no gulps, no outcries; true dignity, a firm, sensible, reasoned, just and masculine style and the greatest economy of gesture. Restraint, sobriety; those must be the marks of your declamation three-quarters of the time.
>
> Vary your tones and accents, not according to the words but according to things and situations. Give employment to your reason, your soul, your entrails, and spare your arms. Learn how to look, learn above all how to listen; few actors know how to listen. Do not sacrifice your interlocutor to yourself. It may bring you a little advantage, but the play, the theatre company, the poet and the public will all lose by it.
>
> Let the theatre have no front or back for you; let it be a place where, and from where, nobody sees you. You must have the courage sometimes to turn your back on the spectator; it is important never to remember him. Any actress who addresses herself to him would deserve to hear a voice from the auditorium saying 'Mademoiselle, I am not here'.
>
> And then, the best advice, even for the success of your acting, is to have good morals. Persevere in this. As there is an infinite difference between the eloquence of a woman of good character and that of a rhetorician who says what he does not feel, there must be the same difference between the acting of a woman of good character and that of a debased one, degraded by vice and parroting maxims of virtue. Also, do you think there is no difference between them for the spectator, to hear an honourable woman or one who is lost to vice?
>
> Once again, do not let yourself be deceived by success. In your place, I would be making experiments, trying out bold effects, developing a style that was really mine. So long as your performance is no more than a tissue of little borrowings, you will be nothing. When the soul grows inspired, there is no knowing what one will do or how one will speak. It is the moment, the situation of the soul, which should dictate; they are the only good masters, the only good prompters.
>
> Adieu, Mademoiselle, keep well; risk boring the Germans[15] sometimes to learn how to amuse us.
>
> *Postscript by Mme Diderot*
> Mademoiselle, do not be so imprudent as to let M. Roger[16]or your mother know what my husband says to you, for he always tells her everything you write to him. Adieu, Mademoiselle, I wish you perfect health and everything that your heart desires and I embrace you with all my heart.

When Jodin received this letter, she may have felt it was prophetic. Diderot's repeated warnings, such as 'have good morals' and 'do not let yourself be deceived by success', proved only too apposite, given the events of August 1766 that we have seen unfold in Warsaw. Diderot's final comment, 'risk boring the Germans', suggests that Jodin was already contemplating a move to Dresden even before her fiasco with Rousselois.

The epistolary gap between July or August and December 1766 doubtless reflects Jodin's disasters in Warsaw. She briefly contemplated a return to Paris and launching herself on the Parisian stage. In any case, the Warsaw adventure was over. Whether or not Diderot had heard about her quarrels with her theatre manager in August and the two libels launched against her, as seems very probable, he remained cautious about her appearing before the hypercritical Parisian public before she was ready, implying that more time needed to pass to allow her past to be forgotten. The encouragement of his letter of May evaporates in December. This lends further weight to the idea that the scandal involving Jodin and Rousselois was taking time to die down and had damaged her reputation not only in Warsaw but also in Paris.

On the domestic front, Jodin's mother, who had finally got rid of her brother-in-law, had taken some lodgings in the hope of her daughter coming to share them. The aggrieved Pierre Jodin meanwhile had written a vicious letter to his niece, trying to cause a rift between herself and her mother. Diderot, who saw Jodin's family relationships as crucial to her moral development, would become increasingly exasperated with Jean Jodin's devious brother:

> [Letter of end of December 1766][17]
> It is very difficult, Mademoiselle, to give you good advice! I can see almost equal difficulty in the two options open to you. It is certainly true that, in a bad school, one learns only what is bad, and that nothing but vice is to be gained from vicious actors. It is also true that you would acquire more here [in Paris] as a spectator than in any part of Europe as an actress. Nevertheless improvements in one's acting come, above all, from one's own judgement, from reason, study, reflection, passion, sensibility and faithful imitation of nature, and there are gross faults which one can cure wherever one happens to be. All it needs is to admit them to oneself and to want to be rid of them.

What were these gross faults to which the actress was apparently prone? There was first of all the 'habitual gulp' mentioned in previous letters and secondly, Jodin's habit of leaning forward on the stage in an unbecoming manner. The 'first public letter' made exactly the same point and it seems clear that Diderot had either read it or had its contents detailed to him. Swaying about unpleasantly, as he put it, did not add dramatic force, it showed a lack of decorum. This was Diderot at his most aesthetically censorious:

> I told you before your departure for Warsaw that you had contracted an habitual gulp, which returned every instant and which I found intolerable; and I gather from some young gentlemen who have heard you that you do not know how to hold yourself on the stage, that you sway about in an very unpleasant manner. What is this all about? It is undignified; just for the sake of vehemence, do you need to throw yourself about? There are well-bred women everywhere whom you might consult and from whom you could learn graceful deportment and decorum.

In your place, I would not be eager to come to Paris until I had made sufficient progress to profit from the lessons of the great masters. So long as I could recognize essential faults in my technique, I would prefer to remain unknown and far from the capital. If there were practical reasons too: if by postponing my return for a few months I could hope for more comfort, a quieter and more retired life, more sustained and uninterrupted study; if I had prejudices to overcome, errors of conduct to erase from people's minds, a reputation to secure, these advantages would decide me. Remember, Mademoiselle, that only the highest talent will outweigh the alarm of the Paris acting fraternity at the idea of contact with you. Again, the public, who seem every day to be losing their taste for tragedy, are a real and frightening problem, both for actors and for authors. Nothing is more common than a disastrous début.

So study, work, get money; rid yourself of your worst faults, and then come here to observe the stage and spend your days and nights imitating good models. You will find some men of letters, and some men of the world, ready to advise you, but look for nothing from actors and actresses. Do they not suffer enough from their unpleasant avocation, without having to give lessons after work, in moments they had intended for pleasure or rest?

Your mother was on the point of buying some furniture; she has rented lodgings, so it all now depends on what you yourself decide. She will not go back to live with your uncle: that man is a pauper himself and would be more of a burden than a support.

I thank you for your good wishes, and return most sincere ones for your happiness and success.

The most significant warning of all, based on Diderot's knowledge of Jodin's past life, and on his awareness of what was transpiring in Poland, was 'that only the highest talent will outweigh the alarm of the Paris acting fraternity at the idea of contact with you'. This constituted a none-too-veiled reference to the disgrace of her Salpêtrière experience as well as to her Polish imbroglios. With Paris ruled out, Dresden was to be the next step in her tempestuous career. In the event, Jodin did not, as Diderot had feared, 'bore the Germans'; on the contrary she seems to have electrified them.

Notes

1. The creation of a 'public sphere' in the eighteenth century has attracted wide attention since the publication of Jürgen Habermas, *The Structural Transformation of the Public Sphere: An Inquiry into a Category of Bourgeois Society* (1962), trans. Thomas Burger and Frederick Lawrence (reprint, Cambridge, Mass.: MIT Press, 1989). This discussion is further indebted to John Brewer, 'This, that and the other: Public, Social and Private in the seventeenth and eighteenth centuries', in *Shifting the Boundaries: Transformation of the Languages of the Public and Private in the Eighteenth Century*, ed. Dario Castiglione and Lesley Sharpe (Exeter: University of Exeter Press, 1995); Dena Goodman, 'Epistolary property: Michel de Servan and the plight of letters on the eve of the French Revolution', in *Early*

Modern Conceptions of Property, ed. John Brewer and Susan Staves (London: Routledge, 1995).

2. Goodman, 'Epistolary property', p. 345.
3. Brewer, 'This, that and the other', p. 15.
4. Goodman, 'Epistolary Property', p. 340.
5. Diderot, *Correspondance*, V, letter 361, pp. 201–4.
6. Diderot, 'Sur les femmes', *Oeuvres Complètes*, X (1772), ed. Roger Lewinter (Paris: Le Club français du livre, 1971), pp. 28–60.
7. Diderot, *Correspondance*, VI, letter 393, pp. 166–8.
8. A hemistich is one half of an alexandrine, preceding or following the caesura. Diderot is advising Jodin to underemphasise the fact that she is speaking verse.
9. See his discourse on 'Mannerism' in his *Salon de 1767*.
10. Diderot, *Corrrespondance*, VI, letter 400, pp. 200–202.
11. This was Mlle Sainval the elder, who made her début on 5 May 1766.
12. Mme Jodin's letter has not survived.
13. Diderot, *Correspondance*, VI, letter 407, pp. 239–41.
14. The letter has not survived.
15. The word 'Poles' has been crossed out.
16. A young friend of Jodin's mother.
17. Diderot, *Correspondance*, VI, letter 426, pp. 377–9.

CHAPTER FIVE

'Une malheureuse passion?'

The distance from Warsaw to Dresden is some five hundred and fifty kilometres. When Marie Madeleine Jodin left Poland for Saxony in the winter of 1766–67 to take up her acting engagement, she would have faced a journey in freezing weather, over poor roads and stayed in worse inns. Eighteenth-century conditions of travel, particularly in the dead of winter, were not for the faint-hearted. Nor was is easy for a woman to travel alone. Well connected or wealthy women could ensure they had an entourage of servants. When Mme Geoffrin visited Warsaw in 1766, for example, she made what was something of a royal progress, being provided with carriages, couriers, and every possible convenience by Stanislas Poniatowski.[1] To travel in comfort at the period required having one's own carriage and servants and taking plentiful supplies, or, failing that, having wealthy friends.

Actors normally travelled together in a convoy of carriages and carts. The experiences of Mrs Jordan, the celebrated comic actress, touring Yorkshire two decades later in 1782–85 would have been typical of the itinerant acting profession: 'The journeys could be arduous over the high and desolate moors or across the flat, windswept East Riding ... walking was part of their way of life.'[2] But not as flat and desolate as the plains of Poland in mid-winter, one imagines. Mode and payment of travel was an important item in actors' terms of employment which normally stipulated that they would be paid travel or removal expenses in the event of their contracts not being renewed.[3] For example, in the terms drawn up by Diderot for Jodin to perform in St Petersburg (an appointment she was not to take up), her travel expenses amounting to 1000 *pistoles* were included.[4] Jodin had forfeited any such payment in Warsaw by refusing to fulfil her contract and was reduced, as we have seen, to appealing in emotive terms to Moszynski and the King. In her letters to Moszynski, before leaving Warsaw, she spoke of the crippling cost of the trip she was undertaking and begged him for funds.[5] Like many in her profession, she was heavily in debt, apparently not having followed Diderot's excellent advice to 'economize, and pay in ready money' (letter of November 1765). The spendthrift behaviour of the acting fraternity was proverbial, hence Diderot's many adjurations to save money.[6] Simply to extricate herself from her Warsaw commitments and to make the journey to Dresden constituted difficulties which account for the often frantic tone of her letters.

Since Jodin could not have afforded her own carriage, she would have hoped to take up a spare place in a gentleman's or woman's carriage if one were available. Such an opportunity, she told Moszynski fell through in the case of the Duc de Corilarive but she had another possibility, though one which involved more expense.[7] She may have decided to travel to Dresden in the company of de Marsan, whom the libel alleged was or had been her lover, and who like Jodin took up an engagement in Dresden in March 1767, having decided to leave Rousselois's troupe at the same time as the actress. He had, no doubt, been rendered uneasy at Jodin's treatment by her manager. One notes too that de Marsan's name did not figure in the list of signatories of Rousselois's letter of accusation against Jodin.

Once safely arrived in Dresden, Jodin signed her contract with the court theatre on 29 February 1767. Her engagement was due to begin on 1 April 1767; de Marsan started his contract on the same date. The two were engaged for a period of two years in the first instance and paid the highest salaries in the troupe, 1200 *écus* per year. As in Warsaw, Jodin was to play queens, noble mothers and leading roles in comedy, de Marsan kings and noble fathers. In conformity with contemporary theatrical practice, the repertoire and roles within it were clearly specified. Actors and actresses were not expected to play roles outside their defined contractual obligations[8] and provided their own costumes. This stipulation partially accounts for the fact that plays tended to be performed in eighteenth-century dress, regardless of the period in which they were set. It would have been far less costly to play Elizabeth of England and Agrippine of ancient Rome if one could wear the same costume for both.

The Court of Saxony when Jodin and de Marsan took up their engagements there, had undergone some reversal of fortune. A succession of wars coupled with courtly extravagance had severely damaged the country and its manufactures. The Seven Years' War had ended in 1763, just before the death of Frederick Augustus II, leaving some 90,000 men dead, the Saxon coinage debased and trade ruined. None the less, Saxony was famous for its opulent court life under both Augustus I and II. Rulers and ministers lived in ostentatious style.[9] At the time of Jodin's arrival, though the finances of the country might have been shaky, there seems to have been no question of sacrificing or making economies in the court theatre.

Adding to the woes of the Saxon Electors was the loss of the Kingdom of Poland. Under Saxon rule from the reign of Frederick Augustus I (the Strong) (1694–1733) and his successor Frederick Augustus II (1733–63), Poland had, as we have seen, elected Stanislas Poniatowski, a Pole and not a Saxon, making the country briefly independent.[10] In 1763 the new Elector of the much reduced Saxony, Frederick Augustus III was in his minority, aged thirteen; Saxony was consequently administered by two regents, Princess Elisabeth, the Elector's mother, and Prince Xavier, his uncle. Xavier had unsuccessfully attempted to unseat his father from the Polish throne and continued to cherish the hope of regaining the crown. When he eventually failed in this ambition and his nephew's assumed power in 1768, Xavier retired to France. His nineteenth-century French biographer writes of him in relation to his military career during the Seven

Years' War: 'each of his campaigns was more marked by his success in love than his successes in war'.[11] As Prince Administrator Regent, however, he did a great deal to revive Saxon industry, encouraging the Meissen china manufacture, founding a school of mining in Freiburg and improving agriculture.

A gloomy assessment of Saxony at this period was drawn up by Count Johannes Bernstorff, the Danish foreign minister, in his instructions to the new Danish envoy to Saxony and Poland, Count Werner von der Schulenburg in 1763:

> The Court where you are going, Sir, to reside on behalf of the King, has been so unfortunate during the War and so little fortunate in Peace; it finds itself so dependent on external forces and so ruined internally, its future is rendered uncertain by the age and fragile health of its sovereign [Frederick Augustus II who died the same year, in 1763], by the discontent which reigns in Poland and by the concerted campaign which appears to exist between the Empress of Russia and the King of Prussia against its interests, its inclinations and its hopes, that you will probably find only languor and perhaps that dissipation which is often the effect of Despair and the palliative and grim remedy of those persons who know no other cure for their evils. I do not think, Sir, that at least initially Dresden will furnish you with a lively scene, nor with examples of an enlightened and flourishing state of politics.[12]

This court, allegedly marked by languor, dissipation and despair, was where Jodin was to perform in the theatre. Coinciding with her journey to Dresden, we discover with some surprise, considering her financial worries on leaving Poland, that she was enjoying unaccustomed prosperity. She had written to Diderot proposing to send him a large sum (12,000 *livres*, the equivalent of about four years of a leading actor's salary) to invest for her own and her mother's future maintenance. This is one of many demonstrations of Jodin's trust in Diderot which his unflattering comments on her character had done nothing to damage. Where did Jodin come by this small fortune? Acquisition of the money in question seems to have pre-dated her relationship with Werner von der Schulenburg launched in Dresden and soon to be publicly acknowledged. The most likely explanation is that she had been paid off by the Polish King. We remember Moszynski's comment in his letter to Stanislas: 'Your financial discovery is a good one.' It seems likely that Jodin in the end received a generous severance payment, partly in compensation for the humiliating scene in the theatre with Rousselois and partly to ensure that she did not create a scandal *vis-à-vis* the King, with whom she had been linked in the 'second public letter'.

We can now turn to Diderot's New Year's letter of 1767 and hear his excitement about his pupil's plans for financial prudence. He finds it difficult to believe that in spite of the *étourdissement* (flightiness) associated with her status as an actress, her passions and her youth, Jodin has begun to think of her future. Could it be true that his heedless, extravagant and passionate pupil should have had 'quelque pensée solide' (a genuinely prudent/sensible idea)? His incredulity was evidently an ironic strategy to test Jodin's sincerity and seriousness. After giving vent to these expressions of amazement, he offered sound practical assistance, seriously pledging his full support for her plans to invest her money. At no stage in this or subsequent letters did Diderot query its source and if indeed arising from a rich protector, he saw her as perfectly entitled to profit from the relationship.

It is in this letter that Diderot made his first proposal for a further advantageous contract for Jodin in Russia at the court of Catherine II. The issue of whether or not Jodin would accept this very flattering offer, which confirms that her reputation as a gifted actress was well established, is a continuing theme of subsequent letters. We will see that Jodin's hesitations in accepting the offer had their basis in her new and tempestuous love affair which she would embark upon in Dresden:

[January 1767][13]
What! Mademoiselle, can it be really true that, despite the giddiness of the theatre, of passion, and of youth, you have had a solid thought, and the intoxication of the present does not prevent you considering the future? But maybe you are ill? Perhaps that might produce the same effect?

I have little faith in conversions, and prudence has always seemed to me the quality most incompatible with your character. So I am baffled. Nevertheless, if you insist on entrusting your money to a poor bankrupt like myself, you may do so whenever you please. I will try to respond to this mark of confidence by looking for some solid and profitable investment for you. Count on my discretion, and count above all on the goodwill of Mme Diderot. We will both do our best. Send me your birth certificate, if you have one; or tell us which parish you were baptized in, so that we can get written evidence of your age and forenames.

No one's private fortune is safe, but I think that, in the all financial upheavals, the King has always respected life annuities in his name. Thus I would give the King the preference, unless you disagree. I am glad to see, from your New Year's letter, that this wise scheme to make sure of an income against all eventualities is not just a momentary impulse but one you mean to persist in. I give you my compliments. We are all at your service, and I in particular feel relieved, having been afraid that, by my silence and delay, I might have made you squander your money and have ruined one of the best notions you ever had. Divest yourself as speedily as possible of that money, which is certainly in the most unsafe hands I know of – your own. If it does not arrive within a month, I shall begin to lose hope.

My wife and child are infinitely grateful for your kind wishes and praises; it will always make them extremely happy to hear good news of you. You know that, so far as I am concerned, if the interest I take in your success, your health, your reputation and your fortune counted for anything, no woman in any theatre in the world would be more honoured, richer and more admired than you. Our French theatre deteriorates every day; nevertheless I do not encourage you to return yet. It seems as if, the rarer talent becomes, the harder people are to please. I am not surprised. The more that praise is deserved, the less are people ready to give it.

The Empress of Russia has asked someone here to form a French troupe
for her. Would you have the courage to go to Petersburg and enter the service
of one the most amazing women in the world? Your answer, please.[14]

The remainder of Diderot's letter was devoted to the art of acting. He advised
Jodin to recite scenes from Racine, as one might one's daily prayers – these
were to be her holy texts. In the light of Jodin's hostility to the Church, we can
read this as a mild anti-clerical joke. In his epistolary voice, Diderot posed as
the omnipresent tutor – 'imagine that I am listening to you'. Knowing her
penchant for extravagant behaviour, he counselled 'tranquil scenes' and the
avoidance of mannerisms. Finally, speaking of the seductive power of Racine's
poetry which he implied dominated the very sense and drama of the line, he
recommended de-poetising the dramatist by refusing to sing the music of his
lines, in order to allow the passion behind them to emerge. Even the great neo-
classical writers of tragic verse could be brought closer to natural speech. In
relation to the grandiose playing often associated with Corneille, he similarly
advocates a 'homely heroism':

I salute you and embrace you from the bottom of my heart. Make sacrifices
to the graces, and above all study quiet scenes; every day, as your morning
prayer, perform the scene between Athalie and Joas; and for your evening
prayer, some scenes between Agrippina and Nero.[15] As your *benedicite*,
repeat the opening scene between Phèdre and her confidante, and imagine
that I am listening. Above all, avoid all mannerism. There are cures for
heaviness, stiffness, rusticity, hardness and lack of nobility, but there are
none for petty mannerism and affectation. Remember that everything has
its own tone. Be emphatic sometimes, since the poet is so. But do not do it
as often as he does, for emphasis is never really natural; it is an exaggerated
imitation. If you observe that Corneille is almost always in Madrid,
practically never in Rome, you will get him down off his stilts; and his
characters, as rendered by you, will have a homely, consistent, honest
heroism without parade, which they rarely do in his plays.
    Equally, having observed how musical, 'singing' and long-drawn-out
Racine's verse is, and how little these cadences correspond to the true voice
of passion, you will learn to curb the excesses of his music. You will bring
him closer to noble and simple conversation; and you will have made a
great step forward, a very difficult one. Since Racine always goes in for
music, the actor becomes his musical instrument; since Corneille is always
on tiptoe, the actor struggles to be as tall as he can. Actors, that is to say,
reinforce the authors' vices, when they should be doing the opposite.
    So here are some precepts for you, Mademoiselle, as your New Year's
gift. Good or bad, I am sure they are new; but I hope they are good. Garrick
once told me he would find it impossible to play a role from Racine: that
his verses were like great serpents, winding themselves round the actor till
he was paralysed. What Garrick felt and said is true. Break the serpentine
coils of the one, and the stilts of the other.

Almost from the moment of Jodin's first stage appearances in April, the dramatic
roles she portrayed on stage and the drama of her personal life coincided. The

Danish envoy to Saxony, referred to above in Bernstorff's letter of instruction, Werner XXV von der Schulenburg, became her devoted and indeed obsessed admirer. On first seeing her perform on the stage, he had become infatuated with the actress. Their passionate and stormy relationship, which was to last for just over two years, marked both their lives. But rather than the usual affair of convenience between actress and wealthy protector, theirs seems to have been a mutual passion, though punctuated by violent quarrels. From the evidence of Diderot's letters to Jodin, it is clear that the relationship was extremely volatile, but also that both parties saw it as a serious commitment. In addition, this very public love affair became a matter of notoriety and scandal in the Saxon court, whose mores can scarcely be described as puritanical.

Schulenburg belonged to a Prussian family in the service of Denmark, his father having been Danish ambassador to France. His family owned extensive estates in Prussia. His father and many of his near relations had been distinguished military men. A Schulenburg connection, Melusina von der Schulenburg, had been the mistress of George I of England and became Duchess of Kendal.[16] Diderot had made the acquaintance of Werner von der Schulenburg through his own bosom-friend F. M. Grimm and was to express his enthusiastic approval of Jodin's new liaison.[17]

How did the two meet? Did Jodin first encounter Werner von der Schulenburg in Dresden or possibly in Paris in the winter of 1766? We know that Schulenburg was in Paris in September 1766 and between January and April 1767, suggesting among other things that his duties as envoy to the Court of Saxony were not especially onerous.[18] Diderot, however, makes no mention of such a return to France by Jodin at this time. Equally Schulenburg could have met Jodin in Warsaw (this speculation is the basis of the idea that he might have been 'l'homme intrepide' (the intrepid man) mentioned by Diderot), but this seems unlikely given the way the relationship took off in Dresden in a highly public manner. Nor is there any evidence of Schulenburg having gone to Warsaw at this time. So we may reasonably infer that Schulenburg first met Jodin in Dresden. What is incontrovertible is that the affair as it unfolded in Dresden in 1767–68 was of a desperately consuming nature. The actress was soon installed in his private mansion and was the recognised 'friend' of a leading diplomatic figure in the court. She rode to the theatre in his carriage, which would have been emblazoned with his crest. They appeared frequently in public together. Neither Jodin nor Schulenburg seem to have been prepared to exercise discretion in the pursuit of their grand passion. This tallies with what we know about Jodin's contempt for public opinion generally. She enjoyed playing queenly roles in real life and revelled in her position as the acknowledged consort of the Danish envoy. Both lovers celebrated their relationship in an extravagant manner, financially and emotionally.

The picture we gain of Werner von der Schulenberg, beyond the respectful official family history, is not exactly reassuring.[19] In spite of the approval accorded to Schulenburg by Diderot and Jodin's mother, his character on closer examination turns out to have been as volatile as Jodin's, though he had the great advantages over her of aristocratic privilege and a private fortune, which he was rapidly to dissipate. He proved himself, quite apart from his relations with the actress, to be lacking in judgement in several crises of his life. As a diplomat, he appears to have been rather idle, and his analyses of Saxon politics were frequently misguided, though he was prepared to admit his errors.

The son of a distinguished German field marshal, Werner XXIV, who had served the Danish monarchy both in battle and as Danish ambassador to France, Werner XXV was born in Paris in 1736 and educated at the Knights' Academy in Sorve, Zeeland. Whereas his older brother, Wolff, followed his father into the Danish army, rising to the rank of lieutenant-general, Werner, destined for the life of a courtier, first undertook a period of study at Leipzig and Göttingen, which he was forced to abandon in 1756 when his father died. He quarrelled with his elder brother, Wolff, over the will, believing that he had not received the legacy informally promised to him. In 1758 he returned to Paris, which he seems to have considered his spiritual home, where thanks to his family connections, he was received in the highest circles and revelled in aristocratic society.

His journal covering these years, written up in 1780 from notes taken contemporaneously, reads like an inventory of important persons of the day, of whom Werner was a collector. He enjoyed the Assemblée du Palais Royal and the entourage of the Duc d'Orléans, picking up gossip about the love affairs of the great in the process. Werner did not only go into society. He also acquired a pleasing mistress, one of the Bellenot sisters introduced to him by a school friend. Commenting on this episode, which in hindsight may have been coloured by his relations with Jodin, Werner recalled: 'This young lady was very lovely and cost me nothing. Both sisters owned property and were not self-seeking [mercenary]. We dined together every evening and never did a foreigner have better acquaintances among the sort of women who ruin so many.'[20]

The following year (1759) Schulenburg embarked on a tour of European cities, travelling to Amsterdam, the Hague and then London, where he was received at court and stayed with the French Ambassador, 'who overwhelmed me with politeness'. His family links with the Duchess of Kendal would explain his flattering reception at court. A dedicated tourist in the eighteenth-century manner, Schulenburg and a compatriot, Dedel, toured southern England in July. They were awarded honorary degrees in law at Oxford, along with the entire Dutch diplomatic legation, apparently another mark of politeness. However, Schulenburg and Dedel, whom the former characterised as 'a very unrefined man' began to fall out, though they continued as travelling companions. After visiting Bristol, Bath and Salisbury, they saw Stonehenge whose 'enormous stones' impressed the young count. Proceeding to Portsmouth, Schulenburg and Dedel quarrelled definitively. The two young noblemen fought a duel in which neither participant drew blood, but the still angry Schulenburg insisted on a re-match, this time in St James's Park, London. Here he was slightly wounded, and as the authorities seem to have got wind of the affair, he retired to Amsterdam, demanding again that Dedel give him satisfaction. Dedel, not surprisingly, did not rise to the challenge. Whether honour was assuaged for either party is not clear, but this is one of a number of acrimonious encounters staged by Werner, indicating the histrionic volatility of his temper, though the only violent dispute recorded with a social equal. Returning to Paris, called thither 'by the memory of "la Bellenot"', he discovered to his immense chagrin that she had taken another lover. Werner, at a distance of twenty years recalled in his journal: 'I was inconsolable.'

Werner's character begins to emerge from these rather fragmentary and unreflective recollections. A wealthy young Prussian aristocrat (though not wealthy enough for his taste), handsome with the long Schulenburg nose (see portrait, Figure 6.2, p. 126), European and/or French in his interests, an antiquarian and art collector, he assumed that his place in the world was made to be easy, expected that the nobility and gentry of every place he visited would make him welcome, and was possessed of considerable charm and social address. He was successful with women, both in society and with the lower ranks. In addition, he was hot-headed and inclined to physical violence. He was subject to bouts of unspecified ill-health and he may, from the tone of his letters, have suffered from melancholia. Like most of his class, he would have seen lavish spending and a grand life style as a birthright. He did not take reverses of fortune easily. He was representative of the rather spoilt, vain, self-indulgent though not altogether unintelligent nobility of the *ancien régime*. That even his mother found his spending habits intolerable indicates that he exceeded the normal bounds of aristocratic licence. However, having by the 1780s sowed enough of his wild oats, Werner finally settled down as a respectable member of the Prussian landed gentry.

Jodin met Schulenburg when he had recently entered on what appeared to be a promising diplomatic career. Thanks to his father's distinguished reputation at the Danish court, Werner, who had already been given the largely honorary title of Gentleman in Waiting to the Danish King ten years previously in 1753, was appointed in 1763 Envoy Extraordinary to the King of Poland and the Elector of Saxony, Frederick Augustus II. He was clearly marked out by his father's old friend, the foreign minister to the Court of Denmark, Count Johannes Bernstorff, for preferment. Throughout his five-year posting in Saxony, Bernstorff fulfilled the role of mentor as well as diplomatic superior for the young count. Schulenburg's eventual failure to achieve distinction as a diplomat was directly related to his passion for Marie Madeleine Jodin and their affair in the hot-house atmosphere of the Dresden court.

As a Prussian in the service of the Danish King, Schulenburg was one of a number of German service nobility in his employ, notably Johannes Bernstorff, Streunsee, the enlightened reformer executed for his affair with Queen Caroline Mathilde (1772), and Count Andreas Bernstorff, the great reforming administrator who succeeded his uncle in the 1780s.[21] In 1763 when Schulenburg was given his diplomatic posting, Denmark with a population (including Norway) of only two million was ruled by an absolute monarch, Frederick V (1746–66). Frederick was succeeded by his son Christian VII, who although already showing signs of insanity when he came to the throne at the age of sixteen, reigned, at least in a titular sense, until 1808.[22]

Horace Walpole described both Christian VII and his foreign minister, on a visit to England at the beginning of Christian's Grand Tour of European capitals with his customary irony, mocking the spectacle of the distinguished elder statesman kow-towing to the diminutive king who was only nineteen years old at the time: 'A grave old man, running round Europe after a chit, for the sake of domineering over a parcel of beggar Danes when he himself is a Hanoverian and might live at ease on an estate he has at Mecklenburg.'[23] Walpole's discomfiture at Bernstorff's obsequious role before the new boy-king, points to the sometimes grotesque nature of court life and etiquette. However Walpole ignored the service ethic to which Bernstorff had dedicated his professional life and the pleasures of directing affairs of state. During his long ministerial career, Bernstorff attempted with some success to steer Danish foreign policy safely by cementing a Northern Alliance (England, Scandinavia, Poland, Russia) against Prussia and to secure Schleswig-Holstein for Denmark.[24] He made efforts, ultimately unsuccessful, to ensure Polish independence from Russia. He was a major diplomatic figure in mid-eighteenth-century Europe and his patronage of and loyal support for Werner von der Schulenburg were important factors in the latter's career, affected as it would also be by the volatile political situation in Denmark after Bernstorff's dismissal in 1771.

Schulenburg's appointment to the double post of Poland and Saxony in 1763 was tantalisingly brief, thanks to the election of Stanislas Poniatowski to the throne of Poland and its consequent de-coupling from Saxony. Thereafter, he remained envoy to Saxony alone. Schulenburg does not seem to have viewed his post with great enthusiasm, lingering in Hamburg for a month or so after his appointment, only leaving when 'obliged to depart for Dresden'.[25] In his initial 'Letter of Instruction', Bernstorff had advised him to observe 'the factions which divide Poland and the risk that this great and beautiful kingdom runs, after being the cat's paw of its neighbours, of plunging into the even greater horror of a civil war'. He commended Schulenburg to apply himself with zeal to uncover the complexities of Saxon/Polish politics. He was to observe the conduct of the Saxon court *vis-à-vis* other German states, in particular whether Saxony attempted to resist Prussian domination, and to write frequent and detailed reports.[26]

From what one can gather in his diplomatic reports and accounts of his travels abroad, Schulenburg seems to have taken his duties somewhat lightly, though falling into fits of remorse when chided by Bernstorff.[27] Many of his reports begin with apologies for 'the total lack of news to be found in Dresden'. By contrast, his predecessor Saint Saphorin, who went on to take up the post of envoy to Warsaw, found no difficulty in submitting detailed letters of political and social information to his superiors. Schulenburg's letters, though they mention manufacture, trade, the visits of foreign dignitaries and military preparations, are predominantly concerned with court gossip and scandal. For example, he commented (in code) in one of his reports to the Danish court in 1766 on the pregnancy of Claire-Marie Spinnucci, mistress of Prince Xavier: 'Mademoiselle Spinnucci, Lady in waiting to Madame the Electrice, who has been indisposed for several months, has reappeared at court a week since. Everyone knows that this young lady gave birth in the Castle itself and with so little dissimulation that she appeared at Court until shortly before her confinement with a figure which left one in no doubt.'[28] The transmission of this very item of gossip, intercepted by Saxon intelligence, could have been one of the factors which resulted in Schulenburg's eventual loss of favour.[29]

Schulenburg may also not have endeared himself to his diplomatic colleagues. He quarrelled with the Danish secretary to the legation in Dresden, Samuel Kirchbergner who in 1765 took six months' leave due to 'illness', and gave in his notice on 26 October 1766 because of differences with the envoy.[30] Schulenburg was able to absent himself from Dresden for extended periods to visit Paris and Italy. In 1766 he took leave for three months to attend to his private affairs which coincided with the Kirchbergner episode and with the period in which the engraver and art dealer J.-G. Wille recalled seeing him in Paris. Yet in spite of a certain air of indolence, Schulenburg's performance as envoy seems to have been satisfactory and was even praised when in January 1765 a quarrel over precedence broke out in the Saxon court. This involved a protest on the part of the foreign envoys who had come to pay their respects to Prince Xavier on New Year's Day and who were turned away because the Saxon ministers, it was claimed, had first rights of audience. The assembled ambassadors expressed outrage, arguing that, as representatives of the crowned heads of Europe, they took precedence over mere ministers. Schulenburg, who remained aloof from this protest on Bernstorff's orders, was congratulated for his tact: 'The King has ordered me to tell you that he is very satisfied with your conduct in this affair.'[31] Schulenburg discovered that this mini-drama over etiquette and precedence in reality exposed rivalries in the Saxon court between, on the one hand, the two reigning regents, and on the other the party of the young Elector headed by the Duc de Courland.[32] Such issues combined with court gossip constituted the core of Schulenburg's diplomatic life in Dresden, until the arrival of the new actors from Warsaw in February/March 1767. Marie Madeleine Jodin was to provide all the drama his life could contain and rather more than he had bargained for.

We may now return to Jodin and her mentor. Only two letters from Diderot to Jodin survive from 1767, the first of January, considered above, and the second probably dating from June or July 1767 which is uncharacteristically terse. It appears that Mme Jodin has joined her daughter for a time, as Diderot sends her his best wishes. Whilst he offers Jodin congratulations on her stage successes (it is unclear whether he still believes her to be in Warsaw or whether he knows that her début in Dresden had gone well), he reminds her above all to cultivate her moral character – 'être honnête femme', by which he did not mean lead a cloistered existence but to show some decorum in her behaviour. Diderot may by this time have heard more about the fracas in Warsaw; it would appear that he was not amused. He continues, however, to promise every assistance in Jodin's financial affairs:

> [June or July 1767] [33]
> I have heard of your successes, Mademoiselle, with the greatest pleasure.
> But in cultivating your talent, try also to have good morals.
> I have not bought the books you asked for, since I have been waiting for
> M. du Molard[34] to let me have some money, which he has taken his time in
> doing. I am so frantically busy that I am forced to write to you in Warsaw
> as if you were living four yards up the street.
> My respects to your mother. Let me repeat, it is not enough to be a great
> actress, you need also to be a respectable [*honnête*] woman; I mean, in the
> same sense as women in other walks of life. (I do not mean anything very
> strict here.) Think, occasionally, of the strange contrast between an actress's
> actual conduct and the edifying maxims she sometimes has to utter on the
> stage.
> A virtuous role performed by an actress without virtue shocks me almost
> as much as the role of a fifteen-year-old played by a fifty-year-old woman.
> Good day, Mademoiselle; keep well and always count upon my friendship.

At this juncture Diderot does not mention Jodin's latest love affair, either because Jodin had not yet told him about Schulenburg or because he was being discreet and feared his letters would be opened by Saxon officials. The story as it unfolded, intriguing partly because of the diplomatic storm which it produced, can be told from a number of differing perspectives. But at the heart of this narrative lies a crucial absence. We have no direct testimony from Marie Madeleine herself, either about what occurred or about her feelings towards Schulenburg. Inferences about the progress of the relationship must be drawn from Diderot's letters, which respond to the apparently very detailed confidences which Jodin made to him; from her mother's postscripts to these letters, expressing delight that she has landed a well-born lover; from Jodin's vastly improved financial position, recorded in detail in Diderot's letters; from Schulenburg's Journal of 1780; his letters of 1768–69 to Count Bernstorff; and finally, an account by the Saxon foreign minister, Baron von Ende about the affair, culminating in a correspondence between Bernstorff and Volkersahn, the Saxon envoy to Denmark, relative to Schulenburg. The yawning gap in Jodin's own testimony can partially be filled by comments in her *Vues législatives pour les femmes* concerning the transience of passionate attachments and the haughty behaviour of the aristocracy.

From April 1767, when her contract began, to April 1768, Jodin appeared on the Dresden stage in the leading roles of Andromaque, Agrippine, Cleopatra and Elizabeth I of England, playing opposite de Marsan. She appears to have had considerable success as early in 1768 the theatre manager, Ferber, began negotiations to renew her contract, evidence that she had performed successfully. Ferber wrote in part:

> I would be most flattered if you could make me the bearer of a satisfactory reply [to the Prince Administrator, Xavier], which would assure us of the pleasure of seeing you perform for a longer period. This would procure for me the double advantage of having rendered a very great service to the Public and to be able to prove to you on every occasion the great esteem with which I am, Mademoiselle
> Your very humble and obedient servant,
> Ferber[35]

Simultaneously, Diderot, ever zealous in his protégée's interests, was engaged in investing her 12,000 *francs* and negotiating a contract for her in Russia at the court of St Petersburg. Her financial affairs, Diderot tells her, are in excellent order. He even goes so far as to offer a modicum of praise: 'you are much wiser than I thought your were' and encourages her as to the honourable status of the acting profession, having in earlier letters done rather the reverse:

> [21 February 1768] [36]
> I have received your letter, Mademoiselle, and the one which will serve to arrange your account with M. Dumolard; also your life-certificate and the very full power of attorney that you have given me to look after your affairs; and the bill of exchange for 12 000 *francs* drawn on Messrs. Tourton and Baur.[37] As this bill does not fall due for a month and a half, there should be time for me to look around and find a suitable investment for your money.
> You are much wiser than I thought you were, and I am delighted to have been wrong. I knew your heart was good; as for your head, I thought that no woman had ever possessed a worse one. Now I am reassured about the future. Whatever happens, you have provided for both your own and your mother's most pressing needs.
> I shall be seeing M. Dumolard very soon. I hope our interview will pass off without disagreeableness, but I doubt it. I am saying nothing about M. Dumolard's uprightness, but I cannot respect a man who diverts money which does not belong to him to his own use. Ninon, though short of bread, would never have behaved thus.[38]

I hasten to put your mind at rest; make haste, on your part, to reply to the propositions I made to you in the name of M. Mitreski, who is responsible for forming a theatrical troupe here. I speak quite straightforwardly, and you know from the value I attach to great talents, in whatever sphere, that I can have no intention to humiliate you.

If I had the soul, the voice and the appearance of Quinault-Dufresne,[39] I would mount the boards tomorrow, and I would think myself more honoured to make even the wicked weep over persecuted virtue than, dressed in cassock and square bonnet, to mouth religious platitudes from a pulpit, only interesting the naïve and credulous. Your theatrical morality belongs to all ages, peoples and countries; theirs changes a hundred times from latitude to latitude. So take a properly high view of your profession; it is one of the roads to success in it. One must be the first to respect oneself and one's activities. It is hard to throw oneself into something that one despises. I prefer preachers on the boards to preachers in the tub.

The contract offered by the Russian court was extremely favourable. Jodin, in spite of her troubles in Warsaw, must have gained an enviable reputation for her acting. And though a relative neophyte, she could already command an impressive salary. Even more intriguingly, Diderot turns out to have been a canny negotiator, suggesting to Jodin that she raise her price before accepting the Russian offer:

Here are the conditions offered to you by the Court of Petersburg. Salary, 1600 *roubles*, worth 8000 *francs* in French currency. 1000 *pistoles* for the journey there, and the same for the return.[40] You would be expected to supply your own French, Roman and Greek costumes, but anything more uncommon would be provided from the court's own wardrobe. The appointment would be for five years. You would have the use of a carriage but merely on Imperial service. Gratuities are sometimes very considerable, but, as everywhere else, they have to be earned. As soon as you receive my letter, let me hear your intentions, so that M. Mitreski can know whether he can count on you or not.

Assuming that the 8000 *francs* and the rest seem acceptable to you, write two letters, one of them dated a week later than the other, in the first of them asking more than you have been offered, and in the second accepting the original offer. Send me them both at the same time; I shall only produce the first to start with. Above all, make yourself clear; neither M. Mitreski nor I could make the least sense of your earlier letters.

Good day, Mademoiselle, you are on the right track; stay on it. Everything that rests with me shall be faithfully done.

It is evident that the early months of 1768 represented a most encouraging moment in Jodin's affairs. She had had a successful year on the Dresden stage, saw financial security within her grasp and was sought after by the Russian court. Her professional future, whichever contract she chose, seemed to be assured. But Jodin did not rush to accept the flattering overtures from St Petersburg, finding it hard to decide about the Russian offer. Her replies to Diderot's letters were confusing. She did her best to delay any decision, either with the Dresden theatre or for the Russian contract, an uncharacteristically vacillating behaviour which may be ascribed to her desire not to leave Schulenburg. Though the St Petersburg offer was extremely advantageous, five years in Russia would inevitably have marked the end of her relationship with the count.

Meanwhile, just as Diderot was engaged in his negotiations with the Russian court, there was a mysterious event in the Schulenburg–Jodin household. Schulenburg's *maître d'hôtel* suddenly and mysteriously disappeared after a terrible row with his master. Such an event in an ambassador's household could, obviously, have more than merely domestic significance and Werner took the butler's defection seriously, keeping his superior, Bernstorff, informed of events. He had an advertisement on the matter placed in the Town Hall, offering a reward of eighteen *ducats* to anyone who could help to trace the absconding butler, but as he wrote to Bernstorff on 27 January 1768, he suspected that the runaway could no longer be in Dresden and had taken refuge in Bohemia. He hoped Bernstorff would not think he had taken this step of pursuing the man for reasons of personal revenge. Writing in a tone of injured pride, he asserted that he, Schulenburg, was 'too much above the insults of such low creatures not to have compassion for a man who might not have foreseen what crimes his bad conduct might lead him into. Who knows, though if "some snares of seduction" had not been laid for him long since?' [41]

This affair of the missing *maître d'hôtel* is the first hint that all was not well with Schulenburg's situation in Dresden, and was to be followed two months later by a shattering turn of events. One evening in March, as Jodin was leaving the theatre after a performance, she was arrested by four grenadier guards, bundled into a carriage and thence into prison. She was given a few days to settle her affairs and then summarily expelled from Saxony. Schulenburg knew nothing of her arrest until well after the event. For the third time in her stormy life, Jodin had suffered a quite staggering blow. What intrigues or misdemeanours had precipitated this disaster?

Her arrest and detention had been ordered at the highest level, by Baron von Ende, Minister of State, the successor to Count Flemming but with whom Schulenburg was evidently not in favour.[42] Von Ende's account of Jodin's arrest and Schulenburg's abrupt departure from Dresden, as written to the Saxon envoy in Denmark (20 April 1768) makes compelling reading:[43]

M. the Danish Envoy, Count Schulenburg, left last Saturday to spend a few months on his estates. The more we have had cause to praise him in his first period as minister to our court, the more reason he has given us subsequently to complain of him. An unfortunate passion which seized him for an actress named Jodin changed him completely. This girl ['*fille*', pejorative] was engaged by our court last year, on the recommendation of the French envoy, Baron de Zuchmantel, as the leading actress in the court theatre. This was also the period that marked a change in M. de Schulenburg. Scarcely had she entered in our service, than he attached himself to her. At first he was satisfied with frequenting her, but soon afterwards he installed her in his official residence and publicly displayed her as his mistress. Their extravagant style of living which they carried on together was incredible and I willingly draw a veil over the scandalous scenes to which they treated the public.

Von Ende alleges that Jodin and Schulenburg not only indulge in 'scandalous scenes' (unspecified), but that Jodin is responsible for Schulenburg's moral deterioration, his debts and his propensity to violence. Most suggestive is von Ende's reference to abusive letters that Schulenburg sent him after the count's rows with his *valet de chambre* and his *maître d'hôtel*. Why should Schulenburg complain to the Saxon minister of state over mere domestic difficulties unless he had, or thought he had, evidence that his servants were spies in the pay of the Saxon court? The minister's expressed compassion towards Schulenburg, 'considering him to be ill and not master of his reason', seems little more than a duplicitous manoeuvre to ward off potential criticism of high-handed treatment. Von Ende continued:

> The Court could not be unaware of these goings-on since they occurred with too much publicity. But since the Court does not claim to mix in domestic affairs, as long as public security is not affected, it pretended not to know anything about it. This actress brought disorder and trouble into the Envoy's household. His finances were so affected that he was often obliged to have recourse to onerous expedients [namely to borrow money]. This put him in a foul humour and not daring to blame the author of his disorders, he dealt ruthlessly with his servants. His former butler, no longer able to bear his harsh treatment, fled, abandoning wife and children, as you will see, Sir, by the accompanying petition. He then maltreated his *valet de chambre* and after having badly beaten him, urged on by 'la Jodin', he had him sent to the Corps de Garde where he wanted to leave him imprisoned for one month on bread and water. On these two occasions, he wrote me notes in the most impetuous and improper style. But considering him to be ill, and not master of his reason, I had the discretion to suppress these missives, whilst merely indicating the impropriety of his actions to him with the greatest tact.
>
> For her part, 'la Jodin', under the protection of M. le Comte de Schulenburg committed a thousand follies. She only performed in the theatre at her own convenience and when the whim took her, mocking her superiors' orders and committed so very many impertinences, both at Court and in public, that in the end matters came to a head and she was arrested. On this occasion, as previously, we exercised all possible tact. In order to avoid any sort of disturbance, we made sure of her person as she left the theatre and took her quietly off to prison, and after having given her a few days to put her affairs in order, had her carried out of the country, an adventure which was not new to her, as she had been dismissed from Warsaw in the same manner.

We note that von Ende had Jodin arrested secretly. He must have feared not only Schulenburg's wrath but also public scandal. He feigns astonishment at the envoy's resulting pique and laments his discourtesy in not bidding a formal farewell to the Saxon court:

> From that moment, M. le Comte de Schulenburg broke off all relations with our Court. And although he has often been invited to dinner and though he has been regularly notified of all our Court galas, he has not reappeared. A few days before his departure, he wrote me a letter, of which I enclose a copy, to announce that he had obtained permission from his king to retire to his estates for a few months. You will judge, Sir, what must have been my surprise, not only that he wished to leave his post without bidding farewell to the Court, but also the improper reproaches that he heaped upon us. Not having been able to dispense with informing Monseigneur the Prince Administrator [Xavier] of the letter, His Royal Highness was indignant, quite rightly, at the conduct of the said Envoy; above all at the inconsiderate and offensive manner of his departure, without the least gesture of attention to the Sovereign to whom he was accredited. His Royal Highness ordered me to respond in the following manner, as you will see, Sir, in the attached letter, enjoining me at the same time to inform you of the above, whilst charging you to carry our complaints to the Minister of His Danish Royal Highness concerning the improper conduct of M. le Comte de Schulenburg. You should let it be known, Sir, that Monseigneur, the Prince Administrator had until now hidden Monsieur l'Envoyé's infamous conduct towards our Court out of consideration for him and even more out of regard for the King his master. But as this Minister had lost all self-control, His Royal Highness could not dispense with demanding equity and justice from His Danish Royal Highness against M. le Comte de Schulenburg.

It was quite an indictment: against Jodin; 'follies', outrageous behaviour in public; leading her lover into extravagance; a frivolous attitude towards her acting engagements; mockery and impertinence towards her superiors: against Schulenburg; losing his reason over a woman; an extravagant style of living; scandalous scenes; financial embarrassments; physical abuse of his *maître d'hôtel* and *valet de chambre*; and rudeness, amounting to *lèse-majesté*, towards His Royal Highness, the Prince Administrator. To top it all, von Ende enclosed a letter received a few days earlier from the missing butler's wife, Anna Burckhardin, giving a melodramatically lurid account of her husband's maltreatment by Schulenburg, detailing his disastrous debts and blackening Schulenburg's and Jodin's characters even further:

> Monseigneur,
> The mode of life which 'la Jodin' led with M l'Envoyé de Dannemarc having begun by separating him from a man who from his early youth served him until he became his butler, obvious proof of his irreproachable conduct until then, and which made me decide to marry him. In the month of January, money not being sufficient to pay the usual bonuses which were due to a good many people, as well as to his own domestics, of which I have the receipts in my hands, as well as the account book, confided to my husband by the Field Marshal, father of this Minister. To get him out of difficulties, I pawned my best clothes [gear]. Nevertheless, this expedient

not having sufficed to pay the dairyman, this Minister took this as an excuse
to thrash my husband, whom I have not seen again, except at the moment
when he took his hat to flee, his face black and blue from the blows of a
cane or whip and an eye from which the blood flowed. By abandoning me
with two little children of whom one is still at the breast, without a penny,
or a bite of bread to eat that day. This was on the eve of Twelfth Night. I
made various attempts to show the account books [to Schulenburg], in order
to have my money refunded, but I was never admitted to see him. I then
sent him two written requests. However I had no reply and I was not
permitted to see him. Learning finally, yesterday, that this Minister was
going to leave today in the afternoon, I straight away sent one of my relatives
to see him to whom His Excellency said that he found my proceedings
extremely impertinent, that he had no account to settle with me but with
my husband, to whom, if he returned, he would pay not only what was
owed him but make him a present of 100 *ducats*. Nevertheless by some
excess of goodness, His Excellency had the aforementioned relation paid
fifty *écus* for my children.

My husband is in Warsaw in Mr de Gastenberg's service. I am owed one
hundred *écus* less two *groschen*. I do not know how to set about regaining
my money and my things.

Dresden, 14 April, 1768   Anna Burckhardin[44]

What is one to make of this remarkable imbroglio? One has the feeling that
there must have been some truth in the accusations against Schulenburg,
particularly with regard to financial extravagance and domestic violence. Further,
knowing Jodin's histrionic temperament, one can well imagine that, as
Schulenburg's much-publicised lover, she may have committed, if not 'a
thousand follies', at least a few and to some extent may have helped to bring
the disaster on herself. It is not implausible that some of these 'follies' and
'impertinences' could have involved Jodin giving free rein to her penchant for
mockery and invective which we have already seen in Warsaw. Whereas von
Ende could have simply arranged for her to be sacked from the theatre, if she
was as flighty as he claimed, this was apparently not enough to convey the
official disapprobation she and Schulenburg had aroused. The fact that the theatre
manager, Feber, was keen to re-engage the actress, however, rather undermines
von Ende's account of her lack of professionalism.

There could very plausibly have been other quite different and political
reasons lying behind von Ende's draconian action. Schulenburg evidently
suspected, as his letters of complaint to von Ende suggest, and which the latter
suppressed, that his *maître d'hôtel*, Burckhardin, as well as his *valet de chambre*
were actually spies planted on him by the authorities. It is quite possible that
Prince Xavier had taken a dislike to Schulenburg, who was inclined in his
despatches to take the side of the Electrice Elizabeth against the Prince, and
suspected him of passing on scandalous gossip about him to Denmark (as in
the Spinnucci story). Alternatively, because Schulenburg in his letters to
Bernstorff supported the joint regency and was sceptical about the succession

of the young Elector, he may have offended the anti-regency faction. In any event it is clear that von Ende had cleverly used Schulenburg's own sexual passion and financial difficulties as a convenient lever to embarrass and thus get rid of him. There may be secrets here still to be unravelled.[45] It is, at all events, a piquant trait in our picture of Schulenburg that he later complained, and seemed surprised, at not receiving from Prince Xavier the usual going-away present given to an ambassador.[46] Throughout this period, he seems to have been sublimely unaware of the disastrous impression he had created in the Saxon court, though certainly alerted by Bernstorff: 'I cannot conceal from you that the Saxon court is laying formal complaints against you.'[47]

While all European courts were accustomed to and tolerant of sexual intrigues and irregular liaisons, the distinction between acceptable and unacceptable behaviour seemed to depend on the issue of discretion and whether the relationship in question had serious political repercussions. What 'everyone might know' (for example that Stanislas Poniatowski had been the lover of Catherine of Russia, or that Augustus the Strong of Saxony was reputed to have fathered over three hundred and sixty children) was not necessarily publicly acknowledged. There were notable examples of sexual adventures in high places which ended in disaster, but these were punished less for the deed than in letting the deed be too generally known and for their probable dynastic consequences. Under this heading, noteworthy cases such as that of Sophia Dorothea, wife of George I of England, divorced by him in 1694 over her affair with Philip Köningsmarck, or Caroline Mathilde, wife of Christian VII of Denmark disgraced and imprisoned whilst her lover, Streunsee was executed, suggest that court circles required a high level of dissembling. Where this failed, ruin followed. Yet Jodin and Schulenburg were not even engaged in an adulterous liaison. For a nobleman to take an actress as his mistress was standard behaviour. Von Ende's expressions of moral outrage have a gloriously hypocritical ring, especially given the more than loose mores of the Saxon and Danish courts. Still, it would appear that whilst the motive behind Jodin's arrest was probably political and directed primarily against Schulenburg, as the latter suspected, what gave von Ende a plausible excuse for his actions was the very public nature of the Schulenburg/Jodin relationship.

Twelve years later Schulenburg recorded the event, not as an attack on Jodin, but a personal insult to himself. The affair still rankled. His account was coloured by the fact that he had long since broken with the actress whom at this latter stage he tended to construct as the author of his other misfortunes. Though written in 1780, this journal entry throws into relief how in 1767–69 he was besotted with Jodin, to the extent of throwing up his diplomatic career for her whereas von Ende emerges as the villain of the piece. Schulenburg wrote:

> Count Flemming became Minister on his arrival from Vienna. He died
> shortly afterwards in 1767 and Baron von Ende was charged with

administering foreign affairs and it was thanks to his initiative [injustice?] that one must attribute the adventure of 'la Jodin', who, being my mistress [*amie*] and known as such, lived in my residence, rode in my carriages and often accompanied me, was, in spite of this seized, after having performed one day at the theatre, driven off in a carriage very roughly by four grenadier guards and taken to prison and then out of the country without anyone saying a word to me about what she had done. As this affront rebounded on me, I thought it appropriate to retire from the Court of Saxony. I asked permission from Count Bernstorff to spend some months on my estates in Brandenburg. [I considered that] I was not obliged to return to Dresden given the lack of consideration shown to me by Prince Xavier on this occasion. Having arrived at Salzwedel [one of Schulenburg's estates], I hastened to ask the King [of Denmark] for the grace to be recalled, which he also deigned to do. I sent my letter of resignation to M. von Ende and took leave in writing from Prince Xavier, who accepted my resignation, but without sending me the gifts usually presented on similar occasions.[48]

Outraged *amour propre* and aristocratic hauteur are the main emotions emerging from this account. He refers to his former mistress as 'la Jodin', not 'mademoiselle'. She figures as simply part of his entourage ['she lived in my residence, rode in my carriages']. The insult was to him, rather than to Jodin, and to some extent, of course, he may have been right. But his insouciance over Jodin's situation, nevertheless, seems chilling. Schulenburg, with hindsight, was attempting to explain his effective abandonment of a promising diplomatic career. Reading the subsequent correspondence between the courts of Saxony and Dresden as well as Schulenburg's letters to Bernstorff it seems evident that Schulenburg never really understood how much official disapprobation he had aroused nor how hard Bernstorff battled to save his reputation.[49] Nevertheless he was grateful not to be obliged to take his leave from the Saxon court in person. 'It would be hard to express to you, Sir,' he wrote to Bernstorff, 'how pleased I was to see that His Majesty did not require me to return to Saxony to take leave and permitted me to do so in writing. This trip would have been extremely disagreeable for me after everything that has happened.'[50] However, he penned another of his intemperate letters in his epistolary farewell, which included accusations against von Ende, further arousing the wrath of Prince Xavier. Schulenburg protested to Bernstorff:

> I don't think I could have said anything that could have displeased His Royal Highness, but in receiving M. von Ende's letter where he gives me notice that complaints have been made against me to the King, I replied that I heard this news with pain but with a tranquil mind because my intention had not been to offend His Royal Highness (Prince Xavier) but to make him aware of the lack of consideration shown to me in the affair in question.

He worried, with reason, that he might have lost favour both with Bernstorff and the King:

Whilst Your Excellency does not wish to pain me by telling me that this odious affair has altered his feelings towards me, which until now have been the happiness of my life, I am not without fear that this may be so and in addition that I may have had the misfortune to displease the King, our August Master.[51]

The affair rumbled on through the summer of 1768 between the two courts with Volkersahn, the Saxon envoy to Denmark, repeatedly receiving instructions from von Ende to ensure punishment for Schulenburg, whilst Bernstorff exerted his most emollient diplomatic skills to smooth matters over. Von Ende demanded some kind of disciplinary action, apparently not in relation to the supposed scandal of his love affair with Jodin, but because Schulenburg had failed to take leave of Dresden in due form, constituting an insult on the part of Denmark to His Royal Highness of Saxony. This lends weight to the supposition that Schulenburg was the real target of Saxon wrath. For his part, Bernstorff responded tactfully to the Saxon complaints against Schulenburg, but attempted to evade the question of punishment. As Volkersahn reported to von Ende on 15 May 1768:

Sir; Count Bernstorff, in speaking to me last Monday at the Court on the subject of M. de Schulenburg, told me that the complaints that I had passed on to him put him in an awkward position. It was clear, as your Excellency yourself remarked, that M. de Schulenburg was ill, that he was completely unhinged in his principles, and that his passion had unsettled his mind. That if it was intended to proceed against him with severity, it would at least be necessary to give him a hearing, and that the case being so bad, any explanation would be hopeless, whereas [if left alone] he might perhaps recover one day from his errors. M. de Bernstorff added that he knew the humanity of our court and that Your Excellency had given such fine proofs of your moderation in this whole affair, that he hoped that you would be satisfied if he, M. de Bernstorff, wrote me a letter in which he would indicate how much M. de Schulenburg's conduct was disapproved of and that the King, to show that his ministers must apply themselves to gain the benevolence and good graces of His Royal Highness and of the Court, had recalled Count Schulenburg, and that his successor had orders to make himself worthy and to merit and by every possible means the kindness of Monseigneur the Administrator [Xavier].[52]

In order to calm the diplomatic waters, Bernstorff had seized on the suggestion, originally propounded by von Ende, that Schulenburg had lost his reason in the violence of his passion. Since it was useless to argue with someone who was effectively mad, it would be better to wait until he was recalled to his normal self, to wit: fell out of love. Bernstorff was happy to make the resignation appear to the Saxon court as a royal reprimand, but at the same time wished to protect his love-struck envoy. Whether Bernstorff believed the von Ende/Volkersahn version of events or Schulenburg's is not known but he was remarkably compassionate towards the latter. Whilst the Saxon court continued to insist on a letter of apology from Schulenburg, Bernstorff clearly felt this could not be demanded, since Schulenburg believed that the apology should come to him from Dresden. As Volkersahn put it to von Ende: 'It seems to me that M. de Bernstorff considers the Count de Schulenburg to be too worked up to be amenable to reason and thus he fears insisting on anything from him, lest Schulenburg have the audacity to refuse.'[53] Had Schulenburg received and refused such an order he would have been in rebellion against the Danish King, an act of treason. Bernstorff evidently feared to push him too far but did finally charge his envoy to make a formal apology, dictating the letter he was to write:

> 2 June, 1768,
> Sir; I have again the displeasure of telling you that the Saxon court is not happy with the letters that you wrote to the Prince-Administrator and to his Minister and that they have informed me of it. I see no other way of your terminating this most unpleasant affair than to write to the Baron d'Ende to express the following: that if in the letter that you had the honour of addressing him, some comments had slipped in relative to what had happened to you, this was not with the intention of reproaching him in the least, but only that it was not possible for you to ignore an affair that had affected you so deeply; that you would be devastated to fail in respect to him in any way ... and that you will never have any other desire than to please him.[54]

Schulenburg followed orders, if reluctantly and grovelled as requested. He continued to insist, however, that he was the injured party.

And what of Jodin in all this? In spite of being kidnapped from the theatre, insulted by the grenadier guards, thrust into prison and summarily deported, her spirits do not seem to have been greatly dampened, or at least not for long. She could not afford the luxury of melancholy, but she was certainly angry, initiating a lawsuit against the Saxon court for unlawful arrest. Cast adrift both from her stage career and from her lover, by July 1768 she nevertheless managed to travel, though with difficulty (involving 'disagreeable incidents en route'),[55] to Schulenburg's estate, Salzwedel in Brandenburg, a distance of approximately four hundred and fifty kilometres. Arriving unexpectedly, she had a rapturous reunion with Schulenburg, though they had quarrelled bitterly prior to the count's departure from Dresden, the latter probably having blamed her for his financial and diplomatic embarrassments. It is striking that neither in his contemporaneous letters to Bernstorff, before Jodin's arrival in Salzwedel, nor in his journal written twelve years later, does Schulenburg show any concern for Jodin's predicament. Nevertheless in the summer of 1768, after their reunion, his views were very different. In a letter of 16 July 1768 to Bernstorff, he saw no incongruity in recommending Pierre Jodin, Marie Madeleine's uncle, to the Danish court, citing as his motive: 'The good [fortune] which I wish for his amiable niece.'[56] One wonders how Schulenburg could have been naïve enough to assume, in the midst of the diplomatic row he and Jodin had unleashed, that the King would give preferment to one of Jodin's relations. Bernstorff, waiting in vain for

Schulenburg's 'return to reason', must have sighed on receiving this effusion. Schulenburg had evidently not 'recovered his reason' and was still passionately in love.

Diderot's letter of 6 April 1768, written shortly after Jodin's arrest, takes up the tale. At this stage, having just emerged from prison (and before embarking for Salzwedel), she had proposed returning directly to Paris and living with the Diderots. Mme Diderot, otherwise a loyal supporter of the Jodins, was not enthusiastic. Much to Diderot's alarm, moreover, Marie Madeleine had already launched a lawsuit against the Saxon court arising from her arbitrary arrest and detention.[57] His reference to the lawsuit exudes caution, since he rightly feared his letter might be intercepted. He realised that the Saxon court could easily extend its enmity to Jodin whilst in France, if she persisted in legal complaints, and that Prince Xavier could arrange to have her arrested via the influence of the Saxon ambassador in Paris. He urged her to settle her financial affairs and return quickly to France.

[6 April 1768][58]
Stop at Strasbourg for as short a time as possible; your affairs require you here.

I have received everything you sent me. I am sending you these two letters, which would otherwise have been too much delayed. I have left Dumolard alone, leaving it for you to deal with him as you please. M. Baur will not take any further action without seeing me.

I hope that after tomorrow at the latest our money will be placed. I could not manage things any sooner since life-annuities on the King were closed when I received your capital.

I have said nothing about your suit against the Saxon court. It is not that I don't see clearly what you feel; but I am afraid you may be taking a false step, perhaps perpetrating a real folly which might bring you worse treatment in Paris than in Dresden. All it needs is for the ambassador to make a complaint to the French court. You have not weighed these things up.

Do not take this as ill will on the part of Madame Diderot, nor any kind of unwillingness to oblige you in everything; but her advice, which seems good to me, is that you should take rooms in a lodging house for a few months, depositing your belongings there, to give yourself the chance to look for a suitable apartment. This is necessary, Easter being over.

I am writing in haste. I am terribly sorry about your 'adventure'; but when you arrive here we can see each other and consult about your affairs.

Bonjour, mademoiselle.

Another word. You will not make a good impression on the French actors [in Paris] by linking up with Ofrene.[59]

Diderot's next letter of 11 July, redirected to Salzwedel, was less sympathetic and more appalled at the news he had undoubtedly garnered about the Dresden episode. He wanted nothing to do with Jodin's lawsuit and protested at his name being used as a character witness, pointing out that his reputation with officialdom as editor of the banned *Encyclopédie* would hardly help her cause.

On money matters he counselled her not to let her mother know how much money she, Jodin, possessed.

Diderot revealed that Mme Jodin had been in a lawsuit too, with Mme Brunet, their erstwhile landlady in the rue Saint Benoit, who was claiming three months' lost rent. Mme Jodin had won the suit, but in retaliation Mme Brunet was busy spreading scandal about her and her daughter. It would seem that Jodin's chambermaid, whom she had brought from France, was an old friend of Mme Brunet and was secretly feeding her gossip about Jodin and her lover:

[11 July 1768][60]
You will never persuade me, Mademoiselle, that the unpleasantness that happened to you *en route* was not brought on by yourself. When one wants to be respected by others, one must show them that one respects oneself.

You have also committed a further indiscretion, in giving publicity to this adventure by legal proceedings. Don't you see that it is a new objection that your enemies will not fail to make against you if, by any unforeseen reason, you unfortunately have to return to your old employment? [Diderot appears to mean that now firmly established in her relationship with Schulenburg, she will have no need to return to the stage. We will see that Jodin had other ideas]. And then, you have made use of my name in a thoroughly scandalous context. It is a name that, if pronounced before a judge, cannot bring any credit to you[61] and can only injure people's good opinion of me.

I have drawn the two hundred *livres* of your pension from the King. M. de Van Eycken[62] has paid the bill drawn on himself, and M. Baur has accepted the bill of exchange you know of. I thus have a good sum of money in my hands, which I will dispose of as you please. I also have the portrait of the Count and the copy of yours.

Whatever you do, Mademoiselle, do not mention this money to your mother. The pension you have granted her will be paid punctiliously; but, being the spendthrift she is, if she knew I was holding money of yours we would never have a moment's peace, and soon you would not have much left. I am still waiting for the contract for your life-annuities; we cannot afford much more delay. It is impossible for me to take care of your affairs if you do not have a deed of attorney drawn up, naming me. I am enclosing a model. See to this without delay.

The owner of the hotel in the rue Saint Benoit wanted to force your mother to stay for three months. There was a lawsuit, and we have won.

The letter concluded with advice on how to proceed in her dealings with Schulenburg. Jodin had evidently told Diderot of Schulenburg's physical attacks on her, evidence that he was violent not only to his servants but also to his lover. Diderot, however, was unsympathetic, suggesting that she had brought this on herself: while it was contemptible of a 'galant homme' to strike a woman; it was still worse for a woman to deserve this punishment. His portrait of a woman in a rage, focusing on physical details ('if your eyes flame, the muscles of your cheeks and neck swell' and so on.) seeks to show Jodin a grotesque view of herself. Such visions of female anger could well have been drawn from his own domestic experience. Diderot complained frequently of his wife's jealousy and its unpleasant consequences for himself.[63] His sympathies, at this juncture, lie almost entirely with 'Monsieur le Comte'. Not for the first time, he urges Jodin to adopt the feminine qualities of gentleness, patience and sensitivity proper to her sex, scarcely the advice of a sexual egalitarian, though perhaps prudent in the circumstances. But it is hard to think of any qualities more foreign to his actress/pupil:

> Be good, be well-conducted, be gentle; an offence given in return for a previous offence makes two offences, and more shame attaches to the first than to the second. If you do not try constantly to curb the violence of your character, you will not be able to live with anybody; you will be unhappy; and, nobody being able to be happy with you, the sweetest feelings for you will be extinguished, and people will flee a beautiful Fury, tired of her tormenting ways. Two lovers who hurl vulgar insults at each other are both equally degraded.
>
> Regard any quarrel as the beginning of a permanent rupture. If you keep pulling strands from a cable, however strong, it will break. If you have had the luck to captivate a man of goodwill, think how valuable this is; remember that gentleness, patience and sensibility are the virtues becoming to a woman and that tears can be potent weapons. If your eyes flame, the muscles of your cheeks and neck swell, your arms stiffen, your voice grows harsh, and your lips utter violent things, indecencies and brutal insults, you are then no better than a fishwife, a creature hideous to see and hideous to hear; you will have renounced the lovable qualities of your sex for the odious vices of ours.
>
> It is unworthy of a gallant man to strike a woman; it is even worse for a woman to deserve it. If you do not improve, if your days continue to be marked by follies, I shall lose all the interest I take in you.
>
> Give my respects to the Count. Look after his happiness, since he looks after yours.

Diderot must have had reason to think that his letter might have gone astray, for he wrote again in five days' time. Meanwhile he had discovered that, instead of listening to his advice not to mention her financial affairs to her mother, Jodin had written her an angry letter, forbidding her to try to get money out of Diderot. From Jodin's commissions to Diderot, it is clear that Schulenburg was supporting her handsomely. They had had miniature portraits made of each other (now, alas, lost) and asked Diderot to arrange for these to be mounted as bracelets:

[16 July 1768][64]
You have written your mother a letter as harsh as it is undeserved. She has won her lawsuit. Madame Brunet does not seem at all an honourable woman. I have drawn your pension from the King. I have received two bills of exchange from M. Fischer. One is for 1373 *livres* 18s. 6d. drawn upon Messrs Tourton and Baur; it has been accepted and will be paid on the 9th of next month. The other is for 2376 *livres* 1s. 6d. drawn on M. Van Eycken, which has been paid. These two sums make 3750 *livres* in all, the equivalent of a thousand Saxon *écus*.

I will have your bracelet made by M. Belle, a friend of mine, whose work and probity I can vouch for. But two things: first, the portrait is much too big, and we shall need to cut it down almost as far as the hat, which will be no harm at all. Secondly, the surround of the portrait and the monogram will be very mean-looking if we spend no more than a hundred *louis*.[65] The craftsman, who is not interested in selling or making a profit, says that to make the bracelets look decent one must spend 3000 *livres* [or a thousand *écus*]. See what you think.

Write to me about this, and give my respects to the Count. Try for God's sake, both of you, to do nothing foolish, if you do not want one to be punished by the other. Love each other peacefully, and do not pervert Nature, or a passion which is less precious for the pleasures it give us than the evils for which it consoles us.

If you decide to spend a thousand *écus* on your bracelets, that will leave me with 750 *livres*, which I will dispose of as you choose. Be lovable, and (above all) gentle, and well-behaved. It is all connected. If you neglect any of these qualities, you will find it hard to have the others.

Mme Jodin (now returned to Paris) added an enthusiastic, ungrammatical and unpunctuated postscript about her daughter's situation, rather in the spirit of Jane Austen's Mrs. Bennett. She was happy to learn that her daughter was 'at the summit' of her desires. She has evidently met the Count, on her visit to Dresden, as she speaks of the portrait's resemblance to him. Her invitation for the couple to stay with her in Paris may not have suited Schulenburg and Jodin's ideas of luxury. In any case they were not to take it up:

Postscript by Mme Jodin
I have read your letter of 21 June which gave me much pleasure to learn that you are well and that you are at the summit of your desires. It is all I wish for in the world to see you in the arms of all you adore he well deserves it. I pray to Heaven for his welfare as for yours which is very dear to me my dear daughter. I have received your portrait from Mme Diderot and have kissed it with tears of joy. Madame Diderot makes me put it in my snuffbox and I have seen Monsieur the Count's which is very like him. I have received from M. Diderot your pension from the King which comes at a good moment I am very comfortable in my apartment thanks to M. Roger's help. Your letters make me hope that you will come to Paris with Monsieur the Count. You need not search for any other lodging than mine for it is very pretty, you can both of you stay there. My God what a pleasure for me if I have the happiness to see you again the hope keeps me alive. I have been to see M. Roger to receive the two hundred *francs* he said he had not received them yet and that as soon as he has received them he will bring them to me. I am not worried. I have heard that your chambermaid writes to all her friends about what goes on in the Count's household I thought I would warn you so take care. I must tell you La Frederique has a *valet de chambre* as her lover she is in great poverty I have told her she shall never set foot in my house. M. Fol and M. Balion send their compliments. Your aunt embraces you with all her heart and Mme Laroche embraces you with all her soul I beg you my dear daughter to write to me before you leave Stettin I hope

you will do me that pleasure. Adieu my dear I embrace you with all my
heart and am your good mother widow Jodin.
    If you wish, give my respects to Monsieur the Count and the Mistress[66]
if you think it proper.

All that summer of 1768 Jodin and Schulenburg remained at Salzwedel. Their
happiness in each other seems to have been complete, but Diderot, as we see
from the two preceding letters, continued to be sceptical about their capacity
for happiness. The couple quarrelled too passionately; their temperaments were
too volatile. Jodin evidently confided the progress of their affair and its frequent
contretemps to him in detail. Diderot for his part attempted to convince her that
she should recognise her good luck and do nothing to alienate Schulenburg: 'If
you keep pulling strands from a cable, however strong, it will break. If you
have had the luck to captivate a man of goodwill, think how valuable this is'
(letter of 11 July). Jodin was to recall this advice many years later: 'How much
consideration, how much deference, living together requires. The least collision
destroys the charm.'[67]
    Whereas Diderot's earlier letters had been primarily concerned with tutoring
Jodin in his theories of acting and urging her to live the life of 'une honnête
femme', this phase of his correspondence constitutes a moving attempt in what
might now be called relationship counselling, an effort to remind both these
passionate lovers that their state was precarious and how much they had to lose
in refusing to find accommodation with one another: 'Try for God's sake, both
of you, to do nothing foolish, if you do not want one to be punished by the
other. Love each other peacefully, and do not pervert Nature, or a passion which
is less precious for the pleasures it gives us than the evils for which it consoles
us' (letter of 16 July). Diderot himself, as we have indicated, was no stranger to
domestic disharmony. A man of amorous temperament, his affairs, first with
Mme de Puisieux and later with Sophie Volland, had, not unnaturally, rendered
his wife Nanette extremely unhappy.[68] Thus Diderot's descriptions of lovers'
rows were based on personal experience as was his rueful estimate of the grand
passion: 'less precious for the pleasures it gives us than the evil for which it
consoles us'.
    But it is not always possible to follow good advice, even from a philosopher.
Jodin and Schulenburg had a variety of pressures upon them: their own tempers;
their free spending habits; Schulenburg's generosity to Jodin which thrust him
ever deeper into debt; his arrogance and jealousy; her refusal to take on a
subservient role in the relationship; her recklessness and finally her desire to
return to the stage. These tensions would be acted out over the next eighteen
months in Bordeaux.

Notes

1. For an account of travel in the best style see Martin, *Une Française à Varsovie en 1766*, pp. 28–35.
2. Claire Tomalin, *Mrs Jordan's Profession* (London: Penguin, 1995), p. 28.
3. See 'Contract de Mlle Jodin', Reglement 1768–70, Ausgemartet ff. J. Kaster, 'Theater u. Musick, 297a, 326, Staatsarchiv Dresden.
4. Diderot, *Correspondance*, VIII, letter 472, 21 February 1768.
5. Jodin Procès 120, 124.
6. See Henri Lagrave, Charles Mazouer and Marc Regaldo, *La Vie théâtrale à Bordeaux, des origines à nos jours*, I (Paris: CNRS, 1985), p. 311 for the improvident lifestyle of actors.
7. Jodin Procès, 123.
8. 'I, the undersigned, agree that I have engaged myself for the good pleasure of His Royal Highness, Monseigneur le Prince Administrateur [Xavier], to play in the troupe of the *Comédie Française* in the service of the Electoral Court of Saxony, the leading roles of queens, the roles of Her mione in *Andromaque*, Agrippine in *Britannicus*, Cléopâtre in *Rodogne*, Elisabeth in *The Count of Essex*. In addition, noble mothers and all roles attached to those functions except five or six which the Court reserves to dispose of as it wishes. I promise in addition to facilitate in every way the success of the performance and to provide myself with equipment [costumes] necessary for my employment; the above to be paid at the rate of 1200 *écus* per year which will be paid by 100 *écus* a month. In addition I will be paid 200 *florins* for my return trip in the event that I should leave the service of his Electoral Highness without a new engagement, and that the director of the troupe which I will be going to join does not pay me my travel expenses. The present engagement will be valid for two years commencing the first of April 1767 and finishing the end of March 1769, so that if the Court is not pleased to prolong my contract, I will be warned a year in advance and I will be free to leave immediately after the closure of the theatre during Lent 1769. For the rest, I will enjoy, in virtue of this engagement, all the advantages attached to His Electoral Highness's theatre and [this contract] will have the authority and value as witnessed by a notary and witness. 29 February 1767.' 326 Contract de Mlle Jodin, Staatsarchiv Dresden, Reglement 1768–70, 581, Ausgemartet ff. J. Kaster, 'Theater u. Musick'.
9. Matthew Smith Anderson, *Europe in the Eighteenth Century: 1712–1783* (London: Longman, 1961), p. 198; E. Weiss, 'Europe centrale et orientale: les Etats Allemands, in *L'Absolutisme éclairé*, ed. B. Köpeczi, A. Soboul, E. H. Balázs and D. Kosáry (Paris: CNRS, 1985), pp. 190–91.
10. These Electors of Saxony and Kings of Poland had, confusingly, different names in their different roles. Thus Frederick Augustus I of Saxony was Augustus II of Poland. Frederick Augustus II of Saxony was Augustus III of Poland.
11. Arsène Thévenot, *Correspondance inédite du Prince François-Xavier de Saxe, Comte de Lusace* (Paris: Dumoulin, 1874), p. 9.
12. Letter of Instruction to Count Werner XXV von der Schulenburg from Count Bernstorff (1763), Landesarchiv Magdeburg: Landeshauptarchiv Aussenstelle Wernigerode, Rep. H. Beetzendorf II, II, no. 214.
13. This letter from Diderot still addressed to her in Warsaw and written in early January 1767, has led scholars to suppose she was still in Poland, but she was almost certainly already *en route* to Dresden, possibly having gone on tour. Diderot, *Correspondance*, VII, letter 427, 'A Mlle Jodin, A Varsovie', Janvier, 1767, pp. 11–14.

14. In 1765 Catherine the Great, hearing that Diderot was badly off, bought his library from him for 15,000 *livres*, appointing him its 'librarian'. In return he performed many services for her, including buying paintings for the Hermitage collection; and in 1773 he would visit her in Russia.

15. In Racine's *Athalie* and *Britannicus* respectively.

16. Ragnhild Hatton, *George I Elector and King* (London, Thames and Hudson, 1978), pp. 48–54.

17. During a sojourn of Schulenburg in Paris early in 1767, he and Grimm had been responsible for saddling Diderot with a Prussian woman painter, Mme Terbouche, who would cause him a great deal of harassment.

18. Georges Duplessis, *Mémoires et Journal de J.-G. Wille, Graveur du Roi*, I (Paris: Jules Renouard, 1857).

19. Johann Friedrich Danneil, the younger, *Das Geschlect der von der Schulenburg* (Salzwedel: 1847), vol. 2, no. 82; Georg Schmidt, *Das Geschlect von der Schulenburg* (Beetzendorf: 1908), pp. 563–5.

20. 'Journal fait par moi à Copenhague, 1736–1780', Journal of Werner XXV von der Schulenburg, Rep. H Beetzendorf II, II no. 118–27 – Sachsen-Anhalt, Landeshauptarchiv Aussenstelle Wernigerode.

21. The preponderance of Germans serving the Danish State in high positions became, however, a focus of criticism. In 1766 Bernstorff was forced to deny allegations that he favoured the recruitment of his fellow Germans and despised the Danes. 'Apologie de Monsieur le Comte de Bernstorff', Privatarkiver, Oversekretar J. H. E. Bernstorff, BXX 5130, no. 63, Statenskancellie for Udenlandske Affairer, State Archive Regi, Copenhagen.

22. Anderson, *Europe in the Eighteenth Century, 1713–1783*, p. 198; Stuart Andrews, *Eighteenth-Century Europe; the 1680s to 1815* (London: Longman, 1965), p. 170.

23. Horace Walpole, *The Letters of Horace Walpole Fourth Earl of Orford*, ed. Mrs Paget Toynbee, VII: 1766–71, letter of 14 August 1769.

24. See 'Introduction', *Correspondance Ministérielle du Comte J. H. E. Bernstorff, 1751–1770*, ed. Peter August Frederik Stoud Vedel, 2 vols (Copenhagen: Jorgensen, 1882).

25. Schulenburg, 'Journal fait par moi à Copenhague'.

26. Letters of Instruction to Count Werner XXV von der Schulenburg from Count Bernstorff, Foreign Minister of Denmark, 1763, Landesarchiv LHA Rep. H Beetzendorf II, II, no. 214.

27. Letter of 9 November 1763 to Count Bernstorff which expresses humble apologies for the lack of style and content of his letters. Statenskancellie for Udenlandske Affairer State Archive Regi, Copenhagen, pa-al 49 Sachsen B.

28. 12 May 1766 to Count Bernstorff, Statenskancellie for Udenlandske Affairer State Archive Regi, Copenhagen, pa-al 49 Sachsen B, 1764–68, no. 133.

29. Anderson, *Europe in the Eighteenth Century*, p. 161 notes the common practice of the interception and copying of despatches of foreign diplomats.

30. Kirchbergner was dismissed with the rank of State Counsellor. E. Marquard, *Danske Gesandter og Genandt-Statspersonale* (Copenhagen, Rigsarkivet, 1952), p. 324.

31. Bernstorff to Schulenburg, 27 April 1765, Rep. Beetzendorf, II, II, no. 214.

32. SKUA, Sachsen B, 19 April 1765 to Bernstorff. Schulenburg sent this letter by private courier and was therefore able to be more frank than in his more official diplomatic correspondence which it was assumed was read by Saxon agents. It was Schulenburg's view that Count Flemming, Minister of State for Foreign Affairs and much attached to the two regents, was being undermined by supporters of his corrupt predecessor, the Comte de Bruhl. On Flemming's death he was succeeded

by the Baron von Ende on whom Schulenburg blamed his subsequent troubles.

33. Diderot, *Corrrespondance*, VII, letter 445, 'A Mademoiselle Jodin', pp. 83–4.

34. Evidently a financial intermediary. Diderot mentions him again in a later letter. We note with interest that Jodin is buying books, rather than merely clothes and jewelry.

35. Letter of 25 February 1768, Karler Theatre, 175, Staatsarchiv Dresden.

36. Diderot, *Correspondance*, VIII, 'A Mademoiselle Jodin', 21 February 1768, pp. 12–14.

37. Bankers.

38. Ninon de Lenclos (1620–1705), celebrated for her *salon*, her gaiety of spirit, and her many lovers. Diderot's comment is rather obscure. Beginning with his condemnation of Dumolard, he then seems to be reproaching Jodin.

39. Alexis Quinault (1693–1767), a famous tragic actor.

40. A *franc* was synonymous with a *livre*. A *pistole* was the equivalent of ten *francs*.

41. Schulenburg to Bernstorff, 7/2/1768, no. 188, SKUA, Sachsen B. The full text of the letter with regard to the butler continues as follows: 'All my investigations in relation to my fugitive butler have until now been unavailing. There is little prospect now that I will succeed in catching him. If he had remained in Dresden and if the government's investigations had been faithfully carried out, it would have been difficult for the man to remain hidden and not to be discovered. I prefer therefore to think that he has taken the decision to retire to Bohemia, as I am told he has. At my request, a poster was put up on the Town Hall promising a reward of eighteen *ducats* to anyone who would give information as to his whereabouts. If I was so eager to apprehend him, this was certainly because of the unfortunate consequences which such an event, if unpunished, brings with it and I am too far above the insults of these vile types not to have compassion on this unhappy man who perhaps had not foreseen what crimes his bad conduct could lead him into and who knows whether he has not long since been caught up by others in seductive snares.'

42. Leopold Nicolaus von Ende (1715–92) became the Saxon court Cabinet Minister and Minister of the Interior and War. He was, therefore, a powerful man. Jodin might have been pleased to learn that in 1777 he too fell from favour, 'following his undiplomatic behaviour in trade with the adventurer d'Aglollo' and as the biographer notes, 'took his departure from the Saxon court in disgrace'. *Allgemeine Deutsche Biographie*, 6, ed. Elben-Fickler (Leipzig: Duncker and Humblot, 1877).

43. The Baron von Ende to M. de Volkersahn, Dresden 20 April 1768, Loc. 2713–85, Dresden Hauptstaatsarchiv; also, for another view: Werner von der Schulenburg, 'Journal fait par moi'.

44. Letter from Anna Burckhardin, 14 April 1768 to the Baron von Ende, Loc. 2713, Dresden Hauptstaatsarchiv. The original syntax has been retained.

45. The Danish diplomatic archive in Copehagen holds no letters from Schulenburg for the month of March, and Bernstorff, in his letters to Schulenburg, referring to his troubles, is careful to limit himself to generalities. He cleared the files of anything compromising to Schulenburg and told him that he had hidden the whole affair from the King. There is no mention of Jodin in the Danish diplomatic correspondence. SKUA Sachsen C, 2 June 1768.

46. Werner von der Schulenburg, 'Journal fait par moi', 1780.

47. SKUA Sachsen C, 30 April 1768.

48. Werner von der Schulenburg, 'Journal fait par moi', 1780.

49. A letter of 13 April 1768 to Bernstorff speaks of Schulenburg's need to re-establish his health, that he has broken up his household and hopes the king of Denmark

will not insist that he returns to a court where he has suffered so much unpleasantness: 'My health which has not allowed me to leave my house for a month has obliged me to write to the Secretary of State Baron von Ende, to beg him to excuse me in this respect to their Royal Highnesses. The first letters which I will have the honour of writing to Your Excellency will be from Saltzwedel where I beg you to kindly send the replies which you deign to make. I greatly desire to spend at least the whole summer quietly there. My health is in fact much more unsettled than Your Excellency may imagine.' pa-al 49 Sachsen B.

50. Schulenburg to Bernstorff, 14 May 1768 at Salzwedel, SKUA pa-al 49 Sachsen B.
51. Schulenburg to Bernstorff, 14 May 1768, SKUA pa-al 49 Sachsen B 1764–68.
52. Juël Dossier, 113, Dresden Haupstaatsarchiv.
53. Juël Dossier, 126, Dresden, Haupstaatsarchiv.
54. SKUA Sachsen C.
55. Diderot, *Correspondance*, VIII, letter of 11 July 1768.
56. Schulenburg to Bernstorrf, 16 July 1768, SKUA pa-al 49, Sachsen B 1764–68.
57. The details of her Dresden catastrophe seem to have been known to Diderot but referred to obliquely. Roth in his Denis Diderot, *Correspondance* VIII did not have access to the Dresden material and could not account for 'la nature de ce "désagrément", ni sur "la circonstance tout à fait scandaleuse"', to which Diderot refers in the subsequent letter of 11 July p. 65.
58. Diderot, *Correspondance*, VIII, letter 476, 'A Mademoiselle Jodin à Dresde', 6 April 1768, pp. 23–4.
59. See Diderot, *Correspondance* VIII, p. 24 note 6 on Aufresne, who made his debut in 1765 (as did Jodin). He suffered the jealousy of his fellow actors who feared him as a rival. He left Paris for Prussia and Russia in the same year. He may have urged Jodin to take up the Russian appointment. Diderot thought that this friendship would do Jodin no good if she hoped to appear on the Paris stage.
60. Diderot, *Correspondance*, VIII, letter 481, 'A Mademoiselle Jodin', 11 July 1768, pp. 65–7.
61. Diderot, as a known atheist and editor of the officially banned *Encyclopédie*, was not in favour with the authorities.
62. The Liège envoy.
63. An echo of the Diderots' unhappy marriage can be heard in Jodin's *Vues législatives pour les femmes*, where she describes how clandestine affairs on the husband's part 'produce a state of civil war which ends by making the husband a stranger in his own house' Jodin, *Vues législatives pour les femmes* (Angers: Mame, 1790), p. 60.
64. Diderot, *Correspondance*, VIII, letter 482, 'A Mademoiselle Jodin', 16 July 1768, pp. 68–9.
65. A *louis* was the equivalent of twenty-four *francs*.
66. Schulenburg's mother? It does not seem likely that Schulenburg would have introduced his mistress to his mother, but it is possible.
67. Jodin, *Vues législatives pour les femmes*, p. 66.
68. Diderot married Anne-Toinette Champion, a lace and linen-maker with whom he had fallen violently in love, in 1741, against his father's wishes. Diderot was a fond father but not a faithful husband. His affair with Sophie Volland produced many of the marvellous letters which fill his correspondence. See Furbank, *Diderot*, pp. 17–22 and 186–8. For a first-hand account of the Diderot household and his other relationships see A. Vandeul, 'Mémoires de Mme De Vandeul', Diderot, *Oeuvres Complètes*, I, pp. 776–801; Ernest Seillière, *Diderot* (Paris: Les Editions de France, 1944), pp. 9–17 gives a sympathetic account of the travails of the Diderot marriage.

CHAPTER SIX

Bordeaux 1768–69

Diderot's letters of the summer of 1768 reveal a good deal of the hopes, fears and tensions associated with Jodin's and Schulenburg's reunion at Salzwedel. Jodin had written him detailed accounts of her difficult trip thither from Dresden and her reception by the lover from whom she would have had good reason to fear she was to be parted for ever. However as Mme Jodin had put it, Marie Madeleine was now 'at the summit of her desires', reunited with Schulenburg in what was hoped to be a permanent rapprochement. On his side, Diderot assumed, as we have seen in his previous letter, that Jodin's position was sufficiently secure as the Count's consort for her to leave the stage permanently.[1] Nevertheless he feared the very intensity of their relationship and was sceptical of their capacity to endure one another for long: 'I can neither approve nor disapprove of your reconciliation with Monsieur le Comte. It is too doubtful whether you are made for his happiness or he for yours.'[2]

The couple decided to flee the rigours of the coming Brandenburg winter and go south to a warmer climate for Schulenburg's health. Jodin persuaded the Count to fix on Bordeaux, rather than some obscure spa town. In his journal of 1780, he was to blame Jodin for what he later felt was a bad decision, claiming in addition that she had followed him to Salzwedel, though not at his behest. But these were the rather jaundiced statements of hindsight. In the summer of 1768, it is clear that her influence over him was immense and that if he was the slave of his passion for the actress, he was a willing slave. The couple travelled to Bordeaux by sea, embarking from Hamburg:

> It was in the month of April of that year [1768] that I left Dresden for Salzwedel where 'la Jodin' came to join me without my having sent for her. Being in very precarious health, I had long since resolved to retire to a hot climate and the provinces of the Midi had been praised to me for the mildness of their climate and as being inexpensive. Were it not for 'la Jodin' I would have gone peacefully to Switzerland, then making up my mind which country would have best suited me and put enough money into life annuities to live agreeably. 'La Jodin' persuaded me to go by sea to Bordeaux, ... which I did, leaving from Hamburg. I embarked with her and in three weeks we arrived in Bordeaux. As the cost of living there is very expensive and as she cost me too much, I perceived that my income would not suffice to live there agreeably.[3]

Looking back over the perspective of ten years, Schulenburg credited Jodin with responsibility for his increasingly precarious financial position. Unlike the delightful Bellenot whom he had known in his youthful Paris days, 'la Jodin' became an unaffordable luxury. But he was without a doubt a willing partner in their joint extravagance. When they arrived in Bordeaux the couple continued the grand manner of living they had adopted in Dresden, buying expensive clothes and jewellery, attending balls and joining in the life of display typical of this wealthy provincial city. In addition, Schulenburg generously settled some 25,000 *livres* on his lover. Economic considerations were to be one of the determinants of this relationship and Jodin's finances are one of the intriguing and revealing aspects of their Bordeaux sojourn, chronicled over the following year in remarkable detail in Diderot's letters.

Why did Jodin persuade Schulenburg to choose Bordeaux for their winter quarters? It was, as he rightly said, an expensive place to live. But far more importantly from Jodin's point of view was the fact that Bordeaux was the French city which had the most flourishing theatre outside of Paris. A prosperous, indeed a wealthy merchantile centre, with a tradition of quasi-independent self-governance, Bordeaux had come under the rule of the Duc de Richelieu in 1758. The Duke, having lost influence at court to the Duc de Choiseul and Mme de Pompadour, was given the governorship of Guiyenne (the province of which Bordeaux was the capital) as a consolation prize. Always a devotee of luxury, gambling and erotic pleasures, Richelieu astonished the Bordelais by importing a style of ostentatious living hitherto unknown in their relatively sober circles. An anonymous contemporary critic commenting on Richelieu's effect on Bordeaux life notes:

> His hotel became a place of bad repute which modesty no longer dared approach without blushing ... The luxury that he displayed made others wish to imitate him. We are all moved to follow dominant influences and nothing is as seductive as the appearance of opulence and the attractions of pleasure. Expenses increased in every family; women, who never cease to be tormented by the desire of pleasing, studied with especial care that refined and expensive art of 'la toilette'.[4]

Richelieu, as a Gentleman of the Royal Bed Chamber had been in charge of the Comédie-Française, taking a detailed interest in the theatre. It was he who had licensed Jodin as an actress in 1765. In Bordeaux, his passion for the theatre, as for women, continued unabated. The twenty years of Richelieu's governorship gave Bordeaux the finest provincial theatre in France as well as the society most oriented towards conspicuous consumption of any outside Paris.[5] Although Jodin had in theory abandoned her theatrical career for her relationship with Schulenburg, it is evident she was still drawn to the stage. In the eighteenth century, it would have seemed to many that the career of an actress with its inevitable insecurities was a poor exchange for the life of ease offered as the acknowledged mistress of a wealthy aristocrat. This was not a period in which women 'chose careers' in the sense that they do today. Some years later Jodin spoke of 'the strong propensity which had always drawn me to the theatre'.[6] Evidently she found it almost impossible to renounce acting even for love and a good deal of money. Ironically, Diderot who had coached her to adopt his dramatic theories and praised the social and moral the value of the art, would attempt from prudential motives to dissuade her from re-launching her career.

Though the famous Grand Théâtre de Bordeaux was not built until 1771, a permanent troupe had been established there in other theatres since 1761. Salaries were relatively high, thanks to the shortage of French actors, many of whom, like Jodin, worked abroad. In the year 1768–69, when she and Schulenburg arrived in Bordeaux, the troupe consisted of thirty-seven actors and singers, twenty-eight dancers and twenty-four musicians, whose huge cost, borne by the city government or *jurat*, was 154,341 *livres* per annum.[7] Thus by any standards Bordeaux boasted a generously endowed municipal theatre. The director, Belmont, a barrister turned actor, had persuaded Voltaire to write a dedication to one of his plays especially for Bordeaux, a distinction which further helped place the theatre on the cultural map.[8] The troupe, however, lacked good tragic actors and was obliged to import prestigious Parisian names such as Mlle Clairon and Lekain for short periods. Though no contract or record of performance has emerged from the Bordeaux theatre archives for Mlle Jodin, we can be certain from Diderot's letters that she appeared with success on the Bordeaux stage a number of times from the spring of 1769.[9]

One of Diderot's worries about Jodin's long-standing ambition to launch herself at the Paris Comédie-Française concerned the notorious difficulty of pleasing the critical, indeed brutal, Parisian audiences who could ruin an actor's career after one performance if they were not pleased with them. Bordeaux, second only to Paris in wealth and sophistication, also boasted turbulent and hypercritical popular audiences. Richelieu, who his enemies complained ruled like a despot, attempted to bring order both to the acting fraternity and to the theatre audiences. He issued draconian regulations, as had the local magistrates before him, but this did not prevent the audiences from indulging in constant interruptions – hissing, coughing, groaning and so on.[10] Mini-riots with populist revolutionary potential were not uncommon. For example, Richelieu, writing to the *jurat* of Bordeaux on 24 February 1769, castigated the magistrates for the behaviour of the crowd: 'Sirs; It seems to me that in the tale you told me of the disturbances which occurred at the theatre, everyone had forgotten their duty, the groundlings more than anyone ... There were groups who partook in a kind of revolt, which [event] has obliged me to call out the troops, in spite of the privileges of the city which believed it would not have to suffer them.'[11] For an actor or actress to succeed with this unruly crowd required nerve as well as acting skill. Even the famous and crowd-hardened tragedian, Lekain, complained of his reception in Bordeaux. Though Diderot was to warn Jodin that pleasing a provincial crowd was not an indication that she would succeed in Paris, he was perhaps unduly pessimistic. To please the Bordeaux public was no mean feat.

During their stay in Bordeaux, Schulenburg and Jodin were presented to the city's notables, including the Duc de Richelieu, to the commander of the

Château de la Trompette and a host of other aristocratic individuals.[12] One person whom Schulenburg does not list in his diary among his collection of notables but whom they would have met at this time and who would reappear in Jodin's life in the 1780s, was Jean-Baptiste Lynch, a Bordeaux magistrate who rose to prominence as one of the Bordeaux Parlement representatives to the court of Louis XVI.[13] Briefly imprisoned during the Revolution, he was elected mayor of Bordeaux under Napoleon, whom he enthusiastically supported. But on 12 March 1814, seeing that Bonaparte's downfall was imminent, Lynch enthusiastically welcomed the English invaders into Bordeaux and switched his allegiance to Louis XVIII. Opinion remains divided on this Gallic Vicar of Bray, whether to view him as a traitor or as a true patriot. When Jodin would have known him he was a rising star in the Bordeaux judiciary and magistracy. It was to him that she would in 1789 send her *Vues législatives pour les femmes* for comment.

Shortly after their arrival in Bordeaux, Jodin began negotiating for an acting engagement. This was not at all to Schulenburg's liking. He missed the importance which he had enjoyed in Dresden as a diplomatic figure, did not relish being known primarily as the consort of an actress, and thought Bordeaux society unexciting. Whereas Jodin seems to have thrown herself into the life of the theatre and perhaps attracted other admirers besides Schulenburg, he found himself immured in a provincial setting without a role and where apart from his name and connections he could have little cachet. Schulenburg's notes on the city characterise it as an uninspiring place, virtually devoid of Roman or other antiquities (in which he was mildly interested) though it did boast some beautiful vistas:

> The city of Bordeaux is only handsome from its harbour aspect. The Place Royale is small, though the equestrian statue of Louis XV which one sees there is very fine. [This was subsequently to become during the Terror, 'la Place de la Guillotine'] ... The building containing the Stock Exchange is very handsome and looks out on the Place Royale. The view from the terrace of the Chateau Trompette is admirable. The Palais Galien is a brick ruin, which may have been handsome once.[14]

These dutifully noted architectural sights were not enough to prevent Schulenburg from becoming depressed and quarrelsome. There was little in Bordeaux to attract him beyond his mistress. She, for her part, showed a propensity to independence which caused the lovers to clash. They lived in the extravagant style expected of the Bordeaux élite which inevitably became a further drain on his not endless resources. The couple's relationship continued to be stormy.

We can now let Diderot take up the tale of their Bordeaux sojourn. His letters to Jodin in Bordeaux have three main themes. Firstly he advises her on how to maintain her relationship with Schulenburg and, as ever, scolds her for her passionate temperament, whilst accepting the Count's outbreaks of violence as the right of his class and sex. Diderot would admit however that: 'he seems to want to ruin the effects of his tenderness and generosity'. Secondly, on family themes, Diderot concerns himself in detail with Mme Jodin's monetary difficulties and feuds in the Jodin family between Mme Jodin and her brother-in-law, Pierre Jodin. Diderot expects Marie Madeleine to shoulder the responsibilities of her wider family, now that she is in prosperous circumstances. Thirdly, Diderot writes at length about her financial affairs and, having become her man of business, invests her rapidly growing capital, offering to invest money for Schulenburg as well.

Diderot's letter of 10 September 1768 opens with a pessimistic assessment of the couple's prospects: 'You have your faults which he is never ready to pardon; he has his, and you have no indulgence for them.' With regard to her mother, having told Jodin in his July letter not to let her mother find out about the money Diderot was investing on their behalf, he berates her in the September letter for being too parsimonious in her mother's support. Springing to Mme Jodin's defence, he offers a detailed accounting of her expenses covering the previous two years. The court case against Mme Brunet, her former landlady, and the rent owed, constitute the major single outlay of 216 *livres*. Feuds continue with Mme Brunet who, we remember, has schemed with Jodin's chambermaid to blacken her character. It is clear that Jodin is now sufficiently well off to promise her mother a yearly income of 1500 *livres*. But Diderot complains that she has so far only received about one third of that sum. The cost of the 'farewell supper for her daughter' probably refers to an party for Jodin two year's previously. Diderot at this stage (September 1768) appears to be making a final and retrospective financial reckoning, by which Mme Brunet, still angry with the Jodin family, would acknowledge payment for this supper and various other expenses. On a personal level, this letter strikes a predominately sombre note: 'try', urges Diderot, having perhaps limited faith in his own advice, 'to profit a little from the lessons of the past for the sake of the future':

[10 September 1768][15]
Mademoiselle,
I do not know whether to congratulate or blame you for your reconciliation with Monsieur the Count. It is too unclear whether you are designed for his happiness and he for yours. You have your faults, which he is never ready to pardon; he has his, and you have no indulgence for them. He seems to want to ruin the effects of his tenderness and generosity. As for yourself, I think it does not take much to ulcerate your heart and make you violent. I would not be surprised if, at the moment when you receive my fine exhortation to peace, you are at war on a grand scale. Thus we must wait and see the success of his promises and your good resolutions. That is what I am doing, without being indifferent to your fate.

I have received your power of attorney; it is all in order. At the moment, I need a life-certificate, duly witnessed. Do not delay an instant in sending it to me. I will send you, by the means you suggest, the portrait and letters of Monsieur the Count. It would be expensive by post.

When your mother read your prohibition to take any of the money I am holding for you, she fell ill. What would you have happen to her? And what is the point of that annual pension of fifteen hundred francs you claim to be giving her, if you divert the larger part of it to your own use? If you do not take care, it is going to be just a show and you will not really be helping your mother at all. Some little calculations will convince you of this and make you see reason, if you really have your mother's happiness at heart.

Study the following carefully:

Paid on behalf of Mme Jodin to Mme Brunet, for rent
and legal expenses .... 216 *l.*
To grocer .... 27 *l.* 10*s.*
To Mme Propice .... 15 *l.*
Supper on the eve of her daughter's departure .... 6 *l.* 12*s.*
To Mme Brunet, for washing blouses .... 1 *l.* 10*s.*
For repairs to Michel's[16] clothes .... 1 *l.* 10*s.*
For necessary expenses, i.e. curtains .... 24 *l.*
For shelves and installing of wardrobes .... 24 *l.*
For removal .... 10. *l.*
For tongs, andirons and table .... 25 *l.* 10*s.*
For kitchen chandeliers and snuffers .... 5 *l.* 10*s.*
For Mme Laroche's rent .... 11 *l.* 10*s.*
For postage .... 4 *l.*

Total 374 l. 2s.

This does not include general subsistence, food or laundry.

Mme Jodin has received, since the departure of
her daughter Mademoiselle Jodin, in cash .... 192 *l.*
Her daughter's pension .... 200 *l.*
From M. Roger .... 100 *l.*

As you explained your intentions to me perfectly precisely, I have asked your mother to wait for your reply to this; she is waiting for it with the greatest impatience.

I do not know where you get this sudden access of tenderness towards Mme Brunet, who tore you both to pieces before the commissioner in the most cruel and disgraceful fashion. There is nothing so Christian as forgiveness of injuries.

I must warn you that your chambermaid is in correspondence with Mme Brunet. Make what use you will of the warning.

As you have not thought to give me your address in Bordeaux, I am writing at a venture.

Another thing; there are no more life-annuities in the King's name; but if your money were ready, I would place it at 6 per cent with the Farmers-general, and this would mean that you retained your capital.[17]

This is something I could also do for the Count, but there is not a moment to lose.

I salute you, Mademoiselle. I beg you to give my respects to Monsieur the Count.

I would like to know that you were both happy. I have no time to moralize. It is gone one o'clock; this letter must be in the post before two.

Diderot's detailed reckonings and instructions to Jodin on her financial affairs, illustrated above, show him in the role of accountant-cum-legal-adviser. He took infinite pains over these arrangements, as over his advice on her relations with Schulenburg. The letter continued:

> P.S. Your power of attorney is not in order. I have noted in the margin what needs to be added. Thus you must rectify this one or have another made, as guided by the marginal notes.
>
> Here also is the life-certificate, which you will need to attach to the new power of attorney which you are going to send me.
>
> Pay attention, Mademoiselle, to the little account of receipts and expenditure that I am enclosing, and judge from it what you need to do for your mother, who is ill, disturbed in her mind, and in urgent need of support.
>
> So no delay please, over all this; and try to be sensible, reasonable and prudent and to profit a little from the lessons of the past for the sake of the future.

Evidently, Diderot was growing more and more involved in Jodin's and her family's affairs. He had become incensed against Jodin's uncle, Pierre Jodin, who had written an invidious letter of complaint against her mother. Moreover he had discovered that the same man was behaving shockingly towards his own daughter, misappropriating the funds that other members of the family, including Marie Madeleine herself, had provided to place her in a convent. Before long, he would confront the uncle with his wrongdoings and throw him bodily out of his house. Diderot, outraged at Pierre Jodin's unscrupulous but insinuating behaviour, had become the champion of the Jodin women-folk.

Like his brother Jean, Pierre Jodin (born 1715) had emigrated to France from his native Geneva in 1759 and though an inventor and artisan of some ingenuity, had got himself into serious financial difficulties. Neither did he have an unblemished record in Geneva, having been obliged to appear several times before the Consistory Court for 'seeming extremely indifferent to Religion'. He had five children by his first marriage and one daughter, Marie-Julie Jodin (born 1749) by his second marriage to his nineteen-year-old apprentice. It was probably Marie-Julie about whom Diderot had become so concerned. In Paris Pierre Jodin presented his invention, *un moulin à lavures* or washing system for minerals, to the Academy of Sciences.[18] Diderot believed that he exploited his female relatives and he was certainly willing to call on his niece's influence with her protector to gain favour with the Danish court. One must also remember that unknown to Jodin and her mother, he was one of the signatories of the *lettre de cachet* which had condemned them to the Salpêtrière.

Schulenburg had written the following testimonial for Pierre Jodin from Salzwedel, 16 July 1768, demonstrating that he was still sufficiently enamoured of Marie Madeleine to ask Bernstorff (16 July) to recommend Pierre Jodin to the Danish King, not reflecting apparently that the relations of a young woman who had occasioned a major diplomatic incident between the courts of Saxony and Denmark were unlikely to find favour at court.[19] This letter, which gives a fulsome testimonial to Pierre Jodin, reflects the affectionate regard in which Marie Madeleine still seems to have held her uncle, a regard which Diderot was at pains to undermine with evidence of his perfidy.

> However terrifying the papers which I have the honour to send Your Excellency prove to be, I dare to ask you, as a particular favour to take note of them. [This refers to Pierre Jodin's list of technical inventions. 'Terrifying' suggests a mild pleasantry by a non-specialist, commenting on something scientific or technical]. You will see there, Sir, in detail the talents of a man famous in the mechanical arts and his reasons for quitting France, to which the court had called him from his native country of Geneva. The good that I wish for his amiable niece has led him to presume with reason that this would be an additional motive to lead me to serve him. As it seems to me that the talents of Sieur Jodin could be useful to the King, my master, I have had the pleasure of proving my zeal to him and at the same time helping an artisan who, I am assured, merits in every respect that one should take an interest in him.[20]

In contrast to this glowing reference, Pierre Jodin, acccording to Diderot, was a man who exploited his sister-in-law and then turned against her when there was no more money to be had and who kept his daughter in penury. The man was an 'out-and-out scoundrel', a manipulator and schemer, 'honeyed and treacherous'.

As far as Werner von der Schulenburg was concerned, however, Diderot held him in high esteem, evident in his next letter of 21 November 1768 which suggests a considerable degree of acquaintance as well as mutual admiration: 'Be sure to remember me to Comte. The best way I have of repaying his marks of esteem is to preach his happiness to you.' Perhaps the most surprising point to emerge is his advice to Jodin not to attempt a theatrical comeback in Bordeaux. Schulenburg disapproved of her wish to return to the stage and in addition, Diderot stressed the likelihood of failure before the volatile Bordeaux audience and pointed out how a public humiliation would injure her with the Count. The maintenance of her relationship with Schulenburg, who was inclined to jealousy, should be her overwhelming priority: 'it is better to suffer than to sow suspicion in his heart'. Not wishing to envisage her any longer as a public figure on the stage, Diderot praised her on the score of her private life, namely her care for her mother. The sum of 22,000 *francs*, given by Schulenburg, which Diderot undertook to invest, would become a solid basis for the family's financial security. He ended this letter on a note of optimism; Jodin had begun to put her affairs in order and to think of the future: a revolution indeed:

> [21 November 1768] [21]
> I am answering your last two letters. I am delighted that your last little commissions have been executed to your satisfaction. I have not been too harsh towards your uncle. Any man who will settle himself upon a woman

and drink and eat and be given hospitality by her and then, when she is no longer in a position to do him these good offices, calumniate her and try to make trouble between her and her daughter, putting her very livelihood at risk, is a base scoundrel who deserves no consideration. Add to that the contempt I feel at his endless lies. When one has the wickedness to do a black deed, one should not have the cowardice to deny it.

Your mother does not see, and has not seen, Mme Travers;[22] she only saw the company that your uncle provided, and it is not true that she has been reconciled with him. M. Roger, who is attached to you, serves you and asks no more than to be helpful to your mother, and who also comes in for abuse in your uncle's diatribe, has been no more resentful than the case demands; at his age, resentment and revenge are much the same thing. In short, Mademoiselle, I have no patience with that honeyed and treacherous sort of person. If you had paid a little more attention to the letter he sent you, you would have recognized its stupid tone of irony, which is more wounding than actual insult. Every step had been taken to prepare his daughter for a less wretched future, and he obstinately refused. He preferred to keep her at home and sacrifice her to his supposed needs. Anyway, you at least have done your duty to yourself and to your niece.[23]

You have another poor relation named Masse, who people say is a decent fellow, and who deserves your compassion. The slightest support would be an infinite help to him. See if you might feel like doing something for him; it would be a good deed. I gave your uncle the last letter you wrote him, but I am still holding a great packet addressed to him, which I kept until you had been told about his behaviour and could tell me what to do with it. You have not replied about this, and the sealed packet is still on my table, all ready to be returned to you or to go to your uncle, as you decide.

Be sure to remember me to the Count. The best way I have of repaying his marks of esteem is to preach his happiness to you. Do everything, Mademoiselle, for a true gentleman who does everything for you. Remember that you are less your own mistress than ever and that the slightest and least outrageous caprice on your part may be, or at least seem to be, ingratitude. He is a person of too much delicacy to withdraw his largesse; you for your part are too sensitive not to feel how much tact your position requires. An ill-bred woman would believe herself free to do as she pleased, and you would become just such a woman did you not realize that at this very moment, your slavery begins. There may be sufferings for you to bear; there should from now on be none for him. He has acquired the right to complain, even without good cause. You have lost the right to retaliate, even when he is in the wrong, because it is better to suffer than to sow suspicion in his heart.

I have received the bill of exchange for twenty-two thousand francs drawn on Tourton and Baur. So have no worries on that score. I am going to have it accepted right away so that we have some ready money and are freer in placing it. It would be very difficult to place it with the King, and there would be great danger in placing it with private individuals. Whatever revolution happens in the government, life-annuities will always be respected; and nobody can fully read the mind of private financiers.

I hesitate to approve of your theatrical plans. I do not see any great advantage in success, and I see a very real danger in failure. What you would lose in the Count's heart by failure is much greater than what you would gain by applause. Mademoiselle, do not deceive yourself: in spite of himself, a rebuff by the public would have its effect on him. That is how men are. I am not surprised at his boredom in a town with so little to suit his heart, his character and his personal qualities. If he offers me the chance to do him any service, be sure that I would most happy to seize it. Everything you foresee about his future seems convincing to me, and I will not pretend otherwise. [Had Jodin, perhaps expressed scepticism about their continued relationship and worries about Schulenburg's extravagant mode of living?] For the rest, I will preserve silence over all this with your mother. I only insisted on including her name in these dealings from a fear which we share: I mean, her pitiable state if she should have the misfortune to outlive you. But since you are giving her a raft in such a shipwreck, I have no further objections, and things shall be arranged as you desire.

I salute and embrace you. The order you are beginning to impose on your affairs, and the long views you are taking, the first time perhaps that you have ever thought of your future, give me a better opinion of your head.

Be wise, and you will be happy.

As buffer and arbiter between Jodin and her mother, Diderot, as the next letter (December 1768) shows, was evidently having some success. He exuded cheerfulness both about Jodin's behaviour and her financial affairs. His letter begins with its meticulous totting up of accounts. At this stage of her career, Jodin had already amassed enough money for a life annuity for herself and her mother, she was paying her mother's expenses and she had commissioned Diderot to purchase for her expensive lace, satin and an elaborate bracelet, all of which he cheerfully did. The fact that Jodin was able to 'splurge' 287.12 *livres* on luxury items suggests that she was leading the high life with gusto. Schulenburg was proving extremely generous, if often temperamental.

Diderot's greatest praise is for Jodin's improved relationship with her mother: 'I love warm-heartedness and integrity in children.' As he did throughout his correspondence, he pursued the goal of encouraging the good nature which he believed her to possess. And in another of his frequent reversals of tactic, having scolded Jodin for being parsimonious towards her mother, he now tells her that he has warned Mme Jodin not, under any pretext, to exceed her income of 1500 *livres* per annum:

[December 1768][24]
Let me begin, Mademoiselle, by rendering my account. We can then talk about other things:

I have received from M. Fischer, in two notes, one drawn on Messrs. Tourton and Baur for 1373 *l*. 18. 6; the other drawn on M. d'Eguien for 2376 *l*. 1. 6; the sum of .... 3750 *l*.
From that sum I have advanced to your mother .... 100 *l*.
I have given her as quarterly allowance .... 375 *l*.
For her rent, due on 1 October .... 75 *l*.
For her debts to the shoemaker, the laundress,
   the butcher, the baker, the grocer etc .... 50 *l*.

Paid for 12 ells of satin that you asked for .... 117 *l.*
For 60 ells of black lace .... 24 *l.*
For the great bracelet and the lock, gold: 1 oz $^1/_2$, at
90 *l.* the ounce .... 96 *l.* 12
For the making of the bracelet .... 40 *l.*
For crystal .... 10 *l.*
    Total...917 *l.* 12
If one deducts expenditure of 917 *l.* 12 from the sum of 3750 *l.* in my
possession, there remains 2832 *l.* 8

    Thus, Mademoiselle, you will see that the sum which belongs to you and
is still in my hands is not as small as you imagined. If you let it be increased
by the fifteen hundred *livres* that I shall receive at the end of December,
from your life annuity on the King, your plans can be safely achieved.

    I cannot tell you how pleased I am by your treatment of your mother. If
you were here, I would embrace you with all my heart, for I love warm-
heartedness and integrity in children. You have explained affairs to her;
fifteen hundred francs net is more than enough to give her a comfortable
existence. I have just told her, with a touch of harshness even, that she will
get no more out of you or of me beyond that amount; and that if, by bad
management or extravagance or the like, she incurs new debts, so much the
worse for her. I hope she pays some attention.

The deplorable Pierre Jodin figures largely in this letter. Diderot characterises
him as an underhand schemer, particularly objecting to his attempts to effect a
rupture between the mother and daughter. On top of his other villanies, Pierre
Jodin has sold whatever Marie Madeleine had given her cousin as a dowry to
enter a convent and the girl is now destitute. Pleading for Jodin to show charity
towards the girl, Diderot paints a telling picture of the actress's life in Bordeaux,
given over to worldly dissipation. 'Extend your hand to that child. You need
sacrifice no more than what a rather sumptuous fancydress might cost your for
a gala ball. Deny yourself a gay outing, a new dress, an expensive caprice, and
your niece will owe you life, honour and happiness.' The emotive contrast
between Jodin's opulence and her starving cousin is worthy of one of Diderot's
drames:

Your uncle, allow me to say, is an out-and-out scoundrel, deciding to cause
a quarrel between you and your mother the moment he was told she could
no longer give him board and lodgings. He blames her for expenses she
made entirely on his behalf, and for keeping company with people she
either never met, or only met through him. I was profoundly indignant at
that letter he wrote you. He is an ungrateful cur. His asking you to be judge
of his conduct and your mother's is an insolent piece of sarcasm which
calls for no answer on your part, or a very tough one. He came to see me a
few days ago. I reproached him with the wickedness of trying to make
trouble between a mother, who had loaded him with kindnesses, and her
own daughter. He defended himself; he piled lie upon lie. I thrust your
letter, or rather the one he wrote to you, under his nose, and he didn't know
what to say. He stammered; and while he was stammering I took him by
the shoulders and threw him out like a beggar.

We have received a fairly large packet for him; but we thought it best not to give it to him until we had told you about him. Be so good as to tell us again what to do about it.

You took pity on his daughter, your niece, and you provided her with clothes and linen and some money to make things easier for her when she entered a convent. The money has been spent, the garments sold, and the poor creature is without clothes, without bread, without resources, dying of hunger in a room where she is imprisoned all alone. Her condition, and what it may lead to, wrings my heart.

It is not a question of the father, who should be left to the fate he deserves; it is not a question of the mother that one should help, who cruelly shuts her eyes to her daughter's plight, when she should be relieving it; it is a question of that child. Mademoiselle, perform a good deed; do an action which you could remember ever afterwards with pleasure. Extend your hand to that child. You need sacrifice no more than what a rather sumptuous fancydress might cost you for a gala ball. Deny yourself a gay outing, a new dress, an expensive caprice, and your niece will owe to you life, honour and happiness.

If you add this good deed to your good treatment of your mother, you will be an object of real respect for me, of greater respect than many women proud of their strict morals and who think they have done everything when they do not flirt.

Give my respects to Monsieur the Count. Create his happiness, since he sees it as his duty to create yours. I salute you and embrace you with all my heart.   DIDEROT

We are always delighted to hear of your successes.

I have given M. Deschamps a packet containing 1 *ell* of crimson satin, 60 *ells* of black lace, a lining of striped taffeta with its wadding, and the linen bodice which can serve as a wrapping.

Item, a little wooden box containing the bracelet portrait of the Count, with its clasp. It was made by M. Hardvillier, as you wished.

P.S. If you want me to send you the money I am holding for you, send me a general quittance up to today's date, so that I can rid myself of unnecessary papers.

Good-day, Mademoiselle. Continue to be generous.

Diderot's next letter (10 February 1769) opens with a further list of Mme Jodin's expenses, explaining how she has disposed of her 1500 *livres*. Jodin herself, enjoying a capital of 25,000 *livres* could look forward to an annual income of at least 2250 *livres*. Thus Jodin was by early 1769 comfortably situated for her future with two life annuities, one for her mother and one for herself.

Diderot's efforts over Jodin's finances and his investment strategy for her and her mother were certainly not unappreciated by Jodin herself. When Diderot arranged for Jodin's annuity in 1769, it was agreed, in the somewhat hypothetical event of her pre-deceasing Diderot or his wife, to mark her debt towards him and his family by passing on the annuity's income. The second life annuity, mentioned above, producing an income of 2500 *livres* drawn up by the notary, le Pot d'Auteuil would be incorporated into the marriage contract of Diderot's daughter, Angélique, in 1772 as part of her dowry provision.[25]

It is clear from Diderot's letters to Jodin in Bordeaux that her financial affairs must have taken up a great deal of his time. He was proverbially generous in his efforts on his friends' behalf. His daughter later recorded somewhat ruefully how he expended his remarkable talents on seemingly peripheral projects, though not peripheral to those whom he helped: 'He believed that the greatest good one could do for mankind was to expand human knowledge and his belonged to everyone ... Three quarters of his life was spent in helping those in need of his purse, his talents and his influence.'[26] His management of Jodin's money was an example of this generosity. It was also true that he was busy investing the money from the sale of his library to Catherine of Russia, so that his work in relation to Jodin's modest fortune ran tandem with his own financial affairs.

We learn from his daughter's marriage contract that Jodin remained grateful for these efforts. On 9 September 1772, Angélique, the sole surviving child of the Diderots' four children, married Abel-François Nicolas Caroillon, like Denis Diderot a native of Langres. Angélique's principal dowry was derived from the sale of her father's library to Catherine of Russia in 1765. However, Jodin's annuity also formed part of the dowry settlement. Article 8 of the marriage contract consists of two paragraphs, the first detailing Jodin's 1769 annuity and its provisions, the second relating to new provisions in 1772. The original document described the beneficiaries of the annuity as Mlle Jodin and M. Diderot (see also Diderot's letter of 15 July 1769). The annuity would be paid during the lifetimes of either Mlle Jodin or Mlle Diderot (Angélique). During Mlle Jodin's lifetime she would be the sole beneficiary. On her death, M. Diderot, if he survived her, would be the sole beneficiary and on his death the annuity passed entirely to Mme Diderot. Of interest too is the stipulation that Mme Diderot, should she benefit, would have unfettered use of the income, 'this income being intended for her subsistence'. It seems evident that Jodin was particularly concerned about Mme Diderot's future, should she survive her husband because Diderot's own pension would disappear with his death (though in the event, Catherine of Russia granted his wife a pension when Diderot died). For either Diderot or his wife to benefit after Jodin's death, it was required that Angélique Diderot would still be living. Clearly the actuarial calculation was that Angélique, as the youngest of the four, was likely to live longer and therefore to allow the annuity to go on functioning for a longer period of time.

In the second paragraph of the document (and this explains why the annuity question was included in the marriage contract), the Diderot parents make over one half of their hypothetical interest in the annuity to Angélique, should Mlle Jodin pre-decease them. In their totality, these arrangements demonstrate Jodin's gratitude not only to Diderot, but also to his wife who had befriended Mme Jodin when she was virtually destitute in Paris. What then would have been the fate of this annuity? Diderot died in 1784. Jodin died six years later in 1790.

Mme Diderot lived on to 1796 attaining the ripe age of eighty-six. She would, unless the funds disappeared in the financial troubles associated with the Revolution, have benefited from Jodin's annuity or at least half of it. From her own mother's experience, Jodin would have understood the vulnerability of ageing widows without independent fortunes.

We can now return to Diderot's business-like letter of February 1769 which sets out the minutiae of the annuity question:

[10 February 1769][27]
Let us begin, Mademoiselle, by settling our accounts.
Given to your mother for her quarterly allowance .... 250 *l.*
Given earlier, to settle her debts, as you instructed ...... 500 *l.*
We have her receipt for .... 750 *l.*
From which you will see that I am still holding .... 240 *l.*

Your plan is for your mother to receive 1,500 *l.* a year. To form this, she has your pension at 200 *l.*, the 300 *l.* credit balance, and 250 *l.* per quarter which she draws here. At her age it is difficult to inspire her with a spirit of economy; but I have taken it upon myself to tell her, on your behalf, that if she contracts new debts, you will not settle them. I report only 240 *l.* remaining in my hands, because I had to take 3000 *l.* and add it to the 22 000 *l.* of the bill of exchange drawn on Tourton Baur, to complete the 25 000 *l.* which, invested in the new life-annuities issued by the King, will bring you in an annual income of 2250 *l.*

Of your two life-annuity contracts, one has been passed to the notary Du Tartre, or his successor Piquet. The agreement has been deposited in his office. You ask for a copy or transcript. There should be no problem about this, I think, and I will see about it right away.

The other contract will go to the notary Le Pot d'Auteuil; but between depositing the money in the royal treasury and the execution of the contract there is always a more or less long interval, which however does not prevent your 2250 *l.* from starting to accumulate. As soon as this new contract is executed, I will not fail to get a copy or transcript and let you have it.

Whatever happens, sleep peacefully. Your funds are secure against all contingencies. The documents which authorize your income are in the public archives. You will find the note of the one at the office of Du Tartre's successor Piquet, and the note of the other, when it exists, at Le Pot d'Auteuil's.

In place of the transcripts, I would give you the originals on parchment, if I did not need them myself. One has to have them to obtain payment at the *Hôtel de Ville.*

I am not surprised that, not being used to business, you do not know these little details. I would not know them myself if looking after your affairs had not given me the chance to learn these things.

Having secured her financial position, Diderot proceeded to imagine what Jodin's ultimate destiny might be. Significantly, his vision does not mention the count. He dreams for her a life of moderation, so unlike her previous existence; reasonable exercise, reading, music, visiting close friends. And no more theatre, dissipation and madcap behaviour. As an example of future paths she might follow, he sketches two contrasting careers of famous women which illustrate possible trajectories for young women from humble origins in eighteenth-century France who possessed both beauty and brains. His first example, Mme Geoffrin (1699–1777), whom we have already glimpsed when she visited Poland in 1766, had the good fortune to captivate a rich man as her husband and employed her wealth and status to become one of the leading *salonnières* of the day. Diderot's second example, Mme du Barry (1743–93), was an even more topical figure than Mme Geoffrin. Of low origins and having led a notorious life, she rose in 1768, through the machinations of her husband, the schemes of the Duc de Richelieu, and her own remarkable beauty, to become Louis XV's mistress. In early 1769, when Diderot wrote this letter, it was public knowledge that she was on the verge of being officially presented at court. The ageing King's infatuation with her was a topic of public gossip. Diderot here highlights Mme du Barry's meteoric rise. But even he could not have imagined her eventual fate. She was to live in great splendour, amass enormous wealth, and to be guillotined under the Terror, condemned as a commoner who had sided with the aristocracy and defrauded the state.[28] In contrasting Mme Geoffrin's and Mme du Barry's lives, Diderot offers his pupil two alternative, if not equally admirable models; Mme Geoffrin, who enjoyed the respect of intellectuals and kings alike, and Mme du Barry, who had capitalised on her sexual attractions. Jodin, he believes, could take either path. He dangles before his pupil the image of her as a puppet of fate, principally because of her lack of self-control. Finally we note that Jodin's proposal to have his portrait painted (pre-empted by Greuze) confirms both her new affluence and her great affection for her mentor:

> So now you are sufficiently guarded against all the mischiefs of life. You possess a respectable income that no-one can deprive you of. I know exactly the life that happiness and reason should now dictate to you, but I doubt if your outlook or character would ever reconcile you to it: no more theatre, no more dissipation, no more follies. A little apartment in wholesome air, in some peaceful corner of the town; a sober and healthy regime; some friends you can depend on; a little reading; a little music; plenty of exercise and walking. That is what you will wish you had chosen, when it is too late.
>
> But let us forget about that. We are all in the hands of destiny, which does what it wills with us and has already tossed you about a great deal, nor seems likely to give you peace yet awhile. You are, unluckily, an energetic and turbulent being, and one never knows where such creatures will lay their bones. You would not have believed it if someone had told you, at the age of fourteen, all the good things and evil things you have experienced up to now. The rest of your horoscope, if one could tell you it, would seem equally unbelievable, but the same is true with many other people.
>
> A little girl went regularly to mass in her ringlets and light silks. She was as pretty as an angel; she clasped the prettiest hands in the world at the foot of the altar. Meanwhile a man of power and influence watched her, grew mad about her, and made her his wife. So now she is rich and honoured; now she is surrounded by all that is greatest in the city, in the Court, in

science, letters and the arts. A king receives her and calls her *maman*.[29] Another, in jerkin and short petticoat, fried fish in an inn; young libertines lifted her petticoat from behind and caressed her very familiarly. She leaves there; she circulates in society and undergoes all sorts of metamorphoses until she arrives at a royal court. Then the whole capital resounds with her name, the court is divided for and against her; she threatens ministers with dismissal; she makes her influence felt all over Europe.[30] And who know what other absurd games Destiny will play? It does what it chooses. It is a pity it so rarely chooses to make people happy.

If you are wise, you will leave Destiny as little scope as possible; you will decide to live from early on as you would wish to have done. What good are all the severe lessons you have received, if you do not profit from them? You are so little your own mistress. Among all the puppets of Providence, it is you whose wires she jerks so bizarrely that I never know where you will be next. You are not in Paris, nor perhaps will you be there very soon.

I have just received a letter from Dresden from that unfortunate Michel. I do not know what he did to displease you, but he seem most repentant at having left you. He would like to return to your service. I can see that he was very attached to you. He seems a decent fellow. He has a wife and children and is in great poverty. Your adventure in Dresden has brought him into bad odour; everyone casts stones at them. He is on the streets. See what you can do for him.

It is very handsome of you to suggest having me engraved; as handsome on your part as it would be vain on mine to accept. But the thing is already done. An artist[31] whom I had done favours for and who esteemed me, made a drawing of me, had it engraved (very skilfully), and sent me the plate with fifty copies. So you have had the grass cut from under your feet.

Good-day, Mademoiselle, keep well. Be prudent; do not jeopardise your own happiness, and remember that the true reward of someone who obliges us is his own little good deeds.

I salute and embrace you. Please give my respects to Monsieur the Count.

Another tantalisingly enigmatic clue about Schulenburg's and Jodin's sojourn in Bordeaux emerges in a letter from the Duc de Richelieu, then at Versailles, to a Monsieur Pinel, *procureur syndic* of the city of Bordeaux, dated 24 February 1769. Much of this letter is taken up with a discussion of public disorders at the Bordeaux theatre, against which Richelieu threatened strong measures (calling out the King's soldiers) and warning the *procureur* that his (Richelieu's) patience was nearly exhausted. The letter ends with an apparently unrelated but intriguing comment: 'I am sure you will agree with me about the question of M. de Schulumbourg [*sic*] and his wig maker. Please give me all the details about this.'[32]

One would be glad to know what had occurred between Schulenburg and his wig-maker to cause him to be mentioned in a correspondence between the governor of the province and a law officer, the *procureur syndic*.[33] In the context of the previous paragraph on civic disorders, the reference has the air of being something more serious than, for example, the non-payment of a bill and must have been noteworthy to attract the attention of Richelieu himself. Had Schulenburg brought a serious charge against his wig-maker, or alternatively, had the wig-maker launched a complaint against Schulenburg? The reference suggests a possible recurrence of the scenes of violence towards domestics enacted in Dresden.

The address of Diderot's next letter (24 March 1769) is 'Mademoiselle Jodin, chez M. Jambellant, saddler, rue Porte-Basse, Bordeaux'. Baulked in her plan to commission a portrait, Jodin instead had had the happy thought of sending the Diderot family a huge joint of ham. Meanwhile, on her own domestic front, it is evident that she and Schulenburg still clash. Jodin had complained to Diderot about Schulenburg's high-handed treatment and of social slights or insults she had experienced in her role as the publicly acknowledged mistress to a nobleman. Diderot, displaying his usual ethical pragmatism, advises her to weigh Schulenburg's many virtues ('les vertus d'un galant homme') against the prejudices to which women are subjected (à la place des préjugés auxquels les femmes sont assujetties'). As on the issue of domestic violence, Diderot proves himself conventional in partitioning prescribed sexual behaviour. As a *philosophe* prepared to question almost everything, he did not fundamentally query the inevitability of gender roles as they then existed, whilst recognising their injustice to women. He counsels a certain ethical pragmatism on the question of relations between the sexes, endeavouring to persuade Jodin to accept the world as it is, rather than as it might be:

[24 March 1769][34]
I am infinitely obliged to you, Mademoiselle, for the enormous ham which you have sent me. It will not be eaten without drinking your health with your mother.

Give my respects to Monsieur the Count, as always.

Cultivate your talents. I do not ask of you the morals of a vestal virgin, but merely those which nobody can afford to be without: a little self-respect.

One must weigh the virtues of a gallant man against the prejudices to which women are subjected. Mistrust the warmth of your head, which will often carry you too far. Likewise mistrust the first motion of your impulsive heart, which will advise indiscreet good deeds.

If you take time to reflect, you will never do evil actions and you will do the good ones appropriate to your situation. You will never be wicked, and you will be good in just measure.

I preach economy to your mother, as best I can; but economy among all the virtues is a matter of character and habit; it is not learned in a moment.

I have just written to M. Vergier, chief clerk of the royal treasury, asking him to enable the notary Pot d'Auteuil to draw up your last contract.

Once this is done, I will send you a copy, together with the earlier one. I have not imagined any anxiety on your part, as I have none myself.

I salute you and embrace you with all my heart.

Jodin's increased prosperity inevitably coincided with Schulenburg's increasing debts, already crippling when he left Saxony. Whether she had any idea of his financial difficulties is not known, but their extravagant style of living as well as the generous sums he settled on her had landed him in serious arrears. Was the affair of the wig-maker an added embarrassment? In any event the couple parted in April 1769, apparently by mutual consent, with Schulenburg leaving Bordeaux for an Italian tour. It may be that, weighed in the balance, Schulenburg's virtues did not, for Jodin, counterbalance 'the prejudices to which women are subjected' and that Schulenburg did not relish his role as the consort of an ambitious actress. The lovers, one could say with hindsight, were too much alike in their histrionic temperaments to bear with one another for very long. It is also clear that Schulenburg's financial position, quite apart from his largesse to Jodin, was fast becoming precarious. Nevertheless, from his subsequent journal entries we see that he did not modify his mode of living significantly on leaving Bordeaux. His journal makes no further mention of Jodin, neither did Diderot, alerted to the couple's parting, refer again to Schulenburg in his letters to Jodin. A stormy relationship had worn itself out.

Meanwhile, Jodin, seemingly not at all cast down by her parting from the Count, made her long-awaited and successful debut in Bordeaux in May 1769. Diderot was pleased, but, as ever, warned her not to be carried away by the applause of a provincial crowd. This letter (11 May 1769) finds him in receipt of a further 4000 *francs* from Jodin, possibly a final gift or payment from Schulenburg. There is also a reference to Jodin's plans to sell her porcelain which was probably acquired during her Dresden sojourn from the Meissen porcelain works and which would have been very valuable. Diderot even allows himself to express guarded confidence in his protégée's future if she espouses 'gentleness and grace', women's best weapons. Again we seem to see the fictional Jodin that Diderot was valiantly attempting to construct , rather than the problematic but genuine woman:

[11 May 1769][35]
Mademoiselle,

I have received your letter of credit for four thousand francs, and this sum has been invested right away. You will receive the income from the first of January of this year.

I am delighted to see you making prudent arrangements.

The first of your contracts has been passed to Du Tartre's office, to which Priquois [*sic*] has succeeded. The second is with Le Pot d'Auteuil. The last is with Regnaud. I will keep an eye on your incomings.

I am very pleased that your début was a success, for nothing but constant applause can compensate you for the fatigue and disagreeableness of your profession. My aim is not to discourage you, or to spoil a moment of happiness; but remember, Mademoiselle, that there is a great difference between the public in Bordeaux and the public in Paris. How often have you heard it said of a woman who sang in private society, and indeed sang very well, that she outdid Le More?[36] What a difference, though, when they appeared on the same platform and one could compare them. It is here, on the same stage as Mlle Clairon or Mlle Dusmesnil,[37] that I would like you to obtain the eulogies from the audience that you receive in Bordeaux. So work. Work without ceasing. Judge yourself severely. Pay less attention to the applause of your provincials than to your own self-criticism. What confidence can you have in the applause of people who do not clap when you yourself know you are playing well, for I am sure you have had this happen to you. Perfect yourself above all in quiet scenes.

Take care of your health. Make yourself respected; show your liking for courteous behaviour; receive it, even if it is only your due, as if it were a favour. Be above insults, and never respond to them. The weapons of women are gentleness and grace, and they are invincible.

The Duc d'Orléans grants no annuities, even to his intimates. Mlle and Mme Diderot are both most glad of your success, and also at hearing from you. If you gain anything worthwhile from the raffle of your porcelain, let me have it right away, so that it can be put out at interest.

I am beginning to feel happy about your future.

Accept my best wishes and the assurance of my very sincere friendship.

Diderot's next two letters are relatively brief. He reassures Jodin over her expressed concerns that funds invested in the French State might prove unsafe. As ever he counsels the actress not to allow applause to go to her head and to moderate her violent character. But he ends his homily with the reflection that he has exhausted his lectures on morals and hopes that her stage successes in Bordeaux will be repeated in Paris. At last, Diderot seems to accept that Jodin was ready to launch herself on the Paris stage. This was an ambition that was to be deferred indefinitely for reasons which had nothing to do with her capacity as an actress but everything to do with her reckless character:

[15 July1769][38]

All your affairs, Mademoiselle, are in perfect order. Do not, I beg you, have any anxiety over the safety of your funds. I have dealt with them as I would have done my own; and when you are back in Paris and I return your certificates to you, you will see that I would never have risked so large a sum on my daughter's head,[39] if it had not seemed a better and more solid investment than any other. Pay no attention to ill-intentioned people who try to worry you. You may sleep in peace; for you to suffer loss, the State would have had to crumble from top to bottom. Up to now annuities have been sacrosanct; the government knows it is responsible for the whole fortune of many who have placed their trust in it, and that in betraying that confidence it would reduce thousands of citizens to beggary – which it has never done and never will do. It is in its interest not to do so, for it would totally ruin its credit. The man I have commissioned to collect your income has lost your life-certificate. As soon as you receive this, would you please send me another as soon as you possibly can? Madame Diderot asks you to let her know the price of the material you sent to your mother.

Work; do not rest on your laurels. Pay less attention to those who applaud you than to those who criticize you. The applause will leave you as you are. The criticisms, if you profit from them, will correct your faults and perfect your talent; make their ill-will your own advantage.

Moderate your violent character. Learn to swallow an insult; it is the best way of rejecting it. If you respond otherwise than with scorn you will be putting yourself on a level with your abuser. Above all, do your very utmost to make yourself agreeable to your colleagues.

I have preached to you so much about morals, and my morality is so easy to observe, that I have nothing more to say on that subject.

I salute you and embrace you with all my heart.

The final letter of the correspondence which has come down to us is optimistic about Jodin's prospects. At long last, Diderot thinks that her Paris début is imminent and justified:

[26 July 1769][40]
Your life-certificate arrived three days ago, and I have already received two thousand eight hundred *livres*, the total of your income. I made haste to let your mother have the sum that you have the kindness to allow her, and I fulfilled that pleasant mission not without preaching my usual little sermon about economy. Tomorrow I will send you the remaining two thousand *livres*.

Paris is not unaware of your success, and I believe the plaudits you received in Bordeaux were sincere, but it is here, I repeat, that I would like to see you showered with bouquets.

I renew my old sermons to you and am,
With every good wish,
DIDEROT

Diderot's growing optimism of July about his pupil was to be short-lived. Jodin still had a shock in store for him. On 15 August 1769, in the streets of Bordeaux, she was alleged to have deliberately mocked a religious procession, refusing to kneel and making insulting remarks, while the Christ figure was born along. As the recipient of a 200-*livres* pension from the government as a convert, she was required to attend such religious observances and to demonstrate an attitude of piety. Was she there with some of her worldly Bordeaux friends who encouraged her penchant for mockery? All we know is that her remarks did not pass unnoticed. Someone in the crowd seems to have reported her words to the *procureur général*, who instantly had her arrested and thrown into prison. She was only rescued by bribes or bail payments. Considering the hideous events of only three years before, when the young Chevalier de la Barre was sentenced to having his tongue torn out and to beheading for 'insulting a crucifix',[41] it was a mad escapade, and Diderot wrote about it aggrievedly to his friend Sophie Volland (11 September 1769):

My actress in Bordeaux would make me furious if I interested myself in her beyond a certain point. Consider that she is the daughter of Protestants and draws a pension of 200 *livres* as a new convert. Well, that 'new convert', who receives 200 *livres* every year for kneeling to the Good Lord, took it into her head to make fun of him when he was passing in the street.[42]

The story of Jodin mocking the religious procession, though uncorroborated, unfortunately rings only too true and reminds one of the 'follies' to which she was prone in Warsaw and Dresden. Diderot's warnings to beware 'the warmth of your head' and 'mistrust the first motion of your impulsive heart' (24 March 1766), his injunctions to exercise discretion and cool judgement, seem once again to have been thrown to the winds. That Jodin should have indulged in even a mildly blasphemous gesture seems plausible given what we know of her rebelliousness during her convent education and her explicit anti-clericalism expressed in her feminist treatise. Enlightenment writers such as Voltaire may have mocked the Church, but they either did so anonymously, or in his case, from the relative safety of the Swiss/French border. But Jodin was not a great person whose fame could guarantee her security. She was fortunate to have left prison at all.

It was also the case that the Bordeaux magistrates had the reputation of being somewhat lax on the point of enforcing morals. A port city, Bordeaux had its full complement of sailors and prostitutes as well as devotees of luxurious living. Over the years the authorities tried without much success to restrain disruptive or immodest public behaviour. And they were not always assisted by their governor. Richelieu had once received a deputation from the *jurat* who complained about the enormous population of prostitutes in Bordeaux and suggested that a certain number should be imprisoned as an example to the rest. Richelieu is said to have replied: 'Why have any exceptions? They all merit an equal punishment, and I want to lock them all up; therefore I will order that the gates of the city be closed.'[43] With such an irreverent governor who could propose, even in jest, to lock all prostitutes within the city, turning it into a huge bordello-cum-prison, the *jurat* faced an uphill battle in enforcing public morality, quite apart from any licentious behaviour of its populace. The magistrates promulgated lengthy orders which tended not to lead to enforcement. In July 1769, for example, just before Jodin's latest adventure, the *Procureur du Roi*, Brochas, had issued a proclamation inveighing against the practice of men bathing nude in the river. The police, he asserted had a duty to watch over the morals of citizens, to punish scandalous behaviour and to inform against any persons giving rise to it.[44] This proclamation did absolutely nothing to curb the enthusiasm of the nude bathers, though it could well have encouraged a bystander to inform against Jodin's ill-judged public comments.

Diderot's exasperation on hearing of his pupil's newest adventure is only too comprehensible. Still, he did not wash his hands of her. In spite of her recklessness, it is clear that Jodin's positive qualities – her warmth of heart, her intelligence and her gratitude towards Diderot and his family – ensured their continuing friendship. Nevertheless, as a result of this new scandal, Jodin appears to have abandoned Bordeaux and her stage career there and taken refuge in Paris where she could live with her mother on their now comfortable income. She remained in close touch with her mentor. Her acting days were not definitively over, however. She was to make two further theatrical appearances before abandoning the stage for good.

The end of the Schulenburg/Jodin affair seems an appropriate point at which to sum up Schulenburg's subsequent career. Having left Jodin and Bordeaux behind in April 1769, he set off on a grand tour of Provence and Italy, visiting antiquities and being received in the best circles. He noted with particular pleasure his success with various distinguished ladies. He travelled in style, showing no inclination to moderate his expenses, in spite of the debts he had contracted in Bordeaux. Still cherishing hopes that he could recoup his position by an official appointment at the Danish court, he wrote to Count Bernstorff, but received no satisfactory answer. As indicated previously, Schulenburg did not seem to have grasped the extent of his diplomatic *faux pas* in Dresden.

On returning to Schleswig and thence to Copenhagen in the autumn of 1769, Schulenburg found the court in a state of disorder, thanks to the mental deterioration of the King, Christian VII. Even worse for Schulenburg, Bernstorff had been excluded from influence by the machinations of the King's favourites, Brandt and Streunsee. By 1770 Bernstorff had tendered his resignation to the King, and Schulenburg, who had not found favour because, as he said, 'I did not pay court in a servile manner to Messieurs Streunsee and Brandt, who were also not very courteous towards me, as I did not attend the private balls and dinners given every evening at court', again requested an official salaried post, this time through Streunsee, but was refused.[45] It is perhaps not only from pique that he declined to participate in the increasingly sordid and decadent court entertainments characteristic of Christian VII's reign.[46] Certainly life at this juncture looked very black for him; financial ruin loomed. Pursued by creditors through the courts, he feared he would be publicly disgraced. An abject letter to his mother (11 March 1770), who controlled the remaining family finances, expresses his total disarray. It would seem that she had declined to bail him out yet again:

Fredericia, (Schlesvig) 11 March 1770[47]
It is with the most profound resignation, my dear Mother, that I received your answer to my last letter. I have nothing to put forward as an excuse for the unhappy circumstances in which I find myself. In any case, here you see me overwhelmed with misfortune for the rest of my life, being absolutely incapable of sorting out my [financial] difficulties. The final date to pay my debts and the delay accorded to me will expire in a few days. The writs against me will be formally transferred to Copenhagen or to Brandenburg and I will be formally tried without loss of time. The consequences are too dreadful for me to mention here. Dishonoured, driven away, ruined, what is there left for me in the world and what should I do? I avow myself, my dear Mother, to be inexcusable and unworthy of your pity.

His mother, gritting her teeth, one imagines, rescued him in this extremity. But four years later Schulenburg's finances had not markedly improved and indeed seemed to have worsened. In a further begging letter to his mother (4 November 1774), expressing repentance and the 'wish to sustain my life as miserably as possible', he added that he had retrenched on his household expenses: 'I have a small and very poor lodging and have sacked my cook, coachman and lackey and have only kept a young lad to serve me.'[48]

Deprived of his cook, lackey, and coachman, Werner presents a pitiable spectacle. His own account of the 1770–74 period in his journal draws a discreet veil over these financial reverses. It was, as it turned out, Schulenburg's good luck that his poverty forced him to remain on his mother's estates in Schleswig during these years. He thus avoided what he rightly termed the 'bloody catastrophe' of the Streunsee era, when in January 1772, a *coup d'état* deposed Streunsee, resulting in his arrest and execution as well as in the disgrace of the Queen, Caroline Mathilda.[49]

Schulenburg eventually returned to Copenhagen in 1775, after his mother's death. Having inherited her estates, he was once again in a position to cut a figure at the Danish court, where he was granted the Royal Order of the White Knight of Dannebrog in 1776. In 1781, at the age of forty-five, he married a commoner, Johanne Marie de Malleville (née Meyer) the daughter of a sea captain and a divorcee.[50] The marriage appears to have been happy and his wife an excellent manager.[51] The journal which he wrote up in 1780, immediately preceding his marriage, represents an effort to gain some perspective on what had been a troubled life, though he skates over many of its more dubious aspects. In this later period, Schulenburg inherited considerable property and became a wealthy landowner.[52] He and Johanne Marie eventually retired to his estates in Brandenburg. Schulenburg died at Salzwedel (where he and Jodin had spent the glorious summer of 1768) in 1810. There in the Marien Kirche, his wife erected a handsome marble monument extolling his many virtues and especially his kindness to the poor.

Notes

1.   See comment of letter of 11 July 1768 in relation to Jodin's plans for a lawsuit against the court of Saxony: 'if by any unforeseen reason, you unfortunately have to return to your old employment'. Diderot, *Correspondance*, VIII, p. 66.

2.   Diderot, *Correspondance*, VIII, letter 493, 'A Mademoiselle Jodin', 10 September 1768.

3.   'Journal fait par moi à Copenhague'.

4.   *La véritable Vie privée du Maréchal de Richelieu contenant ses amours et intrigues* (1791), ed. Elisabeth Porquerol (Paris: Tournon, 1954), pp. 292–93.

5.   Lagrave, *La Vie théâtrale de Bordeaux*, I, p. 319.

6.   *Mémoire sur délibéré. Pour Demoiselle Marie-Magdeleine Jodin, Actrice de Comédie. Contre le sieur Neuville, Directeur du Comédie* (Angers: A. J. Jahyer, 1774).

7.   *Mémoire sur délibéré*, p. 313.
8.   See Lyonnet, *Dictionnaire des comédiens français*, I, p. 141, who comments: 'Protected by the Maréchal de Richelieu, Governor of Guyenne, Belmont gave a certain glamour to the Bordeaux theatre and was considered by his friends to be an erudite bibliophile and a writer of merit.' Voltaire's two letters to Belmont and his dedication are to be found in *Voltaire Correspondence*, ed. Theodore Besterman (Genève: Institut et Musée Voltaire, 1961), LXVII, 13697 and LIII, 10651.
9.   The Bordeaux Archives Municipales, then housed in the Hôtel de Ville, burned down on 13 June 1862. Many of the eighteenth-century archives were particularly badly damaged and remain only as charred fragments.
10.   Lagrave, *La Vie théâtrale de Bordeaux*, I, p. 255. For a discussion of the unruly popular audiences in Bordeaux and the political fears they inspired see Jeffrey S. Ravel, *The Contested Parterre: Public Theater and French Political Culture 1680–1791* (Ithaca and London: Cornell University Press, 1999), pp. 178–84.
11.   Richelieu is referring to the semi-independent status of the city, which had its own law officers and fiercely resented having royal troops brought in. Archives Municipales de la Ville de Bordeaux, FF70, 24 February 1769.
12.   Schulenburg kept lists of important people he met on his travels. 'Noms des personnes que j'avais connu à Bordeaux', Rep. Beetzendorf II, II, Personal archiv 217, p. 25.
13.   He was characterised by a contemporary as having 'a very good reputation, sound morals and was generally liked and esteemed, though his health was poor and his character a bit weak'. Lafaurie de Monbadon, quoted in Bernadette Lynch, *Le Comte J.-B. Lynch, maire de Bordeaux 1809–1815* (Bordeaux: Héritiers E.-F. Mialhe, n.d.), p. 31, to whom the above account is indebted.
14.   Lynch, *Le Comte J.-B. Lynch*, p. 29. The Château de la Trompette was destroyed during the Revolution. Twentieth-century Bordeaux largely turns its back on the river vistas admired by Schulenburg, having transformed the river bank into a gigantic car park. In compensation, the centre of the old town has been beautifully restored and pedestrianised.
15.   Diderot, *Correspondance*, VIII, letter 493, 'A Mademoiselle Jodin', pp. 163–6.
16.   The Jodins' servant.
17.   The Farmers-general were private tax-collectors who bought the right to 'farm' or collect taxes on salt and tobacco (*gabelles*) and a host of household products as well as alcohol (*aides*). The gap between what they collected and what they returned to the state allowed for enormous fortunes to be made. The Farmers-general came to represent one of the most notorious sources of bureaucratic inefficiency and corruption under the *ancien régime*. Diderot, who disapproved of them on principle, was not averse to investing in the funds they managed, for himself or for Jodin (letter of 1 October 1768 to Sophie Volland, noted in Yves Durand, *Finances et Mécénat: les fermiers généraux au XVIIIe siècle*, Paris: Hachette, 1976), p. 191. Thus the life annuity taken out on his daughter's lifetime was assigned to the 'Aydes et Gabelles' and he invested his own money derived from Catherine the Great in the same way. In his discussions with Jodin over her investments, he and she demonstrate awareness of the precarious state of the Crown's finances (Jodin seemingly more pessimistic than Diderot). New life annuities in the King's name do seem to have been reissued in 1769. However, it may be that Diderot refers to these as being synonymous with those of the Farmers-general. Subsequent régimes under the Revolution and Directory did attempt to pay the loans which these investments represented to their *rentiers*. See J. F. Bosher, *French Finances 1770–*

1795: from Business to Bureaucracy (Cambridge: Cambridge University Press, 1970), pp. 238–54; Simon Schama, *Citizens: a Chronicle of the French Revolution* (London: Viking, 1989), pp. 72–7.

18. Eugène Ritter, 'Jean Jodin (1713–1761) et son frère Pierre Jodin', pp. 360–71. Ritter argues, without any convincing evidence, that the wicked uncle of Diderot's letters could not have been Pierre Jodin because the latter was Genevan (therefore presumably virtuous), and supposes instead a ne'er-do-well brother of Mme Jodin. It is hard to see how Diderot's references to a brother-in-law can be to Mme Jodin's own brother, of whom nothing is known.

19. Letter of 16 July 1768 from Schulenburg to Bernstorff, SKUA pa-al 49 Sachsen B, 1764–68.

20. Ibid.

21. Diderot, *Correspondance,* VIII, letter 512, 'A Mademoiselle Jodin, 21 November 1768, pp. 224–7.

22. Unidentified.

23. She would presumably be properly described as Jodin's cousin.

24. Diderot, *Correspondance,* VII, letter 515, 'A Mademoiselle Jodin', December 1768, pp. 237–9.

25. 'Contrat de mariage de Marie-Angélique Diderot avec Abel-François-Nicolas Caroillon', Article 8, Diderot, *Correspondance*, XVI, pp. 119–21.

26. 'Mémoires de Mme Vandeul', Diderot, *Oeuvres Complètes*, I, p. 790.

27. Diderot, *Correspondance*, IX, letter 521, 'A Mademoiselle Jodin', pp. 23–7.

28. Duc de Castries, *La du Barry* (Paris: Albin Michel, 1986), pp. 57–99.

29. Mme Geoffrin, married to a rich manufacturer, was a renowned *salonnière* and visited Poland in 1766 at the invitation of Stanislas Poniatowski, who called her 'Maman'.

30. Mme du Barry, mistress of Louis XV.

31. Jean Baptiste Greuze (1725–1805), celebrated for his genre paintings and portraits.

32. Archives Municipales de Bordeaux MS 656, 'Correspondance de Richelieu', 1199/ 60.

33. The *syndics* were the city representatives under the authority of the lord of the manor or town, in this case, Richelieu. Under the *ancien régime*, the *procureur* was the officer charged with representing to the courts those pleading in their jurisdiction. He was a general law officer, rather than purely a prosecutor in the modern sense.

34. Diderot, *Correspondance*, IX, letter 525, 'A Mademoselle Jodin', 24 March 1769, pp. 41–2.

35. Diderot, *Correspondance*, IX, letter 528, 'A Mademoiselle Jodin', 11 May 1769, pp. 47–9.

36. Catherine-Nicole Lemaure (1704–02), a famous singer at the Opera.

37. Marie-Françoise Marchand, known as Dumesnil (1713–1803), a tragedienne.

38. Diderot, *Correspondance*, IX, letter 538, 'A Mademoiselle Jodin', 15 July 1769, pp. 77–8.

39. This was the *rente viagère* or annuity, discussed above, and the contract (dated 4 July 1769) envisages the income passing on Jodin's death to the Diderots. The phrase 'on my daughter's head' refers to the legal arrangement by which the annuity was to be paid 'on the head of', or during the lifetime of, a given individual.

40. Diderot, *Correspondance*, IX, letter 542, 'A Mademoiselle Jodin', 26 July 1769, p. 87.

41. The first part of the sentence against La Barre was carried out symbolically, but not the second.

42. The only known source for this story lies in Diderot's letter of 11 September 1769 to Sophie Volland, Diderot, *Correspondance*, IX, p. 141. The much-damaged Bordeaux Archives retain no record of Jodin's arrest.

43. *La véritable Vie Privée du Maréchal de Richelieu*, p. 294.

44. For the relatively lax approach to public morals in Bayonne see Josette Pontet, 'Morale et ordre public à Bayonne au XVIIIème siècle', *Bulletin de la Société des sciences lettres et arts de Bayonne*, CXXXIII (1974), pp. 127–44.

45. Werner von der Schulenburg, 'Journal fait par moi'.

46. For an account of the excesses of the Danish court and royal family see P. Nors, *The Court of Christian VII of Denmark* (London: Hurst and Blackett, 1928).

47. Schulenburg, letter to his mother, 11 March 1770 Landesarchiv Magdeburg – LHA-Rep. H. Beetzendorf II, II, no. 214, p. 84.

48. Schulenburg, letter to his mother, 11 March 1770, p. 99.

49. See: Thomas Munck, 'The Danish Reformers', in H. M. Scott, ed., *Enlightened Absolutism; Reform and Reformers in Later Eighteenth-Century Europe* (Basingstoke: Macmillan, 1990), pp. 245–63. For an emotive account of the Streunsee/Caroline Mathilde question, see Lascelles Wraxall, *Life and Times of Her Majesty Caroline Matilda, Queen of Denmark and Norway and Sister of H.M. King George III of England*, 3 vols (London: W. H. Allen, 1864) and Nors, *The Court of Christian VII of Denmark*.

50. Divorce had been permitted in Denmark since the Reformation on grounds of adultery, desertion or impotence. In the case of adultery, only the innocent partner could remarry. Roderick Phillips, *Putting Asunder* (Cambridge: Cambridge University Press, 1988), pp. 51–2, 200. However, Streunsee in 1771 repealed a Danish law forbidding a woman divorced for infidelity from marrying the co-respondent. Nors, *The Court of Christian VII of Denmark*, p. 181. The background to Johanne Marie de Malleville's divorce is not known. The issue is of interest in a broader context, as in her *Vues législatives pour les femmes* (1790), Jodin was to champion divorce, not permitted under French law before the Revolution.

51. The *Status Bonarum*, or yearly account book of 1802 for the Beetzendorf estate (Rep. Beetzendorf II, II, No. 217), is prefaced by the following cheerful ditty by Werner von der Schulenburg adapted from Gluck's *Orfeo and Euridice*: 'Che faro senza Euridice / Que faro senza il mio ben! / Quest-il mio ben / E la cara mi esposa, Johanna Maria Wernerina.'

52. From his mother Schulenburg inherited property in Schleswig: Soegaard, Aaretoft and Maaslev; from his brother, estates in Brandenburg: Winterfeld, Beetzendorf, Rittlebein, Saltzwedel. See Marquard, *Danske Gesanter og Genandt-Stadspersonnale*, p. 324.

Figure 6.1   *Bordeaux, the Harbour*, mid-eighteenth century, after Vernet, in
Bankes's *New System of Geography*.
[Courtesy of the Mary Evans Picture Library].
Bordeaux as Jodin and Schulenburg would have known it in 1769

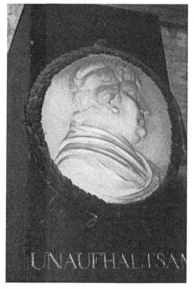

Figure 6.2   Bus-relief of Werner XXV von der Schulenburg from his
funeral monument in the Marien Kirche, Salzwedel.
[Photograph by Eva Bjerregaard, 1999]

CHAPTER SEVEN

London, Angers and the quieter years: 1770–77

Following her arrest in Bordeaux in August 1769, which ended her stage career there, Jodin returned to Paris to live with her mother, as she said: 'in the bosom of my family'.[1] They took up residence in an apartment in the Faubourg Saint-Germain, rue Bourbon Château, near to Diderot's lodgings, rue Taranne. For the next five years she seems to have followed Diderot's prescription for a rational and healthy life, the eighteenth-century 'happy-man' motif, sketched out in his letter of 10 February 1769: 'A little apartment with good air in a quiet corner of the city, a healthy and sober diet, a few reliable friends, a little reading, music, a great deal of exercise ...'. His wish that she should care for her mother and other needy relatives had borne fruit. She maintained her theatre contacts, particularly at the Comédie-Française. She was also free to pursue her intellectual interests. Yet in spite of the fact that Jodin was now financially independent and could afford to leave the stage which had led her into so many scrapes, we will see that the theatre remained an enormous attraction.

Nor were her wanderings entirely over. In May of 1770, following her Bordeaux adventure, she travelled to England, whether on a theatrical tour or in a purely private capacity is not known, and dined with the French envoy to London, the celebrated Chevalier d'Eon, and his friend the radical parliamentarian, John Wilkes. Diderot had given her an introduction to the Chevalier, whilst Wilkes's daughter Mary, then studying in Paris, wrote to her father of Jodin's coming visit and that she hoped he would meet the actress.[2] At the dinner she was persuaded by another guest, the Chevalier de Piennes, to give a dramatic recitation[3]. This meeting, recorded in one of Jodin's rare letters to be preserved, offers us some valuable autobiographical insights and speaks feelingly of her debts to Diderot.

Diderot had met Wilkes during the latter's Paris exile of 1764–68. In May 1770 when Jodin dined with them, both he and d'Eon were at crucial stages of their careers. In April 1770 Wilkes had just completed an eighteen-month prison sentence for libel and was about to re-launch his political fortunes.[4] D'Eon, a military hero and accomplished swordsman, who was Louis XV's personal diplomatic agent in London, was in the throes of the famous controversy about his sex – it was strongly rumoured that he was in reality as woman – so much so that he went into hiding later in the year. Anatomically a man, as was discovered on his death, d'Eon seems to have been willing to lend weight to these rumours which rose to fever pitch in London, with fortunes being staked on his sexual identity. Though living in an age when gambling had attained epidemic proportions, the enormous sums wagered on the question of his true sex were nevertheless astounding.[5]

When it was decided by a court case in 1774 (though without anatomical examination) that d'Eon *was* a woman, s/he became something of an icon for eighteenth-century feminists who argued that her/his worldly success proved women's capacity to play a role in public life. Women who hoped to shine in the male sphere of letters revered him. The historian Catherine Macaulay was a friend and admirer. He was cited approvingly by Mme d'Epinay and Mary Wollstonecraft as evidence of what women could achieve.[6] This admiration for what was believed to be d'Eon's successful masculine disguise is reflected in a little anecdote passed on by the Chevalier de Piennes to d'Eon: 'Mme de Sarsefieds very much wanted you to be a woman *for the honour of her sex* [author's italics]. She wishes to go to England to see you.'[7] In addition to his reputation as a military hero, d'Eon was a bibliophile who possessed a remarkable library with an emphasis on ancient and modern philosophy. More unusually some forty to sixty volumes of his collection were about women, from pious works to feminist pamphlets. While this collection indicates d'Eon's feminine self-identification, it equally suggests his interest in feminist ideas. Jodin had indeed fallen among intellectual sympathisers.[8] The tone Jodin adopts in her letter to d'Eon (she writes to him, she says, to 'relieve her heart') is testimony, too, to the affection that he inspired in his friends and acquaintances.

The social value of friendship emerges as a central theme in Jodin's letter when she praises Diderot as a shining example of friendship in action. Yet what she records of his influence on her life was more that individual benevolence on Diderot's part. The circle of like-minded thinkers represented by Diderot, d'Holbach, Helvétius and the *Encyclopédie* writers generally, whom we identify as constituting the Republic of Letters, were linked not only by radical ideas but by the concept of active friendship or sociability.[9] We have seen in Diderot's correspondence with Jodin how seriously and sometimes no doubt to the recipient, maddeningly, he took his responsibilities as a friend of her father, her mother and herself. More remarkably perhaps, the ethics of practical involvement with which Diderot bombarded her were on the whole taken in good part; Jodin fully recognised his value to her, even if she frequently failed to swallow his energetic doses of moral advice.[10]

From the confiding tone of her letter, Jodin seems to have found in d'Eon a further example of unaffected sociability and kindness:

> Paris, rue de Bourbon-Château, at the corner with the rue de l'Echaudé, in the house of a wine-merchant, Faubourg Saint Germain; 3 July 1770[11]
>
> I have this morning relieved my conscience by writing to M. de Piennes. Now, Monsieur, I shall relieve my heart. Truly, you are very ill fitted to be living where you do. I left you there with much regret. Everyone has rushed to ask me what I thought of London. I replied that it was a superb palace

whose masters were absent and which was occupied by their valets. No doubt M. de Piennes told you of my life and my profession, of which you will I imagine have formed your opinion when, at his insistence, I recited you some lines – a proof of my willingness to oblige rather than of my talent. Well, Monsieur, I owe to the foreign theatre the re-establishment, not of the fortune I might have expected if my father had lived, but at least of a sort of comfortable competence.

The warm friendship which I enjoy with M. Diderot is the consequence of his connection with my father, who was a close friend of his. He is the only one of those who laid claim to this title who justified it by the interest he bore to those who belonged to my father. He has seen your compliments, which he receives with much gratitude. He strongly urged me not to forget to greet you in his name. He congratulated me on having made your acquaintance and that of Mr. Wils [sic] and said to me, with truth: 'Your wishes were well served there.' I replied, 'Only you were lacking, for them to have been fulfilled completely'. We count on you, Monsieur, to send us your *Loisirs*, about which I told M. Diderot.[12] Please remember to keep your word about this, I beg you, and, to be sure they reach me safely, send them by the post or tell M. de Piennes to promise not to forget to bring them. But goodness knows when he will come to Paris. I would rather not wait so long, so do try to find some other means.

I would encourage you to read the *System of Nature*, and even to buy it; it will not disappoint you. Since my return I have not been able to put it down; it amazes me. I think I recognize the method of M. Helvétius in it and will ask M. Diderot to pass on your compliments to him, as I only know him from his works.[13] If you have any more important commission in which I can oblige you, I beg you to ask me and to believe I will perform it with the greatest zeal.

I have the honour to be, with the most distinguished compliments, Monsieur,

Your very humble servant,
JODIN

Jodin's reference to her 'état' translated here as 'profession', may also be rendered as 'status' which in her case had a double significance of which she was acutely aware and which Diderot had frequently emphasised in his letters to her.[14] Her status at birth was as the daughter of a Genevan citizen, a designation conferring considerable prestige. Rousseau provides confirmatory evidence of this in his *Confessions* where he made much of his Genevan citizenship and considered himself to have fallen from his rightful social place on running away from the city in his teens. He was at pains in later life to reclaim that citizenship. For her part, Jodin never forgot, nor did Diderot wish her to forget that her status origin was widely different from her status as an actress: 'You are an unfortunate child but a well-born one' (letter of 21 August 1765). We have seen that in numerous letters (for example 10 February 1769), he shared her ambivalence about the theatrical profession and held out the lure of private life as being more honourable. Jodin's assertion of her rightful social place was to be a central theme of her subsequent writing.[15] Her tribute to

Diderot's friendship for her family demonstrates how he stood by them after her father's death and that in spite of the Bordeaux débâcle, she and Diderot were still on friendly terms. In the worlds she had inhabited from prison to stage to courts, with their rivalries and jealousies, Diderot and his family must have represented a haven of disinterested benevolence for both herself and her mother.

The other intriguing remark in Jodin's letter is her enthusiastic recommendation to d'Eon to read d'Holbach's *Système de la nature*, which had been published anonymously in 1766, but which Jodin had just discovered.[16] Her tentative (mis)attribution to Helvétius was not wide of the mark; both writers were materialists and free-thinkers, neither was d'Holbach's authorship of the *Système* generally known until after his death. What was it about this text that Jodin found so gripping? The *Système de la nature* was a frankly atheistic work, a position impossible to espouse openly under French religious and political censorship in the eighteenth century, hence its anonymous publication. It argued that all human attributes derived from a material basis, that God was a chimera, and that, in contradistinction to Descartes, there were no innate ideas. The book was also strongly anti-clerical, attacking the Church for its resistance to progress and reason.[17] Jodin's admiration tells us a great deal about her interest in materialism and confirms that philosophy was not new. Further her enthusiasm for this text can be directly linked her reported anti-religious outburst in Bordeaux. She evidently rejoiced to find confirmation for her religious scepticism in a seriously argued work of contemporary philosophy.[18]

Following her London excursion in 1770, and her mention in Angélique Diderot's marriage contract in 1772, nothing more is known of Jodin until 1774 when she travelled to Angers in south-western France to perform in the theatrical troupe directed by Honoré Bourdon de Noeuville or Neuville. She was recruited to perform in Angers by Neuville's employer, the entrepreneur Mlle Montansier, a formidable businesswoman whom Diderot could usefully have used to illustrate, in tandem with Mme Geoffrin and Mme du Barry, what a woman from humble origins could achieve in eighteenth-century France.

The daughter of a pin-maker from Bordeaux, Mlle Montansier, born Marguerite Brunet (1730–1820), moved to Paris after her father's death and from the age of eighteen lived as a *fille galante*. For some years she 'kept a house' where her activities were faithfully recorded by the police. Among her many lovers was M. de Saint-Florentin, the official who signed the order to imprison Marie Madeleine and Mme Jodin in la Salpêtrière for 'libertinage'.[19] Unlike Marie Madeleine Jodin and her mother, Mlle Montansier's courtesans and their male clients, wealthy aristocrats and merchants, though under police surveillance, were not arrested. Status privilege operated in the world of the *demi-monde*, just as it did in society at large, a point Jodin would raise in her feminist treatise. The actor Fleury in his memoirs characterised Mlle Montansier as a woman of amorous appetites: 'Since she only knew how to make love, she made this her capital, a capital which brought a good rate of interest from licentious aristocrats.'[20] In fact Montansier was an highly astute woman, rather than merely the good-hearted cocotte painted by Fleury. Like many women emerging from prostitution, she tried her hand at acting, but after an unsuccessful début at the Comédie-Française, abandoned the stage to form her own company. She became an immensely successful impresario, running theatres at Nantes, Rouen, Caen, Orléans as well as, briefly, at Angers. She formed a close friendship with the Queen, Marie Antoinette, who gave her the direction and administration of the royal theatre at Versailles. In spite of these royal connections, she survived the Revolution, though not without a period in prison under the Terror, and went on to own and manage a further series of major theatres. By any standards she possessed extraordinary entrepreneurial skills.[21]

The chief failure of judgement with which it might have been possible to tax Mlle Montansier, noted for her ruthless eye to the main chance, was her long-standing passion for the former army captain turned actor, Neuville. Vain and declamatory on the stage, he attracted the odium of critics such as Grimm who noted his disastrous début of January 1768: 'He showed unbearable conceit and kept his head tucked down into his shoulders which gave him the air of an insolent hunchback.'[22] Offstage he was reputed to be arrogant and aggressive. In 1774 Montansier put her lover in charge of a travelling troupe due to perform in Angers, which turned out to be a short-lived engagement. By 1778 she had made him her business partner and director for the Rouen theatre. Wherever he went, Neuville maintained his reputation for quarrelsomeness and womanising. He was forced to flee Rouen in 1782 following a stabbing incident. The experiences of his theatrical management that Jodin was to recount in Angers seem entirely in character.

On 23 April 1774, Jodin signed a contract[23] with Mlle Montansier to perform the kinds of roles in which she had already starred in Warsaw and Dresden (queens and noble mothers). From her own account, she was head-hunted by Mlle Montansier, who persuaded her to undertake this 'fatal engagement' and overcame her initial reluctance to return to the stage by appealing to her passion for the theatre:

> Acquaintances in the theatre world introduced me to Mademoiselle Montansier, director of a number of [theatrical] troupes. She begged me strongly to join her: she was not surprised by my refusals, but she had the skill to awaken the inclination which had always attracted me to the theatre, which resembles a fire erupting from the ashes. She awoke this inclination in my heart and fanned it by the memory of those laurels which she said I had gathered in several foreign courts. I was sufficiently weak to sign a contract with her on 23 April 1774; I was engaged to play the roles of Queens and leading roles in tragedy, and noble mothers in comedy. We stipulated that the first to break the contract would pay damages of 1000 *livres*.[24]

The quarrel which arose between Jodin and her director, Neville, reminiscent of her imbroglio with Rousselois in Warsaw (also arrogant in his attitude towards his actresses) can be read in two ways: firstly for its considerable anecdotal interest' and secondly as an example of the *mémoire sur délibéré* or *mémoire judiciare*, a popular genre in the late *ancien régime* where courtroom debates were reported like theatrical dramas by participants in the disputes.[25] Jodin's *mémoire*, one of only two known published works by her, was a characteristic example of the genre.

When Jodin told her actor friends that she would be under Neuville's direction, they were reportedly horrified: 'With what dark colours did they not paint him to me; how forcefully they described to me the miseries that this violent, haughty and dishonest man would inflict upon me.'[26] Having belatedly and unsuccessfully attempted to persuade Mlle Montansier to allow her to withdraw from her engagement, Jodin proceeded to Angers on 14 July after a delay occasioned by the period of mourning for the death of Louis XV (10 May) when all the theatres in France closed. Jodin gave her first performance as Aménaïde in Voltaire's *Tancrède* on Saturday 16 July.

Following the Saturday performance, Neuville informed her that she must travel with the troupe that night to Saumur, a distance of about fifty kilometres, in order to perform there on Tuesday the nineteenth. Jodin pleaded exhaustion after her journey from Paris and offered to travel by private conveyance on the Sunday. Neuville insisted that she travel overnight with the troupe in their common conveyance, or he would have her arrested. Jodin, who had stipulated in her contract that she and her mother would travel by private carriage, was most unhappy: 'Mlle Jodin, used to the greater comforts of life, and in spite of the fact that her contract stated that she would be given transport (she and her mother) by royal coach or some other suitable means, was subjected by *le sieur* Neuville to the common rule imposed on the rest of his actors.'[27] Evidently Jodin's new financial prosperity had allowed her to assert her rights to creature comforts. From Neuville's point of view, however, she was playing the temperamental diva, a role, as we know, at which she also excelled.

On arrival in Saumur, Jodin claimed that Neuville insulted her at rehearsal before the whole company but that nevertheless, in spite of feeling ill, she performed her roles both at Saumur and again on returning to Angers. The director's motives, it emerged, in deliberately antagonising his leading lady and star performer were not random malevolence, but based on wounded pique. Jodin, it transpired, had rejected his advances. Her account of his unsuccessful seduction is richly ironic:

> This violent man who persecutes me has not always had these feelings of hatred for me that motivate him now. Director of a theatrical troupe ... he thought that the hearts of his actresses were the tributes that they owed to his greatness. But love is a feeling that cannot be commanded to order; one

must inspire it. I thought that, without failing to honour my contract, I could be an exception to this rule, no matter how universally he thought it applied. Let me not be accused of false pride. Was the spectacle of le Sieur Neuville sighing at my feet enough to make me vain? My rejection [of his advances] inflamed his desires; my disdain made him furious. From this moment he swore my ruin.[28]

The pace of the quarrel quickened. The following Saturday, 23 July, the actors, in accordance with normal practice, met to decide on the play for the following day. In Jodin's words: 'It is an accepted custom that the company's actors meet to decide which plays will be performed first. We perform those which everyone knows [by heart], thus giving the actors time to recall those roles which they remember less well.'[29] Indeed the necessity of retaining a large number of plays in their memory was one of the major challenges facing actors:

> Provincial audiences being small and impatient and many provincial actors lacking in talent, theatre companies could not perform one play over several nights but were obliged to present an extremely varied repertoire. An almost superhuman feat of memory was required to keep enough roles in one's head.[30]

Jodin who had interrupted her acting career for five years declared herself unable to recall the part of Iphigenia in *Iphigenia in Tauris* sufficiently well to perform it. She proposed that they put on Voltaire's *Mérope* instead, but the male lead, in the same position as herself with Iphigenia, did not know the role of Polifonte.[31] The actors therefore decided to present a comedy, *Gaston and Bayard*. At this juncture Neuville intervened, insisting that Jodin play Iphigenia and threatened that if she refused he would have the police drag her to the play. He presumably wanted to discredit her before the Angers audience by forcing her into a lamentable performance. The troupe however ignored his threats and duly put on the comedy as they had agreed.

Neuville retired to Saumur on Sunday 24 July in a sulk, temporarily defeated, but let it be known that Jodin was dismissed, seasoning his remarks (reported back to Jodin) with a great deal of invective and personal abuse. The following Thursday, 28 July, Jodin informed Neuville that she stood ready to fulfil her engagements. He replied that he no longer considered her a member of the troupe. Not to be outdone, on the following day Jodin submitted a plea to the Angers tribunal against Neuville for breach of contract. The case was first heard on Saturday 30 July, but was adjourned to allow her to send to Paris for her copy of the contract. The second hearing, held in early August, was finally adjudicated on 1 September 1774. The court found in Jodin's favour.

Before the court's decision, Jodin had published on 13 August 1774 her *Mémoire sur délibéré, pour Demoiselle Marie-Magdeleine Jodin, Actrice de Comédie Contre le sieur Neuville, Directeur de Comédie*. It was customary for *mémoires* to be written by the barristers acting in a case. This *mémoire* was signed by both Jodin and her barrister, Delaunay.[32] A late nineteenth-century

Angers historian, Queruau Lamérie, argues that the work is certainly by Jodin herself, not her barrister, given the personal details it contains: 'Its dramatic and bombastic style, the terms in which the insults Neuville addressed to her are reported, the praise that she addresses to her own superior birth, education and talents over her adversary can only have been written by a woman doubly wounded in her pride as a woman and as an artist.'[33] Jodin certainly asserts in the first paragraph that the work is entirely her own: 'Reduced to the necessity of defending myself energetically against slander, I come to implore the protection of the Law and to justify myself in the eyes of the Public: I am not eloquent, nor am I a lawyer; I have only the truth at my disposal. I will borrow a pen of no-one.'[34] It is possible to agree that Jodin authored the *mémoire* herself, though taking legal advice from Delaunay, whilst disagreeing with the above strictures about her style. The histrionic nature of Jodin's account is no doubt partly due to her personal involvement, but also shows her to be writing in an already established legal, quasi-literary tradition, which had its roots in melodrama. Sara Maza has demonstrated the heavily fictionalised nature of the *mémoires judiciaires*. Via melodramatic narratives, they painted social archetypes – villains and pure heroines or heroes. These courtroom dramas owed their popularity when published, to their very simplicity. They were, it would not be too fanciful to say, the soap-operas of their day. Maza notes the interplay, so clearly demonstrated also in Jodin's *mémoire*, between the theatre and the courtroom, the technique of the former being applied to the latter.[35]

If we read the Angers *mémoire* in the context of eighteenth-century courtroom dramas, we can appreciate how Jodin as an actress, pleading her case in court, used her dramatic skills to charm and convince her judges. It helped a good deal, of course, that her case for breach of contract against Neuville was reasonably easy to prove. However from a literary or popular culture standpoint, it is her construction of Neuville as a tyrant and of herself as a victim which demonstrates the politicisation of her case. Her self-construction as a hapless weak woman, one could add, is scarcely reminiscent of the tearaway Jodin we have seen in action heretofore. Still, this was not so much an exercise in sincerity as in persuasion. In this courtroom drama, Jodin manipulated her legal audience with skill. Though she may have refused to perform the part of Iphigenia on the Angers stage, in court she played a version of this sacrificial victim to Neuville's Agamemnon.[36] The director appears in her text like a grand seigneur or a tyrannous king unjustly oppressing the weak:

> The integrity of my Judges gives me confidence; ... they will confound the shameless man who profits from the weakness of my sex to crush me. [Then addressing herself:] Dispel your alarms, unfortunate one, are you not under the protection of Justice and of Truth? [37]

It was also true of the genre of the *mémoires judiciaires* that the cases which they recorded describing the downtrodden struggling against his or her betters may in fact have reflected negligible social inequality. The *cause célèbre* of Mme de Saint-Vincent versus the Duc de Richelieu (1774–77), in which a former mistress of the Duke was accused of fraud, was fought out on the rhetorical ground of the helpless woman against the corrupt *grand homme*, whereas there was virtually no social or status distance between them. It may be no accident that Jodin's *mémoire*, also published in 1774, employs many of the verbal strategies that would flourish in the Vincent/Richelieu case of high-life scandal.[38] Certainly Jodin emphasises her intrinsic worth (birth, fortune, talent) against the lack of these in Neuville, painted as a monstrous bully, a tyrant without legitimate power. Yet it would be misleading to imply that the whole *mémoire* is a fiction. It is scrupulous in detailing dates and places. Jodin's contract with Mlle Montansier, reproduced at the end of the *mémoire*, factually clinches her case. But it is the way a contractual and sexual dispute is transformed into a struggle between the weak but virtuous, talented, though well-born woman (fallen from her proper sphere) and the powerful, gross, masculine oppressor, that lends the *mémoire* its status as fiction. This is not to say that there may not have been a great deal of truth in Jodin's portrait of Neuville or indeed in the assertions of her own worth.

After describing Neuville's unsuccessful sexual overtures, the text moves into what one could term the villain mode: 'From this moment he swore to destroy me. Let us carry a torch into his soul, let us unveil his schemes and his shadowy manoeuvres' (*Mémoire*, p. 4). Jodin was no democrat, objecting particularly that a man of such inferior parts should aspire to her love. Neuville 'ought to know the prodigious distance which separates us from the point of view of birth, fortune and, dare I say it, talents'.[39] He used his authority as director to behave malevolently, spreading scandalous rumours about her. Jodin's prose becomes lyrical:

> His mouth, like a rotten sepulchre which spreads corruption everywhere, in its fury vomits all the horrors that could destroy my reputation, my talents and my morals. His speeches were like so many dagger thrusts, all the more dangerous from being made secretly.[40]

This rotting sepulchre then metamorphoses, a trifle confusedly, into a monster of classical antiquity, the Minotaur. Mlle Montansier takes on the role of the seductive Theseus and Jodin, the hapless Ariadne, abandoned on the island of Naxos.[41] This trope is couched in an imagined address to Mlle Montansier, perceived both as Theseus and as an alter ego for Neuville:

> I would say to the demoiselle Montansier, 'You have taken me from my family, my friends and my hopes. You have altered my plans for my life, based on a belief in a contract which ought to be sacred. I have spent more than 4000 *livres* to buy theatre costumes [Can this have been true? Jodin earned a good salary, but it only came to 3000 *livres* per annum.] You have made me leave my own country, you have sent me a hundred leagues from

home under a foreign sky, without resources, without support, to deliver
me to the fury of an inflexible man. *You have abandoned me to my unhappy
fate, as was the unfortunate Ariadne by that ungrateful Theseus* [author's
emphasis]. Oh what would my destiny have been if I had depended only on
our contract! But I threw myself at the feet of Justice. I knew that the laws
come to the rescue of the unhappy, groaning victim, that they avenge honour
outraged and faith betrayed ...[42]

By identifying herself, if improbably, with Ariadne, one of the figures of
mythology most imbued with pathos, Jodin, an actress with a known life of
some scandal behind her, conjures up innocence, defencelessness and herself
as the victim of injustice. In this instance, her theatrical career has stood her in
good stead. Though Diderot had in his third letter warned her not to take her
stage roles into real life, here the possibilities of the court as stage, coupled
with the already thriving melodramatic conventions of the *mémoire judiciaire*,
meant that she succeeded with her judicial audience.[43] It also seems more than
likely that the emotive charge of her *mémoire* as a whole, subsumed in this
image, reflected her experiences of arbitrary power from la Salpêtrière to
Dresden, and perhaps feelings reflecting her parting from Schulenburg.

In her conclusion, Jodin turns a mixture of irony and the rhetoric of
oppressed innocence on Neuville. Responding to his complaint that she, as his
pensionnaire or employee, did not show him enough respect, Jodin ripostes
that she showed him all the respect he deserved: 'I know to what extent this
creature is admirable and what consideration he merits. I will always make it
my duty to give him the proof of those sentiments which he inspires in those
who know him best.' Then moving from sarcasm to pathos she continues:

My heart is incapable of hatred; I pardon him for having sought to destroy
me; his efforts will be powerless, they will be crushed by a truth superior to
his slanders; my conscience, my morals, the esteem in which I am held by
honourable people will compensate for the sorrows he could cause me.
Shame and Remorse will avenge oppressed Innocence and outraged
Honour.[44]

If the *mémoire* is an accurate record of Jodin's court performance, we can
imagine that the judges, who heard a carefully argued case, also experienced
the pleasures of theatrical representation. As far as we know, this Angers
courtroom was the scene of Jodin's last theatrical performance. However we
hold two further clues concerning the temptations to return to the stage that
Mlle Montansier had so skilfully exploited.

The first is an anonymous poem, 'Vers à Mlle Jodin', published in the
Journal de politique et de littérature, Brussels, 1775, in praise of the actress,
urging her to take up her rightful place on the Paris stage. After her stormy
Angers tour, the poem's author, responding to Jodin's expressed intention to
abandon the theatrical profession for good, endeavoured to persuade her that
the Comédie-Française, currently bereft of talent, would welcome her and that

in any case she would find retirement unbearably dull. The verses offer a telling though necessarily idealised portrait of the actress:

'Verses to Mlle Jodin'[45]

Proud Jodin, accept my tribute.
I have not come to praise your beauty.
You despise that sickly and affected tone,
And in order to please you
One must speak as a sensible man.

Already more than once jealousy
Has raised its frightful standard against you;
You make enemies of your admirers
And your success inflames their fury.
Can you be surprised?
A somnolent bourgeois
Dies as he lived, in tranquillity
But for those elevated and transcendent spirits
Who always abandon themselves to their ardent impulses
Their fate must be quite different.
They live far away from well-trodden paths.

It is rare that mortals deign to render justice.
Genius always burns at its own expense
And the heavens allow the palm of talent
To flourish on the steep cliffs of a terrifying precipice.

To shield you from all these evils
What must the shining brilliance of your merit carry with it in its wake?
Do you wish to renounce your noble work?
Unimpressed by the lure of lasting fame
And fearing the cowardice of your enemies
Would you prefer contemptible repose
To the glaring miseries of celebrity?
What can obscurity offer you?
You seek it in vain. The impulse which
Nature printed in your heart, from your earliest years,
Stronger than reason and your most prudent plans
Will make you loathe an obscure existence.

If you can bear the inconstancy of public opinion
Of groundlings led by blind ignorance,
Fly to Paris; the abode of talent alone deserves to be your home.
It is there that you will be able to find
An audience of enlightened good taste.
It is there also that stern criticism reigns
But it is just and you should confront it.
Clairon who formerly captured public approval
Stole away from her triumphs
And no longer wishes to receive the tributes

That Frenchmen lavished upon her.
She allows the days of her beauty to glide away
In the bosom of sweet intoxication
And for her heart, debilitated by lethargy
A moment of pleasure is worth immortality.

Indeed Paris has no more actresses.
Oh sublime JODIN; the moment is propitious.
Melpomene[46] calls you to the honour of her art.
Take the dagger from the hands of Dumesnil![47]

This effusion must have been written not just by an admirer of Jodin's stage performances but by someone who knew her volatile character. Characterising her in a romantic trope as a rare soul ('an elevated and transcendent spirit') whose greatness lies in her capacity to abandon herself to her ardent impulses, the poet alleges that professional and personal jealousies have poisoned her career but even these are a mark of her genius. The image of the palm tree of talent only flourishing on the edges of a fearful precipice, if gorgeously exaggerated, reflects the prototype of the artist cursed by exceptional qualities; gifted souls must court danger and controversy. Such constructions of turbulent genius had become a commonplace of eighteenth-century aesthetics. Goethe's Werther, for example, was an icon of the genius misunderstood by society and Rousseau cultivated this opposition in his own personality. These writers stressed the disruptive potential of genius and the links between the terrible and the sublime.[48] The poet's analysis of Jodin's mercurial character, not as a flaw but as an index of her talent, reflects this aesthetic. Diderot, on the question of genius, had remarked in his essay 'Sur les femmes': 'When they [women] possess genius, I think they bear a more original stamp of it than we do.'[49]

The poet chides the actress for wishing to leave the stage permanently, evoking the example of Mlle Clairon as a dire warning against such a course. The great Clairon, known for her haughty character as well as her superb acting, had retired in 1766, though she had subsequently performed in various private theatricals and in provincial theatres. In 1773 she had become the official mistress of the Margrave of Anspach and left Paris for his court. In the 'Verses to Mlle Jodin', this decision is construed as the betrayal of a fine talent for sensuous pleasures. In contrast the poet invokes the other great contemporary French actress, Mlle Dumesnil, equating her acting style with Jodin's. Unlike Mlle Clairon, whose performances had won Diderot's approval for being highly studied and controlled, Mlle Dumesnil's trademark was an ability to convey spontaneous passion: 'Owing more to nature than to application, Mlle Dumesnil, unequal like all artists who deliver themselves over to inspiration, was only ever excellent in passionate roles.'[50] Voltaire claimed that she made the audience weep throughout two whole acts. Jodin, in being invited to 'take the dagger from Dumesnil' was the recipient of a highly complimentary judgement on her acting style.

Certainly Jodin could not have wished to be linked with any greater names in the theatre than Mlle Clairon and Mlle Dumesnil. She did not, however, take the bait of this poetic flattery and never, as far as is known, appeared at the Paris Comédie-Française. Yet, when in 1774 she left Angers, she was only thirty-three years old and would have had a long theatrical career to look forward to. One can imagine that she was torn between her very real passion for the stage and her awareness of the precarious and scandal-ridden nature of the actor's life. Furthermore she had no financial need to continue in the profession. Thanks to Schulenburg's largesse, Diderot's prudent investments and whatever damages she had won from her Angers court case, she was comfortably off. But though she opted for a life of retirement, it cannot have been without severe regrets.

That the theatre remained Jodin's great love can be gathered from a curious letter she wrote to Stanislas Poniatowski, the King of Poland, in 1777 asking him why he had not put her in charge of his efforts to gather a new French troupe to perform in Warsaw. Her familiar and chatty tone suggests that she was reminding him of a degree of previous intimacy and must add to the earlier speculation that she was his lover in Warsaw. It is not known whether Stanislas replied to this request or whether he and Jodin had corresponded in the interim. We note that in this letter she gives Diderot's house as her return address, indicating that she had remained in close touch with him:

To Stanislas Poniatowski, August 1777[51]
Sire,
I have read in the *Courier de l'Europe* that there is to be a French theatre re-established in Warsaw, that persons were coming to gather a team of actors. I am not in despair that the mediocrity of their talents (for that is all there is in our theatre) may remind you of the pleasure which I had the happiness to give you, and may not awaken in you the desire to see me again. You will find me always entirely ready to satisfy [your wishes]. I am very unhappy that you did not have enough confidence in me to charge me with the choice of actors. You would have been able to congratulate yourself on such a choice. The poor success of those first actors, whom agents, more concerned to further their own interests than your pleasures, took to Warsaw, should have led you to remember my attachment to your majesty and the zeal which I would have brought to execute such an important commission. It is true that you would not have had the actors cheaply, for I would have made every effort to find good ones, and I am certainly a good judge of their talents. Your investment would have been repaid a hundred-fold ... Bad actors are for a man of taste what a bad cook is to a gourmand, who leaves the table hungrier than he arrived.

Three years after her aborted Angers tour, Jodin appears to have wished to follow Mlle Montansier's example and become a theatrical entrepreneur. Though one is not surprised, given her troublesome career in Warsaw, that Stanislas should have ignored her offer, it is clear that the theatrical world still had a powerful hold on the actress's imagination.

It seems appropriate to consider at this point, at the end of Jodin's acting career, the relationship between her performative skills and Diderot's theories of dramatic art, perhaps most fully formulated in his *Paradoxe sur le comédien* (1770–77) but in the process of development throughout his letters to Jodin.[52] Though accounts of Jodin's acting are few, we know that she was applauded by audiences from Warsaw to Bordeaux and that she held leading parts in the theatres in which she performed, suggesting at the very least a successful stage presence. The effect of Diderot's tutelage on her performances is more difficult to judge, but if she was indeed more of a Dumesnil than a Clairon as the 'Verses' suggest, then it would appear that she was not entirely won over to his theories.

A more productive strategy might be to read Diderot's letters to Jodin in the context of his own development as theatre and art critic as well as moral philosopher.[53] His advice to Jodin on acting was partly a genuine effort to help her in her profession, and partly an exercise in articulating his concept of a more naturalistic style of acting. The paradox, which he was to develop in his treatise on acting, lay in the fact that to seem natural on the stage required a high level of artifice and control as opposed to spontaneity. When Diderot scolded Jodin (letter of 1766) about her 'tragic gulp' (*hoquet tragique*) his criticism was based on its affectation, its lack of naturalness: 'Examine men in their most violent attacks of fury, and you will witness nothing of the kind. regardless of the poet's emphasis, stay as close to nature as you can; forget harmony, cadences and the 'hemistich'; have a clear, precise and distinct articulation, and for the rest, consult only feeling and sense.' These parallels between themes, images and expressions that Diderot developed in his letters to Jodin and his *Paradoxe sur le comédien* are sufficiently marked to suggest that for Diderot, Jodin served as a living laboratory or at least a sounding board to test out his theories. His preoccupation with dramatic theory of course antedates his involvement with Jodin but the letters occupy an important place in the development of his aesthetic and moral philosophy.[54] However, as we shall see, the major theoretical shift between the letters and the *Paradox* concerned the role of *sensibilité* or feeling in the actor's art.

One of Diderot's characteristic strategies for teasing out or presenting his ideas was the dialogue, which allowed for the play and clash of opinions as in a dramatic performance. The *Paradox* is in dialogue form and is a text, as many critics have noted, that ranges well beyond the theatre to deal with the meaning of representation in all the arts and arguably with ethical questions as well.[55] Diderot's letters can equally be read as dialogues, but in the case of his correspondence with Jodin (as with Sophie Volland) only one half of the dialogue, Diderot's, has survived. We can be quite certain that Jodin's letters to Diderot must have commented on his instructions in relation to acting. From what we already know of her she was unlikely to have been a passive recipient of any advice and would certainly have discussed his theories whether or not she agreed with them. But what we actually possess are Diderot's impassioned exhortations to Jodin advocating a more naturalistic style of acting combined with greater moral accountability.

The ethical strand of these letters, linked to his aesthetic preoccupations, shows Diderot wrestling with the problem of how to establish firm artistic and moral standards within a materialist or empirical philosophy. From a philosophical perspective, the advantage of belief in the Deity lay in the conception of God as establishing absolute standards of beauty, perfection or goodness. For materialists, once the divine benchmark had disappeared, moral and aesthetic relativism were the logical consequences. Diderot was evidently most unhappy to accept these consequences of his materialist premise. Votaire's cynical quip: 'If God did not exist, we would have to invent him' was effectively a response to the same problem. We have seen that Diderot in his letters to Jodin urges her to adopt firm theatrical and ethical standards. The question which required answering was: 'on what basis?' The *Paradox* attempts to address these questions.

However, initially much of the *Paradox* concerns the role of *sensibilité* (feeling, sensibility, enthusiasm) in artistic performance. It certainly marked a shift from Diderot's earlier belief expressed in *On Dramatic Poetry* (1758) that genius is to be equated with enthusiasm and inspiration, whereas the person of intellect or good sense is incapable of genius. By 1769 (*Le Rêve de d'Alembert*) he seems to have definitively abandoned his theory of enthusiasm, which was little different from the age-old concept of divine inspiration, in favour of his new physiological theory of 'central fibres', an essentially materialist explanation of temperamental difference.[56] This shift had clear consequences for his dramatic aesthetic.

We recall that what Diderot first noted and approved in Jodin's acting was her ability to come out of herself, to surrender to her role:

> I have not heard you often, but I seemed to discern a great quality in you, that one can perhaps simulate by dint of artistry and study, but which one does not acquire; a soul alienated from itself, which is profoundly affected, which is transported to other places, which becomes such and such a person … I have been satisfied when, emerging from a violent scene, you seemed to come back from far away, scarcely recognize the place that you had [in fact] never left and the objects which surrounded you (letter of 21 August 1765).[57]

This 'alienation' was a great natural gift. Nevertheless, and we see Diderot here at mid-point in an aesthetic argument with himself, the greater part of his advice was for her to render her acting a question of conscious control ('study', 'observe', 'imagine yourself without a mirror or an audience'), rather than one of spontaneous impulse. Thus his letters to Jodin, written between 1765 and 1769 can be read as a developmental mid-point in his aesthetic theory. As A.

M. Wilson has remarked, in 1766, whilst writing to Jodin, Diderot suggests that to be sublime requires good sense, intellect *and* sensibility.[58] 'An actor who only has good sense and judgement is cold; he who has only verve and sensibility is crazy. There is a certain temperament of good sense and of warmth which makes a man sublime' (letter of 1766).[59] However, by 1773, sensibility in the *Paradox* has been completely dethroned. Greatness or the sublime are entirely a question of intellect and conscious control.

It is likely that Diderot's revulsion from the cult of sensibility was fuelled not merely by the incompatibility of a materialist theory of the mind/body with a theory of divine possession, but also by his well-documented quarrel with Rousseau. The Genevan philosopher had made subjective feeling (*sensibilité*) the touchstone of both truth and virtue. As Carol Blum argues:

> Diderot, who had been closest to him [Rousseau], was as obsessed with the subject of virtue as Rousseau, but denied a claim to virtue based only on inner sensations of goodness. During his arduous, largely practical, work with the *Encyclopédie*, he had replaced a morality of intention and sensibility with one based solely on socially useful action.[60]

In his letters to Jodin, Diderot had employed wit, persuasion and remonstrance to convince his pupil, a victim of uncontrolled *sensibilité* as he saw it, of the necessity for self-control both in her life and her art. From a philosophical point of view, given Diderot's (and Jodin's) atheism, the difficulty in establishing objective standards in either ethics or aesthetics was evident. The letters themselves and his care for Jodin and her mother are concrete examples of Diderot's commitment to social utility, to the construction, for want of a better word, of goodness. However on the aesthetic front, Diderot would attempt in the *Paradox* to resolve the problem of an objective standard by positing the concept of the 'ideal model', a strategy applicable to both moral and artistic standards.

According to the First Speaker in the *Paradox*, a great actor like Mlle Clairon has a conception or an ideal model of the role she is playing. This model, which sounds indistinguishable from a Platonic archetype, in Diderot's hands becomes not a universal but an individual conception which, if successfully communicated on the stage, attains universal validity.[61] For Diderot, the ideal model was an index of the artist's creativity and intellect. To attain an approximation to that model in performance required the complete domination of sensibility.

We have seen that in writing to Jodin, Diderot linked good acting (on-stage) and ethical excellence (off-stage). In the *Paradox*, however, he argues, seemingly in contradiction with these views, that there must be a complete absence of the self in acting; the actor does not represent her/himself but an ideal character. It would seem to follow that it really does not matter what sort of person the actor is; s/he cannot be a person of sensibility, but must act merely as an instrument 'cold and tranquil' in order to express the passions of others:

'Above all, no sensibility' (*Paradox*, p. 426). Nevertheless, though to be a good actor is not to 'be oneself', the reverse is not necessarily true. Can a bad person be a great artist? As a moralist as opposed to a critic, Diderot wished to see the moral status of actors and actresses improve. In addition he felt there was something repellent in a known scoundrel mouthing lines of morality or heroism. In this sense the private selves of actors did impinge on their performance and helped to discredit what Diderot considered to be the ethical basis of drama: 'What makes me angry is ... that an honourable actor or actress should be such a rare phenomenon ... I think of the influence the theatre could have on good taste and on morality if actors were respectable people and if their profession was honoured' (*Paradox*, pp. 464–5).

Arguing against the eighteenth-century cult of sensibility, Diderot put forward the deliberately outrageous proposition that the less sensibility the actor possesses, the better: 'I want him (the actor) to possess a great deal of judgement; I require that this man be a cold and tranquil spectator [of his own performance]. What I demand is penetration and absolutely no sensibility' (*Paradox*, p. 426). A genuinely sensitive individual who 'felt' his or her part in every performance would be driven mad by such a play of feeling and 'the actor's condition would be the most unfortunate of conditions' (*Paradox*, p. 431). The gifted actor is one distanced from the role being performed. He can bring consistency and perfection to his acting style. Above all he must achieve dominance over his material. Poetry itself, the very beauty and rhythm of lines can militate against the actor's control of his material as well as more naturalistic effects. In an identical image to his warning to Jodin over Racine's seductive verses, Diderot remarks that the actor becomes 'entrapped by the harmonies of [his] verses ... as though by so many serpents whose coils clasp his head, his feet, his hands, his legs and his arms, [as a result] his action loses all its freedom' (*Paradox*, p. 425). Similarly he had written to Jodin in January 1767: 'Garrick once told me he would find it impossible to play a role from Racine: that his verses were like great serpents, winding themselves round the actor till he was paralysed.'[62]

Like the author of 'Verses to Mlle Jodin', Diderot contrasts the acting style of Mlle Clairon, intellectual, controlled and consistent with that of Mlle Dumesnil, spontaneous, uneven if occasionally sublime. Clairon, he asserts, constructs an ideal model of the character she plays in her mind, and strives to conform to it. She achieves consistency as well as perfection. Dumesnil by contrast 'enters the scene without knowing what she will say; half the time she doesn't know what she is saying; but sublime moments do occur' (*Paradox*, p. 248). Then in an echo of his oft-repeated advice to Jodin to cultivate quiet scenes where the real sense of a character emerges: 'It is not in the first gush of fury that characteristic qualities emerge; it is in tranquil and cold moments, in entirely unexpected moments ... It is for sang-froid to temper the delirium of enthusiasm' (*Paradox*, p. 429). Nevertheless Diderot had himself been greatly attracted to the spontaneous in performance and considered himself to be an example of the man of sensibility. In the letter of July/August 1766 to Jodin he had urged her to attempt daring things and to follow inspiration: 'When the soul is inspired, one never knows what one will do, how one will speak; it is the moment, the soul's situation which dictates. These are the only good masters, the only good prompters.' This is a rather different concept from the intellectualised and controlled acting of Clairon. By 1770, if not earlier, Diderot's admiration for enthusiasm or sensibility had cooled markedly. Yet the 'man of feeling' remained at the centre of the *Paradox*, for he is the First Speaker, the advocate, paradoxically, of sang-froid. He even highlights this seeming contradiction. 'It is the special perquisite of the "man of feeling", says the First Speaker ... to be a generous admirer of the qualities he lacks.'[63]

In the *Paradox* dialogue, the Second Speaker, a proponent of spontaneous acting or enthusiasm, suggests a compromise that would preserve *sensibilité* as an aesthetic criterion in acting. His description of those moments of 'delirium' that should be allowed to the actor echoes Diderot's description of Jodin's performances quoted above. It is proposed to 'reserve the actor's natural sensibility, for those rare moments where he loses his head, where he no longer sees the spectator, where he forgets that he is in the theatre, where he forgets himself, where he is in Argos, in Mycenae, where he *is* the very person whom he represents' (*Paradox*, p. 479). The First Speaker interjects sardonically to ask whether the actor at the moment of total identification with his character is not weeping, exclaiming and so on in the poetic cadences and rhythms of the verse. In other words, he cannot be said to be the personage of his role, speaking in his own voice. 'A sensitive actor will perhaps have in his role one or two of these moments of alienation which will be in dissonance with the role, the more powerful they are' (*Paradox*, p. 480). It is as though Diderot, remembering his admiration for those moments of 'alienation' that he had witnessed in Jodin's acting, now rejected the implications of spontaneity in artistic technique. Truth on the stage is the reverse of life as we live it; it is the faithful realisation of an ideal, not a real type: 'What then is truth on the stage? It is consistency of actions, of speeches, of expression, of voice, of movements, of gestures with an ideal model imagined by the poet and often exaggerated by the actor' (*Paradox*, p. 435). Yet the fact that the *Paradox* is in dialogue form seems to indicate that Diderot was, as ever, playing with different possibilities and points of view. He resembles his own characterisation of the great actor: 'What then is a great actor? A great tragic or comic *persifleur* [mocker].' The whole of the *Paradox* can be read as a piece of persiflage, which teases out in dialogue form (namely a little play) the complexities of representation. And though the style of Clairon may be endorsed, the genius of Dumesnil is not derided. The *persifleur* is both self-mocking and profoundly serious.

In the eleven years between 1777 and 1789, nothing more is heard of Marie Madeleine Jodin. This silence could have had a number of causes. She was no longer a public woman, whose name would appear on theatre bills. Her professional existence was over. Living in Paris as a private individual, still in touch with Diderot (until his death in 1784), she was no longer in correspondence with him. We note that his letters to Sophie Volland also ceased when she and her sister moved into Paris in the 1770s. Another reason Jodin subsided into obscurity was that she did not again come to the notice of the authorities. Much of what we know of Jodin's life, as will have been clear to the reader, arises from detailed records of her brushes with the law. We can infer, then, a relatively blameless retirement. She read philosophy, kept abreast of radical politics and studied what came to be called 'the woman question'. What friends or lovers she had, what circles she frequented, we simply do not know.

We may suppose, however, that she kept up her contacts with the theatricalworld and that she rejoiced at the lifting of the status of infamy against Jews and actors, 24 December 1789, giving them *droit de cité*, or full citizenship. nevertheless, actresses, though no longer 'infamous', were, as women, not full citizens. She would have known as well of the disgraceful petition of a group of actors at the Comédie-Française to deprive actresses of their voting powers in the troupe's management and to sack any actresses with morally dubious lives or who had children out of wedlock.[63] This backlash against women may have partly inspired her feminist treatise.

Sometime in 1789, in the early and heady days of the French Revolution, Jodin finished a first draft of her feminist treatise, *Vues législatives pour les femmes* and sent it for commentary to her old friend Jean-Baptiste Lynch of Bordeaux, currently in Paris. The following year she published the complete text including Lynch's reply and her further thoughts on the question of divorce. From this remarkable document, published under her own name, we gain a clear picture of her readings in philosophy and feminism and her attachment to revolutionary ideals. Her life after leaving the stage had evidently been intellectually extremely productive. But she was not to witness the full course of the Revolution. The following year, in August 1790, Jodin died at Fontainebleau at the age of forty-nine. She may have gone there to escape the civil disorders then engulfing Paris. She was buried on 9 August, the ceremony, like Diderot's funeral, conducted by a priest. Her burial certificate does not give the cause of her death which may have been quite sudden, as she was writing the postscript to her treatise in February or March of that year with all her usual energy and panache.[64]

Whether Jodin was reduced to poverty in her last years thanks to political upheavals is not known. Diderot had said that the investments he made on her behalf would survive everything except a revolution in the State, something he evidently did not foresee. The fact that she could pay for the publication of her

Vues législatives suggests she was still well off. We are left with her radical feminist treatise, a testament both to her intellectual life and her political and social opinions. Though it was not Diderot's intention to do so, a large part of his influence on his rebellious pupil was to turn her into a fully-fledged *philosophe*, a process begun in her early youth but encouraged and nurtured by his correspondence. His letters which occupied a pivotal place in her life also charted an important stage in his own theoretical and practical development. If, for Diderot, Jodin constituted a living experiment for his dramatic and ethical theories, it was an experiment, as he recognised, which was by no means within his control. His letters to Jodin represent a remarkable example of moral action at work and of the communication of intellectual and artistic enthusiasms. In reply, her *Vues législatives* may partly be read as a coded acknowledgement of her intellectual and ethical debts to this extraordinary friend, whom, nevertheless she nowhere mentions in her text.

Notes

1. Marie-Magdeleine Jodin, *Mémoire sur Déliberé pour Demoiselle Marie-Magdeleine Jodin, Actrice de Comédie, contre le sieur Neuville, Directeur de Comédie* (Angers: A. J. Jahyer, 1774), p. 2.
2. Wilkes acknowledged having met Jodin in two notes to his daughter, saying that he had passed a most agreeable evening at d'Eon's with several French people; 'the lady to whom Diderot refers was present'. Diderot, *Correspondance*, X, letters of 5 June 1770, p. 65 and 10 July 1770, p. 89.
3. The Chevalier de Piennes was a captain of dragoons, a former comrade in arms of d'Eon's, and depended on him heavily for financial assistance.
4. John Wilkes (1727–97), Whig politician, friend of the Baron d'Holbach at Leyden University in 1744. He published a paper, *The North Briton*, and was convicted of libel. In 1764 he fled to Paris where he was welcomed by d'Holbach and Diderot, not returning to London until 1768. He won the parliamentary seat for Middlesex in 1768, but having surrendered to the authorities (on the libel conviction) began a prison sentence. Parliament falsified his election results in order to defeat him in 1769. Discharged from prison in April 1770, he was elected alderman and became a public hero. He was returned successfully for Middlesex in 1774. *Dictionary of National Biography*, vol. LXI (London: Smith, Elder and Co., 1900), pp. 242–50.
5. See Gary Kates, *Monsieur d'Eon is a Woman: A Tale of Political Intrigue and Sexual Masquerade* (New York: Basic Books, 1995), pp. 182–95. D'Eon lived out the second half of his life as a woman and the fact he was a man was only discovered after his death in 1810. On gambling mania see Amanda Foreman, *Georgiana, Duchess of Devonshire* (London: HarperCollins, 1998).
6. Kates, *Monsieur d'Eon is a Woman*, pp. 196–200.
7. Le Chevalier de Piennes to le Chevalier d'Eon, 27 July 1771, H. 96, Archives d'Eon, Bibliothèque Municipale de Tonnerre.
8. Kates, *Monsieur d'Eon is a Woman*, pp. 151–4.
9. Dena Goodman, *The Republic of Letters: A Cultural History of the Enlightenment* (London: Cornell University Press, 1994), pp. 1–11 and Daniel Gordon, *Citizens*

without Sovereignty: Equality and Sociability in French Thought, 1670–1789 (Princeton: Princeton University Press, 1994): 'The term *sociabilité* was coined in the early eighteenth century and became the slogan of moderate literati who idealised private life and saw reciprocity as the bond among humans in "society". Diderot and d'Alembert included the word "social" as a "term recently introduced in our language" in the *Encyclopédie*' (p. 6).

10. Not all Diderot's experiments of this nature were so fortunate. Famously, his interventions in relation to Rousseau and his attempts to bring Rousseau out of his (as Diderot saw it) misanthropic retirement only caused furious resentment and the end of their friendship.

11. Mlle Jodin to the Chevalier d'Eon, 3 July 1770, Diderot, *Correspondance*, X, 1963, pp. 83–5.

12. D'Eon was an indefatigable writer and was busy with his *Loisirs du Chevalier d'E. de B … sur divers sujets importans d'administration, pendant son séjour en Angleterre*, published in thirteen volumes under an Amsterdam imprint in 1774.

13. Claude-Adrien Helvétius (1715–71), author of the freethinking *De l'Esprit* (1758) and *De l'Homme* (1772). In fact, the *Système de la nature* was not by Helvétius but by the Baron d'Holbach.

14. Gordon, *Citizens without Sovereignty*, p. 3, notes that few of the *philosophes* advocated political equality and most accepted the principle of differential status, e.g. privilege.

15. Carol Blum, *Rousseau and the Republic of Virtue: the Language of Politics in the French Revolution* (London: Cornell University Press, 1986), pp. 24–5 argues that the arrogation of 'virtue' to kingship and equated with blood meant that the aristocracy had a monopoly on identification with virtuous pursuits. Commoners were trained in contempt for their own social inferiority. That there was a disjunction between the theory of aristocratic virtue and its practice was one of the glaring contradictions exploited by the Revolution. Genevan republicanism, which was élitist and undemocratic, nevertheless offered an alternative model of social virtue, hence its attractions to the socially marginalised.

16. The editor of the Diderot correspondence, Geoges Roth, permits himself an astonished and condescending footnote at Jodin's expense at this misattribution: 'Mlle Jodin philosophe! Qui l'eût dit, Qui l'eût cru? Rappelons pourtant que le Système de la Nature n'est pas de "Mr. Elvétius" mais du Baron d'Holbach.' Diderot, *Correspondance*, X, p. 84, note 8.

17. Paul Henry, *Th. D. Holbach, Système de la Nature* (1766) (Hildesheim: Georg Olms, 1966), p. viii. Diderot would write a *Refutation of Helvétius* in 1773, attacking not his materialism, with which he agreed, but his reductionism. P. N. Furbank, *Diderot*, p. 373. Jodin, by contrast, seems to have found Helvétius's *Système* an enormously liberating text.

18. Not all commentators were as favourable as Jodin. Charles Simon Favart, a playwright and poet, wrote: 'It seems to be a distressing book for humanity: its title is *Le Système de la Nature*; this is not deism that one is trying to prove; it is atheism pure and simple. Every day it gains an infinite number of proselytes.' *Mémoires et Correspondance Littéraires, Dramatiques et Anecdotiques*, II (Paris: Collin, 1808), p. 245.

19. See L. Henry Lecomte, *La Montansier: ses aventures – ses entreprises (1730–1820)* (Paris: Félix Juven, n.d.) and for police gossip *Journal des Inspecteurs de Sartines*, pp. 37–51.

20. Bernard, J. A. called Fleury, *Mémoires de Fleury de la Comédie-Française 1757–1826*, 6 vols (Paris: Dupont, 1836), p. 135.

21. See E. Kennedy et al., *Theatre, Opera and Audiences in Revolutionary Paris* (Westport, Connecticut and London: Greenwood Press, 1996), pp. 70–71, Lyonnet, *Dictionnaire des comédiens français*, pp. 460–64.

22. Quoted in Lyonnet, *Dictionnaire des comédiens français*, p. 490. See also M. Aimé de Soland, 'Le Théâtre à Angers en 1784 – Collot d'Herbois et Mlle Marie-Magdeleine Jodin', *Bulletin monumental et historique de l'Anjou* (1858), pp. 375–79.

23. Jodin, *Mémoire sur délibéré*, p. 2. Jodin's contract, appended to her *mémoire*, reads as follows:

   'Contract Between Mlle Montansier and Mlle Jodin'

   We the undersigned, Demoiselle Montansier and Mademoiselle Jodin, presently domiciled in Paris enter into the following agreements: namely that I, Montansier, now agree to engage Mademoiselle Jodin to play in Tragedy all the parts of queens and other leading roles; in Comedy, noble mothers; to furnish herself with costumes suitable for the parts; to follow the Troupe in whole or in part wherever I decide to send it with my employee or associates; to attend rehearsals, performances and meetings at the advertised times or risk a fine. And I, Montansier, promise to pay her 3000 *livres* salary for the theatre year, payable monthly in equal portions, which comes to 250 *livres* per month, which payment will begin on the day of her departure from Paris, which will be a week from next Monday. In addition I promise to give her and her mother transport by royal coach or other appropriate conveyance and to pay for removal expenses. The present engagement will be valid until the Saturday before Palm Sunday, 1775. We wish it [this contract] to have the same validity as though drawn up before a Notary; a fine of 1000 *livres* is payable by the first person to break the contract. Drawn up between us in good faith, in Paris, 23 April 1774. [signed] De Montansier. Jodin

24. This reading has been greatly informed by Sara Maza's *Private Lives and Public Affairs: the Causes Célèbres of pre-Revolutionary France* (Berkeley: University of California Press, 1993).

25. Jodin, *Mémoire sur délibéré*, pp. 2–3.

26. Aimé de Soland, 'Le Théâtre à Angers en 1784', p. 378.

27. *Mémoire sur délibéré*, pp. 3–4.

28. Ibid., pp. 13–14.

29. Aimé de Soland, 'Le Théâtre à Angers en 1784', p. 375.

30. This play was probably *Iphigénie en Tauride* by a former actor M. Guimond de la Touche, first performed in 1757. Diderot gave it a lacklustre review. See Diderot, *Oeuvres Complètes*, III, pp. 213–16.

31. This was the father of Joseph and Pierre-Marie Delaunay, who both became deputies during the Revolution. Delaunay *père* was the *procureur au présidial*. His son, Joseph, joined the Jacobins and voted for the execution of Louis XVI. He was himself executed in 1794. His brother, a barrister like his father, and a political moderate, survived the Terror.

32. Queruau Lamérie, 'Notice sur le Théâtre d'Angers', *Bulletin monumental et historique de l'Anjou*, no. 1100 (1889), p. 28.

33. *Mémoire sur délibéré*, p. 1.

34. Maza, *Private Lives and Public Affairs*, pp. 9–16.

35. Iphigenia was the daughter of Agamemnon and Clytemnestra. Artemis demanded that she be killed as the price for sending a fair wind to the Greeks waiting to set sail for Troy. Agamemnon eventually agreed to have his daughter sacrificed.

36. *Mémoire sur délibéré*, p. 16.

37. Maza, *Private Lives and Public Affairs*, p. 141. *Mémoires* as well as other legal documents could be freely printed under the *ancien régime* and were notable exceptions to otherwise rigorous censorship. Paul Mellottée, *Histoire économique de l'imprimérie: l'imprimérie sous l'ancen régime 1439–1789* (Paris: Librairie Hachette, 1905) pp. 63–4.
38. *Mémoire sur délibéré*, p. 4.
39. Ibid., p. 7.
40. Ariadne, a daughter of King Minos of Crete, helped Theseus to slay the Minotaur by leading him through the labyrinth with a thread of wool. Theseus then fled with Ariadne to Naxos where he abandoned her.
41. *Mémoire sur délibéré*, pp. 10–11.
42. 'Be on your guard against ... speaking with the emphatic tones of the princess one has been playing. When taking off the costume of Mérope, Alzire or Zénobie, hang up everything connected with it on the same peg.'
43. *Mémoire sur délibéré*, pp. 15–16.
44. Footnote 1 to 'Verses': 'Mlle Jodin is an actress distinguished by very rare talents for the roles played by Mlle Dumesnil. She has performed with the greatest success in our different provincial theatres and in Poland. It is to be hoped that in the distressing state in which our theatre finds itself, she would bow to the wishes of her friends who call upon her to fill these roles.'
45. The Muse of tragedy.
46. See Appendix pp. 207–8 for the original French version.
47. As Edmund Burke put it, 'Whatever is fitted in any sort to excite ideas of pain and danger, that is to say, whatever is in any sort terrible, or is conversant with terrible objects or operates in a manner analogous to terror is a source of the sublime.' Edmund Burke, *A Philosophical Enquiry into the Origin of Our Ideas of the Sublime and the Beautiful* (1757) (London: University of Notre Dame Press, 1968), p. 39.
48. Diderot, 'Sur les femmes' (1772), *Oeuvres Complètes*, X, p. 36.
49. Lyonnet, *Dictionnaire des Comédiens Français*, p. 607.
50. Jodin *Procès*, no. 12, 281.
51. An early version appearing in the *Correspondence littéraire* was revised with Grimm as interlocutor in 1773 and the 'play' and 'prologue' added after 1777. The coincidence of timing then is approximate and argues a long period of gestation. See Lewinter, 'Introduction', Diderot, *Oeuvres Complètes*, X, pp. 414–15.
52. A. M. Wilson, *Diderot* (New York: Oxford University Press, 1986), p. 620, notes the shifts in Diderot's aesthetic formulations from his letters to Jodin to the *Paradoxe*.
53. One cannot separate Diderot's theories of drama and painting. His fascination with and knowledge of the imitative arts produced a wide array of writing. For example his first play and its surrounding 'fiction' *Le Fils naturel* (1756) and *Conversations sur le Fils naturel* (1756): *Le Père de famille* (1758) and the essay *On Dramatic Poetry* (1758) pre-date his correspondence with Jodin but laid the groundwork for his dramatic theories. The *Parodoxe sur le comédien* (1770–73) gathers together a wide range of social and aesthetic concerns revolving round the theatre and the imitative arts generally.
54. Wilson, *Diderot*, p. 626, feels 'there is no clash of opinions' between the two speakers of the dialogue. However, the Second Speaker, though dominated by the First and certainly worsted by him, does put up a good rearguard action. In his demolition of 'enthusiasm', Diderot (First Speaker), more in sorrow than in anger, disavows his own formerly held opinions.

55. Diderot, *De la Poésie dramatique* (1758); *Diderot le Drame bourgeois*, ed. Jacques Chouillet and Anne-Marie Chouillet (Paris: Herman, 1980), p. 393 and footnote 123.
56. Diderot, *Correspondance*, V, letter 346, 'A Mademoiselle Jodin à Varsovie', 21 August 1765, p. 101.
57. Wilson, *Diderot*, p. 622.
58. Diderot, *Correspondance* VI, letter 393, 'A Mlle Jodin à Varsovie, 1766, p. 168.
59. Blum, *Rousseau and the Republic of Virtue*, pp. 57–8.
60. For an extended discussion of the 'ideal model' see James Creech, *Diderot: Thresholds of Representation* (Columbus, Ohio: Ohio State University Press, 1986), pp. 62–8.
61. When repeating this image in the *Paradox*, Diderot may have had in mind a drawing of Laocoön by Jean-Baptiste Corneille, used as an illustration of drawing technique in the *Encyclopédie*. Madeleine Pinaut, 'Les Chapitres artistiques des volumes de planches de l'*Encyclopédie*', *Diderot: Les Beaux- Arts et la musique*, Actes du colloque international tenu à Aix-en-Provence 14–16 décembre, 1984 (Aix-en-Provence: Université de Provence, 1986), pp. 67–93. The drawing in question is from Volume III of the *Encylopédie*, 1763.
62. P. N. Furbank, *Diderot*, p. 356.
63. Acte d'inhumation de Marie JODIN, 9 août, 1790, Archives Départementales de Seine et Marne. Her father's name and profession are listed, and her mother's maiden name.

CHAPTER EIGHT

Vues législatives pour les femmes 1789–90

'And we too are citizens'

The last two years of Jodin's life coincided with the early days of the French Revolution. Life in Paris must have been, depending on one's point of view, exhilarating, terrifying, or for the poor, a continuing saga of deprivation punctuated by moments of collective excitement. Public order crumbled. The crowd, always a potent force in Paris street scenes, came to life. The fall of the Bastille in July 1789 and, the series of street demonstrations, as well as uprisings in the provinces, constituted a kind of living theatre, but one with unpredictable consequences. A central impression we can garner from Marie Madeleine Jodin's *Vues législatives pour les femmes*, published in 1790, and reflecting the excitements of the early revolutionary events, is ambivalence. On the one hand, everything seemed possible, including the emancipation of women; on the other, freedom brought with it the fear of licence and mob rule. What would that liberty, which Rousseau had argued was Man's natural state, produce on its restoration to the society of late eighteenth-century France?

In 1788, in response to widespread unrest and economic failure, Louis XVI had called for the reconvening of the Estates General. At the same time he had lifted government and press censorship. The three estates, aristocracy, clergy and commoners, were invited to submit grievances to the King in the form of *cahiers de doléances* (notes of complaint). Their recommendations ranged from proposals to move slaughter houses out of the centres of cities, to the complete reorganisation of the legal and political system. In addition, the lifting of censorship resulted in an avalanche of pamphlets, books and journals, all works publishable for the first time, calling for a variety of social and political reforms, including a significant number of feminist and anti-feminist pamphlets.[1] Among them was Marie Madeleine Jodin's *Vues législatives*, first drafted in 1789 and published in 1790 by Mame, an Angers firm of radical reputation.[2] The National Assembly, formed in June 1789, was charged with drafting a new constitution. It was a time for anyone with a radical social vision or, for that matter, an axe to grind, to launch themselves into print.

In spite of what we now know of the discouraging later history of women's emancipation in France, there cannot have seemed a more hopeful moment than the year 1789 to encourage male legislators to grant citizenship rights to women.[3] Women had participated enthusiastically in revolutionary action and in October brought the King back to Paris, effecting as Olwen Hufton observes:

'momentous political change'.[4] But Jacobin politicians were clearly frightened by the implications of women's involvement in the political process. Jodin, whose treatise was addressed to the Assemblée Nationale, which in 1789–90 was busy drawing up new legislative codes, seems to have been sensitive to the fears of male legislators over working-class women's disruptive potential and therefore proposed to turn them into model citizens, future denizens of the new state to be founded on virtue.[5] Jodin's feminist treatise may be read as an expression of the social and political enthusiasms of the early revolutionary period in France while raising issues which transcend the topical. Two of its main themes: prostitution or, more broadly, the reification of women as paid sexual servants of men; and, conversely, women's untapped potential to regenerate public morals, relate to the concerns and prejudices of the legislators of the Constituent Assembly. Jodin appealed to one of their central preoccupations, namely to ensure that the purpose of political transformation should be the moral improvement of society. In this sense, the *Vues législatives* is imbued with the spirit of Jean Jacques Rousseau.[6]

Jodin's eighty-six page treatise proposed the eradication of prostitution, the establishment of a women's legislature with jurisdiction over women's issues and the institution of divorce. She attempted nothing less than the creation of a valid place for women in the public sphere.[7] Women would form the necessary link between *l'esprit social* which incorporated morality (*moeurs*) and a formal code of laws. (*Vues législatives*, pp. 177–8). The ostensible occasion for the publication of her *Vues législatives* was a resolution, which she quotes on her title page, from the Municipality of Paris in its *cahier de doléances* to the National Assembly to: 'consider means to revive the regulations, which have so far proved useless, for repressing the scandal of public prostitution' (*Cahiers du Tiers État, Municipalité*, Article 34).[8] This section of the *cahier* contains detailed plans for civic improvements in the fields of mental health, public hygiene, public morals and traffic-calming measures ('to control the vertiginous speed of vehicles passing through our streets'). The resolution on prostitution is, significantly, the only specific appearance of women in the whole document. Jodin seizes upon this fleeting, though admittedly unflattering, mention, as an opportunity to make a case for women's citizenship. Confronting the issue of public prostitution, Jodin exploits the Assembly's concern about public morals in order to argue, paradoxically, for the inclusion of women as full citizens, as part of a programme of moral reform. Though radical in its feminist implications, Jodin's *Vues législatives* is also characteristic of the bourgeois moral conservatism of the early revolutionary period. It attacks male absolutism but like most writings of the *philosophes* is not egalitarian, endorsing degrees of status difference in its concepts of social cohesion.[9]

Jodin's title page (see Appendix, p. 176) demonstrates how she wished to inscribe herself as a published author in the public sphere. Many feminist or anti-feminist pamphlets of the period were anonymous. Jodin's was probably the first signed, woman-authored, feminist work of the revolutionary period. The fact that she published under her own name was a significant and defiant gesture. The label of female writer or *philosophe* was still pejorative. She would perhaps have known Restif de la Bretonne's opinion on women writers: 'How I pity a woman author or scholar! ... She has lost the charm of her sex; she is a man among women, and she is not a woman among men.'[10] In her *Vues législatives* Jodin identified herself unambiguously as a *femme-philosophe*, that contentious figure so disliked by Restif, Rousseau and, as she would discover, by her friend Jean-Baptiste Lynch. The impressive list of philosophers, ancient and modern, invoked in her treatise, represents her claim to intellectual authority.[11] Whereas in her *Mémoire sur Délibéré* of 1774 she had figured as '*Marie-Magdeleine Jodin, Actrice de Comédie*', here she forefronts her claim to intellectual seriousness and, via the paternal line, to the honour of citizenship. To this extent she embraces the patriarchal principle. The phrase: '*Fille d'un citoyen de Genève*' (Daughter of a Genevan citizen) confers legitimacy to her voice as a woman speaking for women and additionally establishes her as one who understands, historically and philosophically, the duties as well as the rights of citizenship.[12] The introduction addressed 'to my sex' has as its motto the declaration: 'et nous aussi, nous sommes citoyennes': 'and we too are citizens'. In publishing under her own name as a descendant of citizens, Jodin attempted to authenticate her right to a place in the new social order.

The strong tinge of moral puritanism which colours her pamphlet should not surprise us, though it seems at odds with Jodin's colourful career chronicled in the proceeding pages of this biography. Her condemnatory tone towards sexual licence relates to actual social conditions in late eighteenth-century Paris, to the audience of bourgeois legislators to whom she addressed her pamphlet and to the simultaneous degradation and idealisation of women in contemporary representation. But in comparison with many pamphlets of the period on the subject of prostitution, Jodin's text emerges as decidedly on the liberal wing of the debate. There was ample evidence of aggressive soliciting by prostitutes and open sexual display on the streets of Paris. Complaints proliferated about the shameless behaviour of women engaged in soliciting. In the *cahiers de doléances* submitted by the clergy in 1789, out of one hundred and twenty *cahiers*, eighty-eight mention morals (and their decline) and in eleven, largely urban parishes, the discussion centres on specific measures to curb prostitution.[13] Whereas the clergy had in the past primarily denounced traditional Catholic concerns such as adultery, the focus here turned on the increasingly public spectacle of prostitution, an inescapable aspect of the 'public sphere'.

A pamphlet entitled *De la Prostitution* by Laurent Pierre Bérenger, a writer of moral tracts, is characteristic of the sense of moral panic engendered by the highly visible presence of prostitutes and forms an instructive contrast to Jodin's text which discusses many of the same social problems.[14] Firstly, Bérenger claimed, the sheer number of prostitutes was large and apparently growing. Louis Sébastien Mercier estimated some 30,000 in Paris (a statistic quoted by Jodin), whereas the population of Paris as a whole was somewhere in the range of 500,000.[15] Other writers inflated the number of prostitutes to 40,000 or even 60,000.[16] Bérenger's tract denounced, in turn, child prostitution, the 'plays of the boulevard peopled with little gangrenous prostitutes' and particularly lamented the 'all too frequent displays of public fornication'. As deterrent and punishment, he advocated whipping, shaving of heads and in cases of suborning children, life imprisonment. We note that in Jodin's text there is almost no discussion of punishment, only of reform. Bérenger did recommend opening a hospice for repentant women and making weekly health checks on prostitutes (but not their clients). In common with many writers, including Jodin, he linked the need for moral reform on the streets to the moral regeneration of the state.[17]

Campaigners like Bérenger accepted the assumed necessity of prostitution, but wanted it off the streets, out of public view and preserved for the convenience of male clients.[18] Similarly the *Cahiers du Tiers État* frequently denounced the most public and shocking forms of prostitution without arguing for radical suppression. However female prostitution was more than a scandal that offended public decency. It was credited with contributing to population decline because prostitutes avoided conception whenever possible and men, who could satisfy their sexual needs easily given the availability of women for sale, were not motivated to marry. According to Mercier: 'Why should there not be many bachelors in a city (like Paris) where vice is so easy to find?'[19] On another level, family life was threatened by parents who sold off their children into prostitution.

Overall, writers on prostitution fell into two schools: the punitive, recommending ever heavier penalties (such as branding, corporal punishment and long periods of imprisonment); and the reformist, and even utopian, school. Among the latter, Mercier and Restif de la Bretonne wished to see prostitution sanitised, as for example, in Restif's utopian novel, *Le Pornographe* (1767), which advocated a healthy, non-punitive and voluntary prostitution, institutionalised in a national brothel.[20] For his part, Mercier argued that prostitutes were not essentially vicious, but were pushed into vice by poverty. One practical solution, propounded by the painter Bachelier, director of the Royal Free School of Drawing, was to give working-class girls an artisan's education that would fit them to enter a variety of trades and thereby avoid the necessity for them to enter the oldest and perhaps least rewarding profession.[21] Such writers recognised the economic imperative driving young women into prostitution.

In contrast to depictions of female vice, one finds an alternative discourse on women's nature, stressing essential feminine virtue. It was pre-eminently Rousseau who configured women of the middle ranks as a morally purifying force in society, to be enlisted, subsequent writers would argue, in the process of revolutionary moral transformation. Jodin too has recourse to this trope. Having castigated female immorality, she contends that only women are fitted by their qualities of gentleness and sympathy to assist their fallen sisters. The tradition of women's alleged superior moral excellence, though it could be co-opted for socially conservative ends, also appealed to feminist reformers. Thus the feminist Etta-Palm d'Aelders entitled her work, which appeared shortly after Jodin's text, *A Call to Frenchwomen on the Regeneration of Morals and the Necessity of Women's Influence in a Free Government.*[22] This appeal emphasised the moral influence women could exercise if admitted to public life. Invoking as empirical evidence historical examples of women's achievements, d'Aelders argued for a companionate relationship between the sexes rather than one of rivalry and the formation of women's groups to care for orphans, help indigent women and reform the morals of single mothers. We will find these points greatly expanded in Jodin's treatise with the addition of a philosophical and legislative framework.

Even as outspoken a feminist as Olympe de Gouges stressed the non-competitive aspect of women's desire to serve the state and claimed that their ambition was not to be men's rivals. In her *Project Addressed to the National Assembly, the Day of the King's Arrest* (1792) she declared: 'We will not allow ourselves, Sirs, to enter into competition with you in politics, or in business, our only aim is to make ourselves useful.' She argued that women should be persuaded to leave the public sphere of clubs and assemblies and return to their homes, hardly the most radical of feminist proposals.[23] If this gender conservatism seems surprising coming from the author of *The Rights of Women*, it suggests the weight of opposition feminists encountered to even moderate demands.[24] Did Jodin know or have links with contemporary feminists like d'Aelders and de Gouges? It seems extremely likely. Given the similarity of some of d'Aelders's arguments and proposals to Jodin's, one can suppose they frequented the same radical circles in Paris. Even more striking is the case of Olympe de Gouges, an actress and playwright, who would in all probability have formed part of Jodin's acquaintance in the theatrical world of the capital.

What is additionally clear from the *Vues législatives* is that Jodin was widely read in the debates surrounding women's alleged capabilities, virtues and vices, that she had sought historical as well as contemporary precedents to support her arguments, that she linked the degradation of women in prostitution to the condition of all women and that both her discussions on prostitution and divorce are charged with a passion derived in part from experience. We can reasonably infer a fusion in her *Vues législatives* of her wide-ranging intellectual interests and her traumatic personal life. Her prison sojourn in la Salpêtrière had shown her the reality of poverty and sexual exploitation as it affected women. The acting profession, for all its flaws, had demonstrated how women could exercise authority and experience limited gender equality in the public sphere. From her discussion of divorce, one wonders whether she was not only arguing for an abstract principle but for an issue that may have affected her directly. In any case, for Jodin, the brothel and the sexual double standard were expressions not of masculine desire but of despotism which it was ostensibly the project of the Revolution to abolish.

The *Vues législatives* makes a powerful case for the possibility of transforming the material and ethical lives of ordinary citizens. Those who have shown themselves degraded by poverty and vice can, like the denizens of Voltaire's garden at the close of *Candide*, be redeemed by work and gain self-respect. This, we recall, was very much the theme of Diderot's early letters to his young tearaway protégée in Warsaw. The prostitutes whom Jodin wishes to reform are not to be *repenties* (penitents), but refashioned into persons capable of exercising civic responsibility and even perhaps being worthy of citizenship. Her pamphlet utilises the arguments of many previous philanthropic writers that the cause of prostitution is largely women's economic vulnerability. Destitution, unemployment, late marriage, the dowry system, poor education: all contribute to their marginalisation. The point of eradicating prostitution is not merely to make the streets of Paris safe for unwary pedestrians, but to enable all women to share in the moral and political regeneration of the state. Prostitution affects all women, not only prostitutes, but their sexual degradation, she suggests, also corrupts men. All are members of the same diseased polity which at this historical moment is capable of a revolution in morals. The concept of what it meant to Marie Madeleine Jodin to be a citizen, or alternatively, as she had only too fully experienced in her own life, to be excluded from citizenship, lies at the heart of the *Vues législatives*. The personal had in her case emphatically been transformed into a political vision.

Résumé: *Vues législatives pour les femmes*

Jodin's treatise is divided into two parts. The first launches an attack on public prostitution and on moral decadence generally. The second criticises the law of the indissolubility of marriage and advocates divorce. In relation to prostitution, Jodin argues that the present laws created by men and administered by men (the morals police) are unjust and unenforceable. No amount of imprisonment for prostitutes will change the fact of prostitution itself, which has its origins in poverty. The morals police, who tolerate prostitution in order to fulfil the so-called needs of men, are fundamentally corrupt. All women are tarnished by the obloquy meted out to prostitutes; family life is threatened. Jodin proposes to make women themselves the legislators over women's issues and envisages a female judiciary (of prominent women) to deal with disruptive or criminal behaviour in women. Women, in order to become good citizens, to deserve their inclusion in the republic of virtue, would be obliged to learn to govern themselves.

Jodin's practical plan to implement her proposed reforms involved the setting up of a 'National Tribunal' composed of two 'chambers' or courts: the first, the 'Chamber of Conciliation', to deal with family disputes of all kinds and the second, the 'Civil Chamber', to have jurisdiction over disruptive women. Jodin lists the kinds of misbehaviour the Chamber would deal with which reflects with entire accuracy, her personal experiences (*Vues législatives*, p. 188). It is evident that Jodin was not suggesting that women were not frequently guilty of bad behaviour. The issue she wished to address was the best way of dealing with female delinquency. The Tribunal was envisaged as being more than a court of law and would deal with the social realities of women's lives. It would be housed in a vast *hôtel* where the educational, legislative and judicial arms of this institution would operate. It would contain a hospice for elderly indigent women and workshops for the homeless and unemployed. Emphasis was placed on training and on providing some minimal education. Incarceration, the favoured treatment of prostitutes heretofore, only produced a high rate of re-offending and training in vice. Money currently spent on incarceration would be far better employed by establishing workshops to teach prostitutes a useful trade.

As will be seen, Jodin's ruling themes, the intolerable nature of prostitution and the superior grace and gentleness of women, are both a reflection and rejection of her own experience as a woman allegedly once forced to live by prostitution, and frequently in trouble for her volatile temper. Some of the clauses in what she calls the 'purview' of her two chambers arise directly from her own biography: 'Widows will depose against the bad conduct of their daughters, being unable to control them after their father's death. The daughters will be required to justify themselves.' 'A young woman will not be allowed to enter a convent, even with the intention of taking vows, without having formally declared that it is by her own free choice.' 'The conduct of actresses of all kinds will come under the Tribunal's jurisdiction.' Yet, unlike Jodin's own experience of the legal system in her youth, disruptive women would be accountable in a public court, not subject to unknown accusations to which they were unable to reply.

The problem of prostitution[25]

Jodin shows an equal measure of courage and of anger in her discussion of prostitution. Whether or not she had been prostituted by her mother from the age of fifteen, as her family alleged, her period of imprisonment in la Salpêtrière would have given her all too acute an insight into prostitutes' lives. Her language in respect of prostitutes in the *Vues législatives* is the reverse of compassionate – they are vermin to be cleansed from the streets. But they also constitute dreadful evidence of humiliation and suffering: 'When one considers the mortifications which must accompany their vile mode of life, exposing them to such cruel insults, it is plain that only sheer destitution, or the lack of any foothold in society could lead women to it' (*Vues législatives* , p. 189). Not only should these 'malheureuses indisciplinées' ('unhappy rebels') be reclaimed for the body politic, it follows that to exclude women from citizenship and engagement in a citizen's duties, far from protecting them, renders them ignorant and potentially vicious.

Jodin's opening quotation from the *Cahier du Tiers États* betrays the contradictions which beset sexual morality.[26] The regulations attempting to suppress prostitution have 'until now been useless' and not fully implemented because they are unworkable. A fully functioning morals police and a régime of incarceration of 'public women' ('filles en monde', 'filles publiques') had done nothing to 'repress the scandal of public prostitution'. The resolution in the Paris *Cahier du Tiers États* reflects therefore a failure of public policy. Jodin begins from the position that there is a problem, particularly in the capital, and one that cannot be solved by the police alone:

> In Paris it is estimated that there are thirty thousand prostitutes who have no other means of subsistence than that vice which bribes them. The periodic excursions [by the police] by which they expel three or four hundred a month, or cram them into a hospital [for venereal infections] have no effect on lowering numbers or on correcting vice, since a similar number continues to flourish at all periods (*Vues législatives*, p. 185).

Prostitution not only degrades women, it infects the whole community: literally with disease and symbolically with hypocrisy and deceit. The humiliating treatment of prostitutes by the police, who simultaneously tolerate their existence out of deference to male desire for easy sexual gratification, whilst subjecting women to surveillance and harassment, further demonstrates that male authority is not capable of dealing with the issue. The legislators need to understand: 'that the opprobrium with which under the present system a portion of our own sex seems to be sacrificed to the incontinence of yours is an outrage to Law and destroys the respect belonging to the sacred titles of "Citizenesses", "wives" and "mothers"'.[27] Thus Jodin takes it as read that the low esteem in which women are held stems from their use as paid sexual servants to men. Prostitution therefore is not an exceptional situation; it represents in acute form the condition of women's servitude to male despotism. The reform of prostitutes is her passport for women's eligibility to citizenship.

Replying to those who would sanitise prostitution, Jodin refers to Restif de la Bretonne's suggestion in his utopian novel *Le Pornographe* for the creation of state-run houses of prostitution. Such institutions rather than answering inevitable 'needs' in men, create instead unhealthy sexual appetites. *Le Pornographe* called for licensed brothels in which the women inmates were there by choice, were well treated and untainted by moral reproach. Jodin's scepticism about Restif de la Bretonne's utopian scheme is instructive. Women in his utopia are still hired for sex by men, even if they live in materially privileged conditions. Read in conjunction with his other writings on women, for example: *Les Françaises* (1786), *Les Gynographes* (1777),[28] as well as his pornographic novel *l'Anti-Justine* (1798), Restif's social ideal emerges as the complete, though voluntary, sexual submission of women to men. Male authority is legitimised by women's willing enslavement. As far as power relations are concerned, Restif de la Bretonne creates a Sadean universe without the cruelty (hence his title, *l'Anti-Justine*). Nevertheless, Jodin may have been indebted to Restif for her idea of a tribunal for women. The purpose of his tribunal, however, was to teach young women 'complaisance and submission' to their future husbands.[29] Jodin, far from attempting to strengthen male authority, as we will see, radically undermines it.

Another aspect of Jodin's attack on prostitution, more fundamental than its bourgeois Puritanism, lies in a semantic issue, but one with practical consequences. The term *fille publique*, or woman for sale, was an emotive signal to all women of what was meant by women operating in the public sphere.[30] If the expression *fille publique* meant someone who was universally an object of public contempt, then it followed that women's best refuge from such public contempt was the private sphere of the family. Women, in short, were not welcome in the newly-created, bourgeois public sphere. Jodin advances two propositions to undercut this dichotomous understanding of women's role. Firstly, public and officially-tolerated prostitution is not separate from the private sphere of the family and corrupts it. Secondly, until women reclaim the public sphere, in the honourable sense of civic participation, they will continue to be morally degraded and will undermine the efforts of legislators to create a virtuous Republic.

We hear in the rhetorical violence of Jodin's language ('vermin', 'the extermination of prostitutes') an echo of the bitterness of her early humiliations in la Salpêtrière prison. In contrast to this world of licentiousness, Jodin, paraphrasing *Émile*, Book V, returns to Rousseau's conception of innate female modesty as the defining mark of femininity: 'that powerful motive/spirit of beauty' which has been everywhere denatured in contemporary society'. Those women, who have abandoned modesty, have taken over the masculine role in sexual conquest: 'That sex, [the masculine] which alone is destined for the attack' (another *Émile* echo) has been forced on the defensive. The effect of banning women from public life in the honourable sense of civic participation has been to condemn them to a degraded public role which, paradoxically, undermines virility.

Jodin characterises prostitutes, not in a complimentary sense, as a potentially revolutionary force, a trope that was to become a standard image of 'les classes dangeureuse' of nineteenth-century moral reformers. She was not alone in fearing that sexual licence fuelled mob excesses. A *cahier* of 1789 deplored 'the loss of the feeling of respect and subordination in the ranks of the people and the frenzied licence of the boulevard theatre, which leads to the insubordination and ruin of servants and working men'.[31] Her authoritarian and sexually conservative message co-exists with her call to allow women to develop their potential in the civic space (*civilisation*). By pointing to the failure of male jurisdiction over women, to corrupt police and their ineffectual efforts to control or eradicate prostitution, by showing how working-class women of the street were harassed and imprisoned by the *police des moeurs*, whereas the better-off courtesans were tolerated, Jodin convincingly appeals for a new dispensation for women, dedicated to governing themselves, since male authority in this area is corrupt, inconsistent and ineffective.[32]

The philosophical dimension and the problem of Rousseau

In the political context of the late eighteenth century, for Jodin to argue for the eligibility of women for full citizenship required that she demonstrate their capacity for moral perfectibility. Whilst agreeing that many women fell far beneath this standard, she argued that women's debased condition was not the sign of a debased nature, but of living in an unnatural situation. In other words, she applied Rousseau's analysis of social decadence in the *Discourse on Inequality* to women's experience. In this she showed herself both a disciple of the Genevan philosopher and a powerful dissenter from his construction of ethical gender difference.

Rousseau's attraction for women readers in the eighteenth and nineteenth centuries is well documented and has presented something of a problem for later feminists, given his fear and loathing of women as expressed in *Émile* and his adulation of maternal femininity in *Julie ou la nouvelle Héloise*.[33] His conviction that morality required freedom, but that women were too dangerous to be free, led him to construct an alternative morality to the autonomous independence of Émile for his heroine, Sophie. What are vices in Émile, as Mary Wollstonecraft pointed out in *A Vindication of the Rights of Women* (1792), are virtues for Sophie. Yet Wollstonecraft, in criticising Rousseau from a feminist standpoint, was the exception rather than the rule among women contemporaries. Nor was it only women who were mesmerised by Rousseau. Carol Blum has written persuasively of the revolutionaries' identification with the virtuous persona of Rousseau (most marked in Robespierre) and demonstrated how Rousseau's language of a monolithic virtue permeated the thinking of the revolutionary period.[34] Jodin's *Vues législatives* emphatically bears the marks of a personal identification with Rousseau. She identified with him as a daughter of a Genevan citizen and probably also as someone who had suffered considerable social opprobrium. Like Rousseau, her concept of citizenship as well as her conviction that she deserved to be a full citizen derived from the Genevan model. The language of her treatise, aimed at the members of the Constituent Assembly, explicitly evokes the vocabulary of the politics of virtue so characteristic of the *Social Contract*. In a radical departure, however, Jodin did not endorse Rousseau's negative judgement on women in public life.

The twin planks of Rousseau's conception of a reformed society, as envisaged in *The Social Contract*, are liberty and virtue. We abandon our primary liberty in order to seek security in society, but also in order to govern ourselves freely. He develops similar arguments in *Émile*, whereby Émile's education allows him to assent freely to the moral life mapped out for him by his tutor. To be free and self-motivated meant, as Rousseau argued, to be on the path of social virtue. In Rousseau's case, as is well known, the great exception to the human goal of liberty, which would lead to virtue, was the education and position of women. As expressed most succinctly in Book V of *Émile*, women, who are like men except for their sexuality, are nevertheless defined almost entirely by their sexuality.[35] Because their passions are so powerful, women require a regime of continuous restraint from infancy in order to fit them for their social, maternal role. Women are not to be regarded as moral beings in the same sense as men. On the one hand, Rousseau restores women to original sin, making them responsible for his version of the Fall, on the other, and this is what made his writing so seductive to women, he gave back to women their rights to sexuality and passion.[36] The fact that Jodin centres many of her arguments in relation to *Émile* suggests that she too felt the attraction of Rousseau's account of femininity. But more crucial to Jodin's understanding of Rousseau is *The Social Contract*. Here the case made for liberty as necessary for full humanity is powerfully made. Passages such as:

> To renounce freedom is to renounce one's humanity, one's rights as a man and equally one's duties. There is no possible *quid pro quo* for one who renounces everything; indeed such renunciation is contrary to man's very nature; for if you take away all freedom of the will, you strip a man's actions of all moral significance.[37]

and his assertion of the moral legitimacy of political freedom clearly found an answering echo in Jodin's understanding of women's subordinate position. However in Rousseau's formulation, 'man', as we know, turns out not to be generic. Indeed, following the logic of his own position that constraint precludes moral accountability, in *Émile* he was forced to invent an alternative morality for women. What are vices in men (vanity, artifice and so on) are central feminine virtues. It was to this sexual double morality that Mary Wollstonecraft in her *Vindication* directed her most caustic attacks.

In spite of her frequent citations of Rousseau in a positive vein, it becomes evident that Jodin's project in the *Vues législatives* is nothing less than a repudiation of his concept of separate moral/sexual spheres whilst employing the hegemonic discourse of republican virtue. For example, the sub-title to her preface, 'And we too are citizens', was a direct challenge to Rousseau's definition of woman, excluded by him from the 'city', the public space, and relegated to the private sphere. Though appearing to endorse a separate-spheres ideology in her plan for a legislative body to deal exclusively with women's affairs, Jodin was in fact offering a critique of the failures of male authority in relation to women and proposing to dismantle this authority in both the private and the public spheres. It was an extremely tall order to convince the male audience of the Constitutional Convention to whom she addressed her treatise, a legislative body imbued with the concept of manly republicanism, of the value of stripping away the *puissance maritale* and male prerogatives generally. This is not of course how she described her project. Instead she appealed to the legislators to effect radical moral change on society by carrying through a Rousseauistic agenda.

Though claiming ethical equality with men, Jodin nevertheless indulges in courtly commonplaces to describe women, for example: 'the attractive half of this great Empire', 'the weaker sex'. Women, whilst striving to assert their rights, are described in terms of their feminine charm and alleged weakness. One of the problems in interpreting the *Vues législatives* lies in judging whether Jodin's characterisation of women renders them essentially or contingently different from men and the extent to which such difference would affect a theory of rights. It will be argued here that Jodin does challenge notions of necessary sexual inequality. Fundamentally the language of feminine weakness appears to be a manoeuvre to convince potentially hostile male legislators of the need for reform without alarming them. In this strategy Rousseau is co-opted as her philosophical ally only to be subverted with his own arguments.[38]

Jodin's rhetorical ambivalence noted above re-emerges in her construction of woman's nature. Dualist mind/body arguments coexist with seemingly materialist propositions. This ambivalence in argument does not dampen Jodin's own anti-clericalism and her almost certain atheism. In an age when appeals to a rational supreme being were one of the validating principles of philosophic discourse (as in Wollstonecraft's *A Vindication*), the Deity in Jodin's treatise is conspicuous by its almost total absence.[39] Jodin's Bordeaux adventure when she mocked a religious procession was a dramatic sign of her imprudent anti-clericalism We have seen that she read materialist philosophers like Helvetius and d'Holbach. She also, as is evident in her discussion on divorce, loathed the Church with a Voltairean fervour. Whilst there may be confusion in her account of the mind/body problem, she does not seem to have accepted notions of an immortal soul, or of God, and ridiculed the Church's emphasis on the afterlife.

Yet the materialist reading of woman as pure body was, as Geneviève Fraisse reminds us, the central plank of a philosophic and medical discourse which was to dominate nineteenth-century French views on women, with questionable results for their advancement.[40] Materialism, focusing, as Diderot did in 'Sur les femmes', on women's apparent greater emotional fluidity linked to their physiology, was more likely to support arguments in favour of the lesser rationality of women and thus their incapacity for public life. Cartesian idealism, by contrast, was more friendly to the idea of the equality of minds, since minds were independent of bodies, as Jodin must have realised when she quoted (though without attribution) Poulain de la Barre, the seventeenth-century Cartesian feminist (italicised in the following passage):[41]

> The love of country, of liberty and fame, animates our sex as much as yours, Messieurs. We are not, on this earth, a different species from you. *The mind has no sex any more than does virtue* but vices of the mind and the heart belong almost exclusively to yours ... (*Vues législatives*, p. 181).

However, seemingly contradicting this idealist position, Jodin also invokes Rousseau's key concept of innate female modesty, or *pudeur*, as fundamental to women's nature or at least to their situation. As is evident, ascribing innate virtues to women (gentleness, modesty and so on) could be and often was invoked to exclude (or shelter) women from the alleged corruptions of the public sphere by confining them to the home. One could suggest, nevertheless, that Jodin is not entirely inconsistent in arguing for mental or spiritual equality and gender-specific qualities. She distinguishes in effect between modes of behaviour which are sexually congruent in a socio-historical sense (men's aggression versus women's modesty) and intellectual capacity which allows individuals to range beyond the limits of their sexual identity.

Attacking those who assume that women's bodily weakness makes them unfit for public life, Jodin shows the absurdity of this argument on two grounds. In the first place, physically weak men do not forfeit the rights they possess by virtue of birth or intellect: 'Such a ridiculous system would deprive delicate princes of their crowns, courageous actions of weak individuals like Turenne would be negated as would the sublime and universal spirit of Voltaire, issuing from a frail body' (*Vues législatives*, p. 182). Condorcet had dealt briskly with this pseudo-problem: 'Why should beings, to whom pregnancy and passing indispositions are incident, not be able to exercise rights, of which nobody every dreamt of depriving people who have the gout every winter, or who easily catch cold.'[42] Secondly, women's weakness is partly a function of their sedentary lives: 'If the excess of humidity, Plato said, which soaks up women's vigour and makes them softer than men was dried out by moderate exercise ... their bodies would become more agile and more robust' (p. 182). Plato was not, of course, a materialist, but what is significant about Jodin's borrowing of this medical model is that women's greater physical weakness is constructed as socially based; it is a contingent rather than a necessary quality.[43]

Jodin asserts women's historical achievements in order to illustrate what a reformed public sphere might hold. What exceptional women (Elizabeth I of England, Catherine II of Russia) have already shown themselves to be, many more women could become. Women's capacity for patriotism, coupled with humanity, can be demonstrated to contradict the charge that they are incapable of serious political and social commitment. Citing an unidentified 'modern writer'[44] (Antoine Léonard Thomas), Jodin drops the language of complaisance and flattery towards her male audience:

> A modern writer has dared assert that women can scarcely understand a political idea, if in the least wide-ranging and difficult, though he grants them admirable notions of domestic order and economy. He adds that, though strangers to patriotism, they are firmly attached to the gentle pleasure of sociability (*Vues législatives*, p. 181–2)

Women, like men, are capable of vice and virtue. The qualities of each sex are complementary to and necessary to the other. Women have particular gifts for what Jodin terms the civic virtues and are suited to legislate over domestic morality, because they are more rooted in a civil and domestic society. Women are not in competition with men: 'These ridiculous debates over superiority are a travesty of nature. You [men] are born to be our friends and not our rivals' (*Vues législatives*, p. 183). Throughout this part of her argument, Jodin invokes Rousseau to demonstrate that her scheme for a moral jurisdiction for women follows his agenda for a moral state founded on political liberty.

Though calling to her aid the empirical demonstration that women are capable of a public role to make a more convincing case for their eligibility for citizenship, Jodin couches her appeal to the legislators primarily on the maternal domestic ideal. In her plan, women would shoulder a maternal role within the public realm. The importance of the maternal ideal to revolutionary thought, exalted by Rousseau in *La Nouvelle Héloise* and *Émile*, can scarcely be overestimated, but in the eighteenth century it was normally confined to the domestic sphere.[45] The maternal icon achieved hegemonic status – indeed part of the obloquy meted out to decadent aristocratic women (especially Marie Antoinette) on the one hand, and to prostitutes on the other, stemmed from the fact that they visibly violated this ideal of maternal virtue. Jodin, apparently a moderate royalist in her political views, appeals to the King, but not, significantly, to the Queen, already discredited as the mother of her people, to allow women to take on the role in society at large that they hold in their families, to extend the maternal role to the public realm.[46] Paternity and maternity come together to save the State:

> The King, who in his paternal goodness summoned the enlightened élite of men now engaged on that great task, [reform of legislation and the State] cannot forget that we women form part of his great family. He cannot be unaware that fathers take charge of the education of their male children

and leave that of their daughters to the mother. We demand, with the confidence that his justice inspires in us, to be subjected to the same maternal authority, the one assigned to us by nature and implicit in the relations of the sexes (*Vues législatives*, p. 190).

Jodin fully accepts that women's condition is to have duties peculiar to their sex; namely, maternity. But it does not follow that women are restricted to the private sphere.

Having completed her *Vues législatives* by 1789, Jodin sent it to her old acquaintance from her Bordeaux days, Jean-Baptiste, Comte de Lynch (or Linch), now *Président aux enquêtes* of the Bordeaux parlement. One cannot be surprised that this devout Catholic, to be imprisoned under the Terror, though awarded the mayoralty of Bordeaux under Napoleon, should prove unenthusiastic about her proposals. Lynch replied courteously, but with patronising complacency. Jodin, nettled by his reply, chose to include his unfettered expressions of masculine prejudice in her text. Lynch had written:

> I would not dare assure you that the august Assembly will adopt your plan, but I am sure it will appreciate it. Your plan does honour to that sex which knows how to instruct and to please, and whose lessons have far more power over us than those of cold Philosophy (*Vues législatives*).

Lynch told her that he greatly disliked the idea of women, 'the most lovable half of humankind', intervening in government. That would not make for their happiness, he wrote, 'nor for ours'. Ambition and the struggle for reputation on the public scene were designed for men, not for women, who, in their own modest private sphere, had 'a surer and more glorious' way of contributing to human good. Whilst agreeing with Jodin's analysis of present-day moral decline, Lynch suggested that reform must come from changes in the law carried out by male legislators. It was the role of mothers to teach their daughters morality, economy and the love of domestic life.[47] Men must take responsibility for society's moral decline and in doing so would bring about women's reform. Lynch objected particularly to interference in family life and thereby with the authority of the husband: 'Why a Tribunal to reconcile us with our wives?' What Jodin was in fact advocating with her women's jurisdiction over women was the abolition of the father's absolute control over his daughter and a husband's over his wife. Lynch had grasped that what might seem like modest proposals for dealing with family disruption would in fact mean the overthrow of patriarchal authority.[48] Finally, though complimenting Jodin on her graphic depiction of the evils of prostitution, gambling and pornography, he warns her against ambitions to surpass men in the arts, in government or in literature. Women will be happier if they work for the happiness of their families and of society, without any thoughts of ambition or worldly recompense.

Lynch's suggestion that if women trained their daughters properly for domestic life, marriages would be happy and there would be no need for Family

Courts of Conciliation provided Jodin with a platform to argue for the introduction of divorce into French law: 'To make marriages easy and happy; that is the thing, Monsieur, that seems to me most difficult of all if Divorce is not established, for indissoluble marriage is an unnatural bond which almost always ends up a burden to those who have contracted it' (*Vues législatives*, p. 193). Before 1792 divorce was forbidden under French law, though in most Protestant European countries it was permitted in some form and even in Catholic Poland. In France, both the Church and the State enforced the doctrine of marital indissolubility, though in cases of extreme matrimonial cruelty on the part of the husband, judicial separations were possible. Husbands had the right to 'moderate punishment' of the wife, either in terms of corporal punishment or incarceration in a convent. Judicial separation, though providing protection for wives in the worst cases (and it was relatively rare), did not allow remarriage.[49]

What is most significant in Jodin's advocacy of divorce is not the originality of her arguments but the extent to which she shows herself informed of the debate in favour of reform. All the major *philosophes* had advocated divorce. Diderot discusses it in his *Supplément au voyage de Bougainville* and Montesquieu in *Lettres Persanes*. The article on 'Divorce' in the *Encyclopédie*, by Boucher d'Argis, whilst ostensibly neutral on the issue, showed the French law of indissolubility as an exception to historical and even contemporary precedent. Even where Jodin does not refer to philosophical sources, it clear that she has read these and similar works, such as Cerfvol's, *Mémoire sur la population*.[50]

Writers who argued for divorce were not anti-marriage; indeed the proposals in favour of divorce coexisted happily with the cult of family life. They argued that indissolubility of marriage was contrary to nature, that it was contradicted by historical precedent (Jewish and Roman law), that it did not seek to promote human happiness and led to population decline. Jodin took much of her material from the *Encylopédie* article 'Marriage' which, while explicitly endorsing Catholic marriage, gave it a historical reading, thereby undermining the Church's claims to its sacramental and eternal status. The topic of Catholic marriage led Jodin into an anticlerical polemic, even more outspoken than her denunciation of prostitutes and the police in Part I of her treatise. She blamed the example of the Church's emphasis on celibacy for the disinclination of non-clerics to marry and asserted that the present-day Church was primarily concerned with worldly pleasure and political power:

> As enlightenment spread, the ministers of the Church found a new freedom. Like Gods, they descended from their seraphic throne to commune with shepherdesses. Soon they insinuated themselves into the boudoirs of our Sovereigns and of our belles, taking possession there. It is thus that the lure of an indefinite liberty, cloaked with a sacred mantle, propelled them into every kind of human enjoyment ... (*Vues législatives*, p. 197).

While it is true that to accuse clerics of lubricious behaviour, combined with furtive ambition, was the stock-in-trade of contemporary anti-clerical rhetoric, one can surmise that her strictures against the Church arose in part from the memories of her terrible early convent experiences.

Indissolubility of marriage was also against nature: 'At this moment when the Rights of Man, too long ignored, are the object of a new Constitution designed to restore them, none is more important than the one claimed by Nature: the liberty to dispose of one's own person' (*Vues législatives*, p. 198). Whereas superficially, Jodin's discussion of divorce is not directly focused on women's rights, it becomes increasingly clear that its implications particularly concern women. For example, 'the liberty to dispose of one's own person' was precisely that which the law did not accord to women, only to men. Fathers had control over their daughters until marriage, and husbands thereafter. Divorce, by curbing the *puissance maritale* of husbands over wives, had come to be seen as a feminist issue.

The final section of Jodin's treatise (the 'Postscript') attacks a review by Marmontel (an otherwise fairly liberal commentator), which in its turn attacked a book on divorce, advertised by the *Mercure de France* in early 1790, Hennet's *Du Divorce* (1789), which was to become the blueprint for subsequent legislation.[51] Ridiculing Marmontel's assertion that bad marriages were their own punishment for the partners, Jodin speaks indignantly in the first person on behalf of both wives and husbands and constructs a graphic genre scene of marital disharmony:

> What! Am I to be ashamed of not still loving a husband who poisons my life with miseries of every kind? Am I to kiss the mouth which abuses me, the baleful eye which threatens me, the hand which batters me! [Then changing roles from wife to husband] Am I to cherish the faithless woman who lords it in my household, who receives rivals and corrupters in my absence, who maltreats and neglects my children, who ruins me, wrecks my days, and, as the mistress of some great man, has me imprisoned? (*Vues législatives*, p. 203)

Like Hennet, Jodin specifies the need to protect the interests of children and to ensure equitable settlement of property. But the most striking aspect of this section with its dialogic structure is its impassioned tone. Jodin was able, speaking to an intellectual adversary, to drop the language of courtly flattery and come out fighting.

The *Vues législatives* was conceived by its author as a practical plan for the social and moral reform of prostitutes, whose lives she had known only too well during her prison sojourn. However, she broadened her agenda to call for women's rights as citizens, following the logic of Rousseau's views that one cannot demand morality of persons who have abrogated their liberty. She asked for the inclusion of women in the legislative process, offering a replication of 'separate-spheres' domestic ideology in the public sphere. Yet the implications for paternal authority by the admission of women to the responsible public sphere as legislators, even if 'only' over women, were radical. A woman's legislature would in theory legislate exclusively for women, but in practice, as Lynch foresaw, would be involved in complex aspects of social and legal policy. Both the idea of a women's legislature and that of divorce reform implied allowing women to control their own lives in a heretofore unprecedented fashion and massively weakened *la puissance maritale*. Though in her rhetoric Jodin attempted to appeal to the male members of the Constituent Assembly, it is scarcely surprising that both her tactic of flattery and her rational arguments failed. The fate of women's emancipation after the early flourishing of women's journals and the militancy of revolutionary women is well known.[52] Nascent feminism was effectively crushed by the law of *4 Prairial, An III* (1793), when women were ordered back to their homes and were forbidden to assemble in public in groups larger than five. Nevertheless, Jodin's arguments in favour of divorce turned out to be on the winning side in revolutionary-legislative terms. The law of 20 September 1792, passed two years after her death, legalising divorce, was the most liberal in Europe, until its repeal in 1816 under the Restoration.

Jodin's practical agenda which she hoped would fit women for public life was congruent with what would become the ambitions of many nineteenth- and early twentieth-century feminists who were to pursue motherhood and education as the route by which women might be admitted to citizenship, as the maternal teachers of their children. She applied Enlightenment principles of justice and human rights to that one half of the human race unaccountably overlooked by the new legislators of France. As Condorcet would remark in his *Admission des femmes au droit de cité* (1790): 'It was the strongest proof of the power of habit, even among enlightened men, to see the principle of equality of rights invoked in favour of three or four hundred men deprived of it by an absurd prejudice, yet forgotten in regard to twelve million women.'

Jodin's treatise broadens our understanding of the social and gender composition of the Republic of Letters and demonstrates that a feminist agenda was securely in place in the early days of the Revolution. Her *Vues législatives* was the work of woman who had experienced public life on a number of levels, as a 'libertine', as an actress and as the mistress of a wealthy Prussian aristocrat. All of these categories involved risk and humiliation, though also excitement and a degree of freedom. Nevertheless, she aspired to transform the contemporary definitions of the public sphere for women.[53] An understanding of Jodin's career and of her *Vues législatives* contributes to historians' efforts to reclaim the European Enlightenment for feminism.[54] While she decried the practical effects on ordinary women's lives of police harassment and marital oppression, she also insisted that women must attain a better moral standard to qualify for citizenship. In this she showed herself to be both the faithful disciple and the disobedient daughter of Jean-Jacques Rousseau.

Notes

1. For discussions of this literature and the lifting of censorship see Jane Abray, 'Feminism in the French Revolution', *American Historical Review*, 80: 1 (February 1975), pp. 43–62; Benabou, *La Prostitution et la police des moeurs*, pp. 442–505; Paule-Marie Duhet, *Les Femmes et la Révolution 1789–1794* (Paris: Julliard, 1971); Madeleine Gutwirth, *The Twilight of the Goddesses: Women and Representation in the French Revolutionary Era* (Rutgers: Rutgers University Press, 1982); Elizabeth Racz, 'The Women's Rights Movement in the French Revolution', *Science and Society*, 16 (1951), pp. 151–74; Schama, *Citizens, a Chronicle of the French Revolution*, p. 297. The following are a sample of feminist and anti-feminist pamphlets appearing in the early revolutionary period: Esprit Michel Laugier, *Tyrannie que les hommes ont exercée dans presque tous les temps et les pays contre les femmes* (1788); *Requête des Femmes pour leur admission aux Etats-Généraux* (n.d.); *Très-humbles remonstrances des femmes françaises* (1788), *Motions adressées à l'Assemblée Nationale en Faveur du sexe* (1789); *Epitre aux françoises sur l'Assemblée Nationale* (Amsterdam: 1789); *Réclamation des Courtisanes parisiennes adressées à l'Assemblée Nationale* (1790), a male-authored anti-feminist satire.
2. Jodin may have made contact with the firm of Mame when she performed in Angers in 1774. C.-P. Mame used as his crest the Masonic insignia. He would have formed part of the Masonic circle of nobles, lawyers and businessmen who made up the hundred or so members of the Angers Masonic Lodge which constituted the intelligentsia of the city. Delaunay, Jodin's barrister, was probably also a member. *Histoire d'Angers*, ed. François Lebruin (Toulouse: Prevat, 1975), pp. 127–31. For the history of printing houses and the importance of Mame, see Henri-Jean Martin and Roger Chartier, eds, *Historie de l'édition française* II (Paris: Promodis, 1984), p. 293.
3. For example, although universal male suffrage was introduced in France in 1848, French women were not granted the vote until 1944.
4. See Olwen H. Hufton, *Women and the Limits of Citizenship in the French Revolution* (Toronto: University of Toronto Press, 1992), pp. 2–18 on the 'engendered crowd'.
5. See Abray, 'Feminism in the French Revolution', pp. 43–62, Louis Devance, 'Le Féminisme pendant la Révolution française', *Annales historiques de la Révolution française*, 229 (July–September 1977), pp. 341–76. For the timing of women's petitions see Duhet, *Les Femmes et la Révolution 1789–1794*, p. 57. For the theme of moral reform in relation to political change in the context of Genevan republicanism and its relevance to revolutionary thought, see Richard Whatmore, 'The Political Economy of Jean-Baptiste Say's Republicanism', *History of Political Thought*, XIX, 3 (Autumn 1998).
6. See Blum, *Rousseau and the Republic of Virtue* for the impact of Rousseau on revolutionary thought.
7. See Habermas, *The Structural Transformation of the Public Sphere*.
8. 'Cahier du Tiers-Etat de la Ville de Paris', *Archives Parlementaires de 1787–1860*, 1e série, 5 (Paris: Paul Dupont, 1879), p. 290. For further background and

documents on the *cahiers de doléances*, see John Hardman, *The French Revolution Source Book* (London: Arnold, 1999), pp. 75–123.

9. See Gordon, *Citizens without Sovereignty*.

10. Restif de la Bretonne, *Les Françaises*, I, pp. 172 and 77, quoted in Pierre Testud, *Rétif de la Bretonne et la création littéraire* (Geneva: Librairie Droz, 1977), p. 619.

11. Among the philosophers and other writers cited or paraphrased in the *Vues législatives* are: Lycurgus, Delisles de Sales, Lord Chesterfield, Bayle, Voltaire, Plato, Rousseau (most frequently), Montesquieu, Aristotle, Bacon, Montaigne as well as quotations from *L'Encyclopédie* and a host of literary references.

12. Vernière, 'Marie-Madeleine Jodin, amie de Diderot et témoin des Lumières', expresses approval but also astonishment with reference to Jodin's learning. 'Aucun ridicule dans cet étrange ouvrage qui est un authentique précurseur du féminisme moderne. Mlle Jodin connaissait admirablement son sujet, et l'expérience de sa rude vie lui avait inspiré tardivement quelque sagesse. Mais ce qui dans cet ouvrage nous étonne, ce n'est pas seulement son style, c'est la très sérieuse culture qu'il traduit' (p. 1773).

13. Benabou, *La Prostitution et la police des moeurs*, pp. 442–3.

14. Laurent Pierre Bérenger, *De la Prostitution: Cahier et doléances d'un ami des moeurs*, adressé spécialement aux députés de l'ordre du Tiers-Etat de Paris (Paris: au Palais Royal, 1789).

15. E. J. Hobsbawm, *The Age of Revolution 1789–1848* (New York: Mentor Books, 1962), p. 26.

16. Benabou, *La Prostitution et la police des moeurs*, p. 447.

17. Bérenger, *De la Prostitution*, pp. 27–9.

18. Benabou, *La Prostitution et la police des moeurs*, pp. 443–50.

19. Quoted in Benabou, *La Prostitution et la police des moeurs*, p. 450. Louis Sébastien Mercier was a prolific playwright and author of numerous works on Paris, among them *Le Tableau de Paris*, 2 vols (London: 1781), *Les Entretiens au Palais Royal de Paris* (Paris: Chez Buisson, 1786).

20. Diderot had reviewed *Le Pornographe* in 1769 and remarked that it was an excellent book to read on the toilet (or *chaise percée*). Diderot actually calls it 'un excellent livre de garde-robe', a reference to where the *chaise percée* was commonly kept. Diderot, *Oeuvres Complètes*, VIII, pp. 279–80.

21. Jean Jacques Bachelier, *Mémoire sur l'éducation des filles*, présenté aux Etats-Généraux par M. Bachelier (Paris: Imprimérie Royale, 1789).

22. *Appel au Françoises sur la régénération des moeurs et la nécessité de l'influence des femmes dans un gouvernement libre*, lu à L'Assemblée fédérative des amis de la vérité, 30 décembre, 1790. Etta Palm d'Aelders (born 1743) was of Dutch origin and settled in Paris in 1774. She headed a women's delegation to the National Assembly in 1792.

23. Olympe de Gouges, *Projet adressé à l'Assemblée Nationale, le jour de l'arrestation du Roi* (Paris: 1792), p. 16.

24. de Gouges, *Les Droits de la femme* (Paris: 1791).

25. On prostitution in eighteenth-century France, see Benabou, *La Prostitution et la police des moeurs*; D. A. Coward, 'Eighteenth-century attitudes to prostitution', *Studies on Voltaire*, 189 (1980), pp. 363–409; , A.-J.-B. Parent-Duchâtelet, *De la Prostitution dans la Ville de Paris* (Paris: J. B. Ballière, 1836); Mercier, *Le Tableau de Paris*.

26. *Cahiers du Tiers États*, cited by Jodin on her title page to *Vues législatives pour les femmes*.

27. [Jodin's note] 'Everyone knows that the police regard prostitutes as a necessity in great cities. Is not to tolerate them in a sense to sacrifice them to these pretended "needs"?'

28. Full title, *Les Gynographes où ideés de deux honnêtes femmes sur un projet de réglement proposé à toute l'Europe, pour mettre les femmes à leur place, et opérer le bonheur des deux sexes* (The Hague: Gosse et Pinel, 1777), *l'Anti-Justine*, par M. Linguet (Restif de la Bretonne) (Paris: au Palais Royal, 1798). For a more favourable analysis see Pierre Testud, *Rétif de la Bretonne et la création littéraire*.

29. Restif de la Bretonne, *Les Gynographes*, p. 508.

30. See Carol Pateman, *The Sexual Contract* (Cambridge: Polity Press, 1988) for the ambiguous position of prostitutes who made contracts, though as women they were excluded from contractual obligations; see also Jo Labanyi, 'Adultery and the Exchange Economy', in *Scarlet Letters: Fictions of Adultery from Antiquity to the 1990s*, ed. Nicholas White and Naomi Segal (Basingstoke: Macmillan, 1997), pp. 98–108. One may note additionally that the expression 'femme en monde' to refer to prostitutes was another linguistic marker defining the moral status of any woman entering the public sphere which also rubbed off on actresses.

31. Cited in Albert Babeau, *Paris en 1789* (Paris: Firmin-Didot, 1889), p. 495.

32. See the *Journal des Inspecteurs de M. de Sartines*, Première Série, 1761–1764, where the life of the better-off courtesans and their aristocratic lovers is reported in indulgent detail.

33. The vexed relationship of eighteenth-century women writers to Rousseau, a combination of enthusiasm and disapproval has been traced by a number of writers, among them Campbell Orr, 'Cross-Channel Perspectives', in *Wollstonecraft's Daughters*, pp. 1–42; P. D. Jimack, 'The Paradox of Sophie and Julie: Contemporary Response to Rousseau's Ideal Wife and Ideal Mother', *Women and Society in Eighteenth-Century France*, ed. E. Jacobs, W. H. Barber, J. H. Bloch and F. W. Leakey (London: Athlone Press, 1979); Lynda Lange, 'Rousseau and Modern Feminism', in Jacobs, *Women and Society in Eighteenth-Century France*, pp. 95–111; Sara Ellen Procious Malueg, 'Women and the *Encyclopédie*', *French Women and the Age of Enlightenment*, ed. Samia I. Spencer (Bloomington: Indiana University Press, 1984), pp. 250–70; Gita May, 'Rousseau's "Anti-feminism" Reconsidered', in Spencer, *French Women and the Age of Enlightenment*, pp. 309–20; Gilbert Py, *Rousseau et les éducateurs* (Oxford: Voltaire Foundation, 1997), pp. 338–405; Joel Schwartz, *The Sexual Politics of Jean-Jacques Rousseau* (London: University of Chicago Press, 1984); Sylvana Tomaselli, 'The Enlightenment Debate on Women', *History Workshop Journal*, 20 (1985), pp. 101–24; Mary Trouille, 'A bold new vision of woman: Staël and Wollstonecraft respond to Rousseau', *Studies on Voltaire and the Eighteenth Century*, 292 (1991), pp. 293–336.

34. Blum, *Rousseau and the Republic of Virtue*.

35. For a classic exposition of this point see Genevieve Lloyd, *The Man of Reason* (London: Methuen, 1984), pp. 58–63; Py, *Rousseau et les éducateurs*, Chapter 9, locates Rousseau's views on women in the context of eighteenth-century medical discourse.

36. Py, *Rousseau et les éducateurs*, p. 340. It is hard to agree with Py, however, that to tax Rousseau with misogyny is an anachronism and that his views on women simply reflected medical discourse. Condorcet, for example, living in the same cultural climate, did not espouse comparable views. Rousseau's overwhelming fear of women and hence his belief that they required restraint is well expressed in the Bacchic passage in *Émile*, Book V: 'Women so easily stir a man's senses and

fan the ashes of a dying passion, that if philosophy ever succeeded in introducing this custom [women as sexual aggressors] into any unlucky country ... the men, tyrannized over by the women, would at last become their victims, and would be dragged to their deaths without the least chance of escape.' Jean Jacques Rousseau, *Émile* (1762), trans. Barbara Foxley (London: Everyman Library, 1969), p. 322.

37. Jean-Jacques Rousseau, *The Social Contract*, trans. Maurice Cranston (1762) (London: Penguin Books, 1968), p. 55.

38. Rousseau's famous dictum that men must be forced to be free underlines an authoritarian strain in Enlightenment thought which Jodin shares. The assumption underlying the *Vues législatives* is that liberty, as defined by the social contract or what Jodin calls the 'social pact', will result in the pursuit of virtuous social ends. The anxiety that this after all might not be so accounts for the heavy directiveness of such educational works as Rousseau's *Émile* (1762) or Mme de Genlis' soon to be published *Adèle et Théodore* (1792), where an education for freedom is in fact highly prescriptive and the pupil's free choice manipulated to give the 'right' result.

39. Jodin does once refer obliquely to God in a quotation from Delisle de Sales, as the 'Orderer of Worlds', but she is quoting someone else, not speaking in her own voice.

40. Geneviève Fraisse, *Reason's Muse: Sexual Difference and the Birth of Democracy*, trans. Jane Marie Todd (London: University of Chicago Press, 1994).

41. François Poulain de la Barre, *De l'égalité des deux sexes: discours physique et moral où l'on voit l'importance de se défaire des préjugez* (Paris: 1673), p. 109; Diderot, 'Sur les femmes', *Oeuvres Complètes*, ed. Roger Lewinter (Paris: Le Club français du livre, 1997), pp. 29–60; Lisa Gasbarrone, 'Voices from Nature: Diderot's Dialogues with women', *Studies on Voltaire and the Eighteenth Century*, 292 (Oxford: Voltaire Foundation, 1991); Hufton, *Women and the Limits of Citizenship in the French Revolution*. On the feminist implications of Cartesianism, see Marc Angenot, *Les Champions des femmes* (Quebec: Presses de l'Université de Québec, 1977), pp. 58–65; Siep Stuurmann, 'Seventeenth-Century Feminism and the Invention of Modern Equality', paper given at the 'Feminism and Enlightenment: 1650–1850' seminar, Institute of Historical Research, University of London, 2 December 1998.

42. The Marquis de Condorcet, 'Condorcet's Plea for the Citizenship of Women', trans. John Morley, *Fortnightly Review*, 13 (1 June 1870), reprinted in Susan Groag Bell and Karen M. Offen, *Women, the Family and Freedom: the Debate in Documents*, I, 1750–1880 (Stanford: Stanford University Press, 1983), p. 99.

43. Jodin took this Platonic reference from *La Galerie des femmes fortes* (1647), by the Jesuit Father Pierre le Moyne, p. 47.

44. This was Antoine Leonard Thomas, who wrote a patronising essay in defence of women, *Essai sur le caractère des femmes* (1772), reprinted in *A. L. Thomas, Diderot, Madame d'Epinay: Quest-ce qu'une femme?*, ed. Elisabeth Badinter (Paris: P.O.L., 1989).

45. For a fuller discussion of the maternal ideal, see Campbell Orr, 'Cross-Channel Perspectives', in *Wollstonecraft's Daughters*, pp. 10–11.

46. See Lynn Hunt, *The Family Romance of the French Revolution* (London: Routledge, 1992), pp. 17–51 and 89–123.

47. Lynch echoes the near-universal rhetoric of maternal roles in the late eighteenth century which owed so much to Rousseau. See Gilbert Py, *Rousseau et les éducateurs*, p. 385; 'Mary Jacobus, 'Incorruptible Milk: Breast-feeding and the French Revolution', in Sara E. Melzer and Leslie W. Rabine, eds, *Rebel Daughters:*

Women and the French Revolution (Oxford: Oxford University Press, 1992), pp. 55–75.

48. For the issue of paternal authority, see Abray, 'Feminism in the French Revolution'.
49. For this and the following discussion relating to divorce law and the debate surrounding it, see Phillips, *Putting Asunder*, pp. 159–75.
50. Cerfvol, de [pseud.], *Mémoire sur la population* (London [Paris]: 1768).
51. Jean-François Marmontel (1723–99) was an enormously prolific writer and journalist, best known for his *Moral Tales*. His review of this anonymous work on divorce appears on pp. 18–36 of the *Mercure de France* for February 1790. It refers to Hennet's *Du Divorce*, 1789, which was the first work in France to publish detailed proposals for divorce legislation. See Phillips, *Putting Asunder*, p. 173.
52. See, for example, Devance, 'Le Féminisme pendant la révolution française', pp. 341–69.
53. Though Jodin's treatise seems to have been ignored after its publication, its arguments seemingly too radical for the moral conservatism of the ensuing revolutionary phase, echoes of her work continued to be heard in the twentieth century. In a letter to Felicia Gordon, Odile Falieu, Conservateur en chef de la Bibliothèque-Musée de la Comédie-Française (30 September 1998) noted: 'You will be pleased to know that Mlle Jodin's speech ("To my Sex") was read aloud on 1 December, 1987 in the Colbert Auditorium of the Bibliothèque Nationale by Catherine Ferran, member of the Comédie-Française, in the context of "Recitations of Oratorical Pieces".'
54. Karen Offen, 'Reclaiming the European Enlightenment for feminism: or prologomena to any future history of eighteenth-century Europe', *Perspectives on Feminist Political Thought in European History*, ed. Tjitske Akkerman and Siep Stuurman (London: Routledge, 1998), pp. 85–103.

Figure 8.1 *Shaving Heads of Prostitutes*, eighteenth century.
[Courtesy of the Mary Evans Picture Library].
'When one considers the mortifications which must accompany their vile mode of
life...' (*Vues législatives pour les femmes*).

Appendix

LEGISLATIVE VIEWS FOR WOMEN
ADDRESSED TO THE NATIONAL ASSEMBLY

BY MADEMOISELLE JODIN

Daughter of a Citizen of Geneva

'The Paris Assembly will consider means to revive
the regulations, which have so far proved
useless, for repressing the scandal of
public prostitution.'
(Cahiers du Tiers État, page 67)

MAME, Printer to the Department of Maine and
Loire, Rue S. Laud.
ANGERS
1790

TO MY SEX

'And we too are Citizens'

Now that the French have declared their zeal for the regeneration of the State and for basing its happiness and glory on the eternal foundations of Virtue and Law, the thought has struck me that my sex, which constitutes an attractive half of that fair Empire, could also claim the honour, and even the right, of contributing to the public welfare; and that in breaking the silence to which politics seems to have condemned us, we could usefully say: 'And we too are Citizens'.

As such, have we not our rights as well as our duties, and must we remain purely passive at a moment when all fruitful thinking about the public good must also touch on this delicate point, the happy bond which attaches us to that good? No, there is a plan necessary to the health of our Legislation; and this plan, founded upon ancient and pure foundations, shaken by the vicissitudes of time and the alteration of manners, can only, it seems to me, be revived by ourselves.

I mean to do no more than announce this plan. The programme is a simple one; it invites my fellow Citizenesses to take part in an undertaking altogether worthy of them and of the motives which led me to conceive it. Happy woman that I am! Able to pay to my country the debt, not of talents, but of the heart; and to my sex, that of my esteem.

LEGISLATIVE VIEWS FOR WOMEN

At a time when true Philosophy is beginning to enlighten all minds, when the defeat of Despotism leaves the prejudices which owed their existence to it helpless and without defence, shall the weaker sex, excluded by force from public deliberations, demand its inalienable rights in vain? Shall that essential half of Society not have any share in the legislative Code proclaimed in the name of Society as a whole? I can picture the reason and equity which animate the august Assembly of Representatives of the Nation, amazed that these questions have not been raised before, hastening to welcome them. So let us obey the general impulse which directs all ideas towards the goal of liberty regained, a liberty usurped by oppression from all of us equally.

If it is true that our condition imposes on us duties peculiar to our sex, in addition to those entailed by the title of Citizens, we shall need a legislative Code independent of the one we share with the entire mass of Citizens – just as each different section of a general Administration requires its separate protocol. Let us therefore calmly and wisely examine the Code which it behoves us to make our Legislators adopt, and search out the source of those disorders which have tarnished our glory and tainted our original Virtues. These disorders derive less from the imperfection of our Nature than from the negligence of the Laws, which have encouraged licentiousness in manners, so leading to the scandal of public prostitution – a thing especially debasing to this sex, which will always be a pliable reed in the hands of the Law, directed to Virtue by its activity and to degradation by its indifference.

Do you wish to raise us to great things? All that is necessary is to excite our emulation. Now, this can only be brought about by a new mode of political organization – one which grants full rights to opinion and frees us from the species of tutelage which, in a sense, separates us from public concerns, leaving us linked with them only by our heart's vows and irresistible attraction to that imperious sex which enslaves our wills as it does our affections. But whilst the subordination thus inseparable from our condition bends us under its Laws, it has not succeeded in stifling our sense of our rights. We claim them today, Sirs, when a new scheme of Legislation is to consider the bonds connecting us with civic harmony. If our private advice has benefited you, when esteem and love have admitted us into your confidence, what even greater advantages will you not derive from our gratitude (for we shall have to owe it to your goodwill) when you restore to us the rights which are ours by Nature and by the social compact.

We therefore hope, Sirs, that this argument will persuade you to consider, together with us, the plan of a Legislation especially designed for us. To reform the one governing us today is all the more important in that the vices entailed in applying it would be an invincible obstacle to the general happiness which, at the present moment, is so keenly exercising your zeal and enlightened views.

We will point out to you first of all that the opprobrious manner in which, under the present system, a portion of our own sex seems to be sacrificed to the incontinence of yours is an outrage to Law and destroys the respect belonging to the sacred titles of 'Citizenesses', 'wives' and 'mothers'.[1]

Public continence and sober morals are for the body politic, as for the physical body, the source of their force and energy. It is fathers, recognized as such by the Law, who make Citizens, and it is Citizens who make the State. Nevertheless your cities, and above all the vast enclosure of your Capital, contain almost nothing but courtesans; your families die out in the obscurity of a sterile celibacy; by such dark dealings, the hospitals are thronged with anonymous humans, disavowed by the laws, expelled by Society from its bosom, and left to perish by the barbarous desertion of the authors of their being.

'If Modesty is anterior to Law', a philosopher has said,[2] 'and if the Orderer of worlds has provided our world with this feeling as a protection to weakness against force, or even if modesty does no more than heighten the sweet and pure pleasure essential to human happiness, how important it must be to restore it to your hearths and homes.'

It is through the loss of its morals that Rome came to bow her proud head beneath the yoke of Peoples it once had conquered. In all countries, the most licentious classes are always those of the highest or the lowest rank. Happy mediocrity was always the pure refuge of public morals and national reputation; it is there one finds chaste wives and tender mothers, in a word true Citizenesses.

Who, at this very moment, has just reproduced before our eyes the patriotism of ancient Rome? It is not the haughty Nobility, it is not the proud and rich, it is the modest citizenry, the children of talents and arts; it is Virtue herself in her pure and primitive simplicity. Let us be just, however, and admit that that same Nobility and (perhaps too much envied) Wealth only needed a sign to display the most generous emulation and prove that, in all French hearts, love of the Fatherland is a sacred fire that nothing can quench and the least breath is always sure to kindle. We therefore need not think the reform of the highest class a problem: a wise policy, able to regain for public opinion the dominion it should never have lost, will soon have brought this class back to the paths of decency, I might almost say of Virtue.

But to restore decency among the People, who are deaf to all morality once they have broken the curb of subordination, thenceforward becoming strangers to all proper feeling and all social observance, one needs to remove from them the tempting objects which perpetuate licentiousness and incite to shameful excess. The essential object of the first reform, therefore, must be the extinction of prostitutes, who destroy for the People the very notion of modesty and the principles of all physical and moral vigour; women who, often, render those condemned by poverty to the plough or to the battlefield unable to fulfil the duties of their condition.

The need to remove the audacious vice I am denouncing from public view will come home to you the more if you observe that among no people has it produced more excess and scandal than among ourselves; nowhere has the instinct of modesty, that powerful ally of beauty, been more generally perverted; nowhere else do women, whose first duty is to be discreet and reserved, so brazenly provoke the other sex, one that was formed by Nature for attack but that our unbridled behaviour puts upon its own defence.[3] How indignant should decent women be at this inversion of the natural and social order since you too, the members of the other sex, are revolted by it!

In Athens, where courtesans had more prestige than anywhere, they were only tolerated if they offered intelligence and talent in lieu of strictness of morals. Will you, Sirs, be less delicate than this People to whom you have so many affinities?

We have seen, in the *Pornographer*, a scheme to confine these fecund sources of corruption and moral ruin to a single quarter of the town, so as to segregate them from the young, whose earliest thoughts and earliest looks they soil.[4] But in our climes, where men are rarely driven by the restless physical needs engendered by the heats of Asia, and where what leads them to haunts of debauchery and calculated obscenity (more adapted to excite them than to satisfy them) is less such needs than a disordered imagination and the habit of vice, one should proscribe all such facilities, which are only adapted to titillating the deadened senses of old age. The age of vigour and pleasure has no need of such a stimulant, which can only be dangerously inflaming to youth, with its easily stirred flesh, and liable to lead it into destructive overindulgence.

Is the fact that our happy climate gives the two sexes only moderate and delicate desires a reason to overturn this salutary order of Nature? Born to the gentler enjoyments of love and pleasure, ought we to regret the lack of its excesses and furies?

Must we accept the theories of those Legislators who think that prostitution is a necessary evil and is the only protection for modesty? Hardly so. For Sparta, where the Virtue of modesty was, as it were, proscribed, is the one place where one did not see the open scandal of those unfortunate women, reduced by a combination of vices to the last degradation. Moreover though it seems, judging from Lycurgus' Laws, that he did not consider propriety the safeguard of chastity, it remains true that, by proscribing the one, he did not succeed in preserving the other. The first of these Virtues, therefore, is, after all, the guardian of the second. This is so much the case that even the Spartans did not enjoy an unspotted reputation and merited the keen jibes of the satirical Martial.

Another source of evil, not less pernicious for another sort of women, and no less in urgent need of reform, is the privileges granted by your police to our modern Lais's – women who, under the protection of nefarious bargains with the authorities, make their houses into a rendezvous for every sex, age and condition, an abyss where those rash enough to let themselves be ensnared lose their morals as well as their fortune. That species of women, accustomed to all risks, finds no problem in assuming a grand name and a livery; and this glittering masquerade, concealing their baseness from inexperienced eyes, is a further snare, often not recognized by their prey till they are securely caught. The lucre gained from this profession is so great that women of position and repute do not blush to join it, to rescue their shattered fortunes or, by a show of luxury, to sustain (though really to degrade) their good name.

It is not for us, Sirs, to enquire whether gaming-clubs are absolutely necessary to great cities and to your Capital; but we believe it our duty to invite you to consider the fatal idleness of those men who pass their days and nights there, having nowhere else to alleviate their crushing uselessness.

A third source of national immorality is the tolerance by the police of the obscene prints with which your public squares, your promenades and your quaysides are covered. These objects, gathered from all quarters, corrupt the eyes of infancy, presenting it with the idea of vice and justifying its turpitude. Let us leave to courtesans, to the unhappy creatures in whom all the springs of Nature have grown slack, these miserable refinements of an expiring pleasure. If they can still make some impression on jaded hearts, what a conflagration must they not produce in those who need no more than a spark to ignite them?

We see respect for public morals violated, equally, in art galleries, where it should be protected by a prudent selection of the subjects exhibited. The purpose of all the imitative arts, destined to perpetuate virtuous and heroic actions and to reproduce before us the varied scenes of Nature, ought to be as pure as Nature herself in her noble or her smiling scenes. They ought to join in reinforcing national morals and Virtues and not in degrading them by compositions which cannot excite admiration without offending decency. Seeing the loves of Paris and Helen, the picture for which Zeuxis chose his models from the most beautiful of the daughters of Greece, would not a modest wife be tempted to cover their nudity with a veil?[5]

Shall I speak of our innumerable little theatres which, lacking the dignity of the National one, attract an audience by licentiousness? Shall I speak of that mass of Citizens incapable of enjoying a sweet and pure morality, a modest and delicate enthusiasm, people whom Thalia could not please if her festivals were not orgies and her gaiety the most shameless cynicism? In such theatres, it will soon be impossible to use even the least discreet equivocation. None of the imitative arts is safe from the general contagion; dancing, that art which causes us to wonder, with thoughtful enjoyment, at the finest potentialities of a supple and vigorous body, is sometimes prostituted in the very sanctuary of taste and made to reproduce movements and postures fit for the den of the vilest debauchery.

Such, Sirs, believe me, are the sources of the corruption of our morals. This is what causes the degeneration of a nation and transforms a proud and courageous people into an inert and enfeebled multitude, too weak to break the fetters of despotism and prejudice.

'Parisian women', says Jean-Jacques, 'accustomed to seeing men everywhere and to mixing with them, have the same pride, the same audacity, the same way of looking and, very nearly, of walking.' Why did he not say the same Virtues, the same courage, the same elevation? He would have been more rightly praised for this. Milord Chesterfields [*sic*] was no more just in regarding French women as overgrown children, to be amused with toys, vanity and gallantry.[6] Bayle defends us against these detractors when he says: 'The whole war they wage against us is no more than telling us things they do not believe.'

We have this advantage over you, Sirs, that we women of letters have never dipped our pen in the gall of satire. Dignifying ourselves with your Virtues, adorning ourselves with your glory, we are not so inconsistent as to divert you from the rugged paths where a noble ardour leads you, by ascribing the virtuous principles which motivate you to vanity. It would not be difficult, by a misuse of wit, to wither your laurels by a cruel analysis of the actions of legendary heroes. That heroic deed of Horatius, for instance, so celebrated in history, might be considered as no more than the action of a clever and lucky soldier, who owed his triumph more to the overconfidence and negligence of his enemies than to his own courage. A Brutus and Manlius, who condemn their own children to death, against the advice of the Senate and despite the People's prayers, might seem like barbarians rather than ardent Citizens. Scaevola might seem a madman, deadened by rage to his own pain, and the Deciuses and the Curtiuses as fever-victims, throwing themselves out of the window in a transport of sickness.

If all that is needed to be counted a hero is to kill oneself, how much stronger are the rights to this title of Thisbe, the tender Sappho, the ill-starred Hero, the unfortunate Jocasta, the daughter of King Belus who throws herself in a river to save Lavinia from suspicion, Sophonisba and Dripetine, who kill themselves so as not to be captured by the Romans, etc.

Love of country, of liberty and of glory animate our sex as much as they do yours, Sirs; we are not, on this earth, a different species from yours. The mind has no sex, any more than does Virtue; but the vices of intelligence and the

heart belong almost exclusively to your sex. It is painful for me to declare this
harsh truth, but one is sometimes allowed to take one's revenge. A modern
writer has dared assert that women can scarcely understand a political idea, if
in the least wide-ranging and difficult, though he grants them admirable notions
of domestic order and economy. He adds that, though strangers to patriotism,
they are firmly attached to the gentle pleasures of sociability.[7] Who then has
given this writer the measure of our abilities, for him to circumscribe them so
boldly? Such an opinion is the product of mere prejudice; it is the natural result
of despotism and of the yoke imposed on us by an imperious sex which, in the
dawning of the world, found itself stronger than the companion bestowed on it
by a kindly Nature and therefore decided it must be superior in everything. If
the qualities of intelligence and courage depended on the strength or weakness
of muscles, such a ridiculous theory would pull the crown from the head of
delicate princes, placing it on the thick skull of a Swiss or a Hollander. The
courageous deeds of the physically weak, such as the valorous Turenne and
many other warriors, and the sublime and universal genius housed in a frail
frame like Voltaire's, refute that miserable hypothesis.

Moreover, we should be as robust as you if, from an early age, we were
trained in painful and laborious exercises. 'If', says Plato, 'the excess of humidity
which weakens the vigour of women, making them softer than men, were dried
by moderate exercise, reducing their complexion to a more just and exact
equality, their bodies would be more agile and more robust.'[8] 'We have seen
women', says Le Moine, 'who have freed nations from oppression, have driven
victorious armies from captured cities, have given force and courage to defeated
kings and restored lost crowns and fallen thrones. The miracles achieved from
time to time by the hands of women prove that these hands, more tender though
they be and more attuned to wool and silk, are no less fitted for great actions; a
long skirt does not impede heroic Virtue or prevent it from pursuing glory.'[9]

The modesty assigned to women by Nature and the Laws confines their
Virtue to the shadows. Their first duty being to be heard not seen, they are
forced to perform behind the curtain. They cannot appear on the world's stage
until special circumstances call for their presence; then they appear with as much
dignity as the most experienced men.[10] In what genres have they not distinguished
themselves? Many are famous in *belles-lettres*; the names of Giovani, Desroches,
Barbier, d'Aulnoy, de la Suse, de la Sablière, Lambert, the celebrated Agnesie,
Villedieu, Deshoulières, Sévigné, Genlis, Beccary are known to all.[11]

We deserve no fewer eulogies, and no less censure, than yourselves, Sirs.
Some women are the shame of their sex, some are its glory; nothing will curb
the former in vice, nothing will arrest the latter in the painful path of Virtue.
Your sex is not more free than ours from this contrast; for what motives, then,
could you pronounce a *nolle prosequi* on this demand of ours to the right to
contribute with you to the public welfare, in the legal sphere which concerns us

alone? One sex has not been appointed the oppressor of the other, and these ridiculous debates about superiority offend against Nature. You are born our friends, not our rivals, and we emulate you. To reduce us to slavery is to abuse a force which was given you to defend us; it is to deprive Society of what gives it charm and life. It is to imitate Orientals who, combining brutal passion with a sense of their own weakness, put women in chains, to prevent women doing the same to them. Those arrogant masters, victims of their own jealous tyranny, search in vain for true feeling, which, like the delicate pleasure which goes with it, is only to be found where there is liberty.

The empire which we wield through beauty is only given us for the good of the human species. The character of the male, destined to strong actions, has a roughness which it is our task to correct; a gentleness in our manners, even more than in our features, is designed to soften that natural pride of yours which otherwise degenerates into ferocity. From every point of view, man would be less perfect, less happy, if he did not converse with women. He who is insensible to commerce with women, who refuses it, has an inflexibility that renders his very Virtues dangerous. Charles XII is proof of this. His great qualities would not have troubled Europe had he lived more with women; their Society would have softened his wild courage, and he would not have refused to see the Countess of Königsmark, when she came to him with proposals for peace.[12] In our absence, Sirs, your imagination is inactive, your productions are without grace, your philosophy is sombre and harsh; in your absence, ours become too frivolous. It is by commerce with you that our talents and qualities develop and acquire solidity. From this exchange of mutual aid there flows a happy concord which brings both of us nearer to perfection, the faults of one sex correcting those of the other, and in this way women, whatever you do, will always be central to life in Society. Your having charge of public affairs only reinforces our value. The human species conducting itself more by the heart than by the mind, the direction of public affairs, whoever is responsible for it, is always influenced by what is loved. Accordingly, Sirs, you will always do what we want. Where women command, men reign, and when women reign, they prove that they possess the science of government in the highest degree.

The English were never so powerful as under the reign of Elizabeth. Women in France, though excluded from the throne, have none the less played their part in government during various royal minorities. Queen Blanche proved that she deserved more than a mere regency; her maxims are the Code of good kings.[13] Catherine II, reigning in the north at this moment, will be the model for conquerors. Though the snarls of jealous pride endeavour to tarnish the splendour of her great qualities, she will none the less occupy an honourable place in history! The men of Rome, too jealous of their own authority, allowed women no part in government; but in France, where custom and Nature grant them an influence, one could not fail to benefit by entrusting to them Legislation on manners and morals, the more so that 'the question of morals', as Jean-Jacques observes, 'is not regulated like matters of individual justice and strict Law. If the Law ever has an influence on morals, it is when it is drawing its force from them.'

If, Sirs, our annals prove our aptitude for all that can make our talents useful to the public good, it is particularly to the civic Virtues that they should be applied, since these Virtues are better protected by our sex than by yours, distracted as your sex is by restless ambition, blinding it to what is actually around it.

Women, being sedentary by habit, devote themselves entirely to the place and the duties assigned to them. As a result, they have more respect for their sovereigns, more submissiveness towards their superiors, more respect for their equals, more compassion for the unfortunate, more attachment to their relatives, more attentiveness to their children, more love for their spouse. If one doubted the last, it would suffice to read the history of all nations to convince oneself; women carry conjugal love to great heights of heroism. Hipsicrates, Chelone, the Roman Sulpicia, Alcestis, Portia, Artemis and Arria are the first who present themselves to my memory, without speaking of the wives of Malabar, for their religious prejudices might be held against me. Women, like men, prefer to kill themselves rather than outlive their honour. Evadne, Comma, Lucretia, names consecrated for many centuries, Clusia etc. leave no doubt of this. If the Virtues have decayed, they can be reborn from their ashes, the same fire is still in our hearts. Be to us what the husbands of those illustrious women were, and you will find us as devoted as they.

'If you want to know men,' said the celebrated Citizen of Geneva, 'study women. In every country, in every state, in every condition, the two sexes have so strong, so natural, a connection that the morals of the one always determine those of the other.' If you take firm hold of this truth, Sirs, if you study all the various social networks where, in varying degrees, the subtle influence of women is felt; if you calculate the evil and the good which result from their presence in Society; if you look back to those times when they assigned ranks and distributed prizes – you will hasten to grant them this honourable ascendancy which, making your Laws more effective, and perhaps more just, will revive in them those Virtues which are the measure of yours. If moral Laws derive their force from opinion, it is on women that they will have most sway. If some vestiges of Virtue remain, it is among women that it will be found, since shame, modesty, gentleness are Virtues natural to us, which nothing can destroy in our sex as completely as in yours. To correct morals, says Montesquieu, you must first possess them. Which of the two sexes, therefore, is the more fit to revive them, according to this theory, if not the one which has retained more of them; the one which, suffering the full rigour of the Law, is singled out for public disgrace for a temptation common to both sexes; the one, finally, to which you are subordinated both by

Nature, who depends on uniting our desires with yours, and by Law, whose function it is to sanction this? To want to satisfy one's desires without the consent of her who has kindled them, says Jean-Jacques, is the audacity of a satyr. The Virtue most indispensable to women, the one which gives them the greatest moral claim on you, is modesty; here lies the 'point of honour' for our sex, as bravery is for yours. Our ancestors referred all Virtues to those two headings: courage in men, chastity in women. A woman without modesty, they would say, will trouble a State as much as she does a private circle.

What would they think, therefore, of the shameful disorders your police system has allowed to grow up, to the detriment of that Virtue? It has been calculated that there are thirty thousand prostitutes in Paris, possessing no means apart from what vice can procure them.[14] The periodical raids, in which three or four hundred are seized in a month and crowded into a prison, do not achieve their purpose, any more than they redeem the women themselves, for their place is soon taken by as many again. A clumsy procedure of this kind will not destroy this vermin engendered by centuries of corruption. It is not by great acts of authority, or covert police activity, or the venal and unfeeling application of ordinary Law, that Society will cultivate the fruits of women's civic sense. Legislation on these matters calls for a delicacy incompatible with the spirit of conventional Law. It requires responsiveness, and sympathy for the weak; a feeling approach and farseeing views; a supple and pliable hand, which restrains without heavy-handedness, animates without effort, commands without superiority, is firm without rigour, corrects without causing offence, threatens without antagonizing, and persuades with those graces of manner that can win over the most rebellious individuals.

If it is true that finesse and tact of this kind call for flexibility rather than force, must not one look to women to supply them? Morality is the more their speciality in that they are born to it; it is they, Sirs, who teach you the first elements of moral behaviour and stamp you with the traits of character which will decide your glory, your Virtues and your destiny. They engrave your duties upon your soul; they weave the bonds which attach you to Society; they prepare your daughters for the intimacies of marriage. Thus to make them Legislators on morals would be to restore them a right which Nature assigned to them and of which only an ill-conceived political system has deprived them.

The setting up of a female jurisdiction would not be an innovation; history offers examples from all over the world. The Ethiopians put the administration of their provinces in women's hands; according to Mandesto,[15] it is women who govern in the isle of Borneo, their husbands being merely the most distinguished of their vassals. In the West Indies the Achinois are always governed by a queen, in Virtue of a Law which one might call anti-Salic and which forbids a man to mount the throne. Many countries are administered solely by women. In the island of Formosa the sacerdotal ministry is exercised by them. Aristotle tells us that they took a large part in government among the Spartans. Among the Peoples of Germany they were represented in all councils. Have the goodness to remember, Sirs, that the women of Gaul had such a high reputation for justice that it was enacted that if a Gaul offended a Carthaginian, the case should be judged by Gaulish women. The Gauls, divided into sixteen cantons, had for a long time a general council of women, chosen by the various districts. A similar tribunal functioned in Greece. In Ireland, women established themselves as a Senate in each province, without the Parliament in Dublin regarding this as a breach of its dignity. France herself offers examples of women's courts.[16] Though the one which existed under Charles VI was only for enjoyment and entertainment, it had a real influence on manners and morals. Cardinal Richelieu thought highly enough of it, and was sufficiently aware of its political value, to try to re-institute it, but in his day morals were no longer what they had been. Grown degenerate, women lost the sway given them by religious opinion in the age of chivalry and came at last to that degradation which places them under the bold and unskilful hand of the Law.

At this moment when the happiest revolutions are in the making and when, tired of the political vices and excesses caused by the decay of Law and morals (destroyed, like human beauty, by the ravages of time), you are attempting to restore these latter to their first vigour (under which our ancestors saw the honour of our sex flourish, for their esteem equalled their love), we hope that, touched by the truth of these remarks, you will ask us to collaborate with you in your great work of renovation, taking charge of all that concerns our sex's morals, which are the rampart and defence of yours. If order, the foundation of Society, depends especially on the Virtue and decency of women, if regard for this constitutes their honour, as your 'point of honour' is courage, and if your Laws refer matters of masculine honour to a unique and supreme tribunal,[17] why should we not have ours too? Is it because, from fear of our severity, preference is given to the present system, which allows your sex free play to its criminal passions, loading all the opprobrium on to ours? No, a motive so injurious to its glory cannot be at work in the virtuous and heroic men today who compose the august Assembly to which we appeal: men immune from all seduction and over whom our charms have no power, in whom love lights no fire and who, for that very reason, can count it as a patriotic duty to offer us national restitution.

Already my soul, inspired with the sense of their equity, takes a leap into the future; already I see, rising above the piled ruins of despotism and prejudice, the majestic tree of liberty, its branches sheltering the whole of Society; already I see the debased jurisdiction [of the morals police], which gave protection to scandalous disorders for its own profit, replaced by an august College, able to revivify public decency and, by its prudent dispositions, to recall to order those unhappy rebels against discipline who are the shame of one sex and the destruction of the other.

Project for a National Tribunal, concerned exclusively with, and presided over, by women

Mode of Organization

Two methods suggest themselves for creating this tribunal: the first requires two divisions, one entitled the Chamber of Conciliation, and the other entitled Civil Chamber.

Fifty women would sit in the Chamber of Conciliation, eighty in the Civil Chamber; these women would be chosen from among Citizenesses noted for their reputation for morals, Virtues and talents. To say as much amounts to naming them.

Purview of the Chamber of Conciliation

I. Examination of Separation cases, such as could only be brought before ordinary Courts on appeal. It will easily be seen that the intervention of this Chamber would frequently prevent Lawsuits which bring shame and ruin upon families, as in the recent case of Madame de Kornmann.[18] Husbands, on bringing their complaints before this Tribunal, would often receive benefit from a gentle reprimand, an adroit exploiting of their embarrassment, and from fear of publicity.

II. Submission of the motives for a voluntary marital separation to this Tribunal, which would rule on the form it should take and would minimize motives which damage a woman's public reputation.

III. Widows will depose against the bad conduct of their daughters, emancipated after their father's death. In the case of mothers' authority being too weak to control them, the daughters will be required to justify themselves.

IV. A young woman will not be allowed to enter a convent, even with the intention of taking vows, without having formally declared that it is by her own free choice. This usage will prevent the abuse of authority which often leads fathers and mothers to compel their daughters, either by ill-treatment or by direct command, to take the veil, in order to improve the prospects of a son, a nephew or other object of their predilection.

V. Brothers and sisters, and male and female cousins, will not be allowed to sue in the regular courts without prior deposition regarding their motives at the Tribunal, or having appealed against its decree.

VI. All disputes between the two sexes will be submitted to the Tribunal.

VII. Promises of marriage, made before the legal age of majority, which would be harmful to a young man's social position or that of his family, will be annulled by the Tribunal if the young woman is clearly shown to have acted the part of seducer. In the contrary case, she will be authorized to pursue her rights in the superior Courts. If the young man is the older by as much as two years, this will be regarded as a presumption against him.

Purview of the Civil Chamber

(This second division will concern itself solely with matters of public scandal.)

I.   Abuses of confidence committed by women who form liaisons under a veil of decency.
II.   Violent quarrels in private households, testified to by neighbours.
III.   Rash words and behaviour of women designed to foment quarrels between men.
IV.   Women caught in disgraceful activities in public places.
V.   Promissory notes signed thoughtlessly before the legal age of majority and later challenged by the debtor.
VI.   Refusal to return jewels or other such objects taken contrary to the wishes of the owner.
VII.   Too frequent card-parties in the same house, arousing suspicions that its mistress is running a gambling establishment.
VIII. The conduct of actresses of all kinds will come under the Tribunal's jurisdiction.

All the suits brought before this Tribunal will be investigated and pleaded to by means of simple depositions without charge to the parties concerned, or by counsel chosen from the same sex as the plaintiff or defendant. All judgements will similarly be without fee and be purely correctional.

Location of the Tribunal

A very large *hôtel* will be required, of which the main building will be allocated to the Court of the Tribunal. Of two other subsidiary buildings, forming its wings, one would be assigned to the elderly sick and poor, the other would house workshops for unemployed women and offer lodging to the homeless.

In 1787 M. Faydit de Tersac, parish priest of Saint Sulpice, as enlightened as a Legislator as he was virtuous as a pastor, saved four or five thousand members of his parish from the horrors and dangers of poverty.[19] Their industry, together with support from benevolent people inspired by his zeal, brought in enough to meet the full cost of the establishment.

Who could take these benevolent Virtues further than an august Tribunal presided over by the Dames de France, whose humanity keeps them continually engaged in philanthropic work – among them Madame Elizabeth,[20] whose

Virtues have always shone with the same lustre, and Madame la Duchesse d'Orléans,[21] whose very name brings a tear to the eye of the poor, both in country and in town! If to these princesses one adds women whose Virtues are their prime claim to the honour of membership of this Association, what resources would the maternal hands of this august Court not offer to the poor!

To the right to punish must be joined the wish to reform. The secret of success, here, is to distinguish the guilty person who has been driven to crime by the imperious law of necessity from the one who resorts to it from natural bent. It is not surprising if a man, sentenced to the galleys and losing all his links with Society, should on his return commit new crimes, often greater than the ones for which he was first condemned – finding, as he does, no support in the legal system which blasted his reputation or in the human community which banished him from its bosom. Such is the fate of women whom the authorities lock up in a hospital. They come out poorer and more corrupt: poorer, because they have spent all they possessed there; more corrupt, because when vice comes into contact with vice, the result is brazen shamelessness. In this licentious captivity, many of these women, still at the tender age at which bad impressions could be reformed, but hardened by the maxims of those who led them astray or by the desertion of those who suborned them, lose all self-respect and self-control.

I have already said that it has been calculated that there are thirty thousand prostitutes in Paris, with no source of subsistence apart from vice. Among this number there are many whom lack of employment or situation leads to a total moral dereliction, but who could be rescued, by our establishment, from the abyss of prostitution to which they are miserably reduced.

If the King has sacrificed, and still sacrifices, large sums for a Royal School of Music, a nursery for children destined for public entertainment, supplying it with numerous Masters, how much greater a claim on his benevolence would be a refuge for poverty and a shelter from crime: a place where there would be no excuse for idleness and vice and where manufacture in wool, linen and embroidery, as well as training workshops, would give occupation to the vermin who infect our streets, our gardens and our public squares, and would offer them the education which ought to be the birthright of all – I mean reading, writing and the rules of trade. These unfortunates need no more to lead a decent existence, perhaps, than a modest subsistence and a secure roof over their head. When one considers the mortifications which must accompany their vile mode of life, exposing them to such cruel insult, it is plain that only sheer destitution, or the lack of any foothold in Society, could lead women to it. The State would be saved the cost of the hospitals where these unfortunates are now herded, to no good purpose other than to line the pockets of Administrators, the penalties inflicted on offenders against public decency rendering them unnecessary.

Disciplinary methods will be a matter for discussion in the Tribunal, if such should be established.

Second manner of proceeding towards the creation of the Tribunal

The most desirable plan would be to appoint for the coming month of May
[1790] an Assembly of the élite of women from our Provinces, who, coming to
join those appointed by the Capital, would collaborate with them in drawing up
our Laws. The devising of these would be the more satisfying in that such an
array of enlightenment would ensure that they were wise. However well
conceived a plan devised by a single individual, it will always be inferior to
one improved in the light of discussion. It should be with the shaping of our
statutes as with those of the Nation generally. The King, who in his paternal
goodness summoned the enlightened élite of men now engaged on that great
task, cannot forget that we women form part of his great family. He cannot be
unaware that fathers take charge of the education of their male children and
leave that of their daughters to the mother. We demand, with the confidence
that his justice inspires in us, to be subjected to the same maternal authority, the
one assigned to us by Nature and implicit in the relations of the sexes.

Letter to the Author from President Linch[22]

I have read with the greatest interest, Mademoiselle, the work which you have
had the kindness to send me. The subject and the author excited my curiosity as
greatly as the performance has satisfied it.

I would not dare assure you that the august Assembly will adopt your plan,
but I have no doubt it will be glad to receive it. It does honour to the sex which
has the art of instructing and pleasing and whose lessons have so much more
power over us than those of cold Philosophy.

You kindly ask me my opinion; I shall tell you it frankly.

Your project is excellent as regards our present state of morality; but if I
had the honour to be one of the Legislators of the Nation, I would make it my
aim to render it useless by transforming our morals through the instrument of
good Laws.

To make marriages easy and happy, to abolish idleness, to cause celibacy
to be a matter for scorn: these in my opinion would be the proper means to
adopt.

If mothers would apply themselves to giving their daughters good ideas of
morality, would teach them to despise luxury and to found their happiness on
the tranquil and sweet pleasures of the household, they would be making a
great step towards reforming our manners.

Nevertheless you must not imagine I make your sex responsible for our
low morality; I am convinced on the contrary that men, in purifying their morals,
will bring about the reform of women's.

I dislike the idea of your Chamber of Conciliation. Why a Tribunal to reconcile us with our wives? Would it not be better to prevent us quarrelling? Your Civil Chamber should be without functions, or we shall be without happiness.

You will tell me, Mademoiselle, that my ideas of order and perfect union are metaphysical and too elevated for humanity; that according to my views we could also abolish Tribunals. No, but before we set up Tribunals, let us frame good Laws.

It would be worthy of your pen to precede your project for a Tribunal with a species of moral Code suited to the most lovable half of humankind. No one is better fitted than yourself to execute this interesting project.

You paint with great skill the horrors of prostitution and the dangers of corrupt stage performances; you prove splendidly that your sex is the emulator of ours in all genres. But do not make it ambitious to surpass us in the arts, in government, in literature. This is not what will make for its happiness, nor for ours. Rather tell it that it has a different path to the same end, and a surer and more glorious one than ours. We men chase after the (often illusory) recompense of a brilliant reputation, whereas women devote themselves both to the happiness of individuals and of Society without ambition and for no reward save their own inward satisfaction.

I have taken the liberty of giving you my opinion with frankness. You wished for it, and it is a sure testimony to the value I place on your confidence in me and of the sentiments with which I have the honour to be,

Mademoiselle,

Your very humble and obedient servant,

LINCH

Paris, 14 November 1789.

Reply

Everything under your pen, M. le President, moves swiftly and soars confidently over the most delicate point in our Legislation, the reform of morals. Thus the methods you propose offer me a large field for comment.

I know that your talents will give you an infinite advantage in this combat of opinions; thus it is less to maintain, than to correct, my own that I shall risk defending it.

'Change morals by the influence of good Laws', you say, Monsieur? But while our moral habits defy the Law, and while the executive is weak, we must rebuild morality in order to see the Laws observed and respected. May I remind you that before raising a great building an architect takes soundings of the ground, to be sure it can bear the weight? The wise teacher does not begin by drawing up Laws, however good in themselves; he first of all considers whether those they are aimed at are capable of observing them.

It is certain that good morals on the part of a People were always the foundation of Laws and the guarantee of their effectiveness. 'Plato', writes Rousseau, 'refused to give Laws to the Arcadians and the Syrians, because they were rich and could not reconcile themselves to the principle of equality. That is why, in Crete, one sees good Laws and bad men.'[23]

The French run no risk with regard to the second but certainly do so regarding the first. If anything weakens the parallel, it is the progress of enlightenment, which, having made such advances here, disposes our fellow-countrymen to co-operate by a unanimous will in reforming the vices of their Legislation, for which they generally feel the necessity. But however resigned they may seem to the sacrifice of their prejudices; of their wealth, unjustly gained at the expense of the People; and of their hereditary titles, honours and privileges, which created an inequality shocking to Reason; it is to be feared that the fervour of the initial moment, the effect of an irritation which united all classes against a Despotism oppressive to all of them equally, may weaken and that a reaction may recall them to that the spirit of domination, which powerful groups naturally tend to usurp and increase.

Already you will have observed the exclusion introduced by the decree of the silver *marc*, restricting eligibility for a post under the Administration.[24] One might add the rejection of juries for civil courts, which leaves the new judicial bodies with the all the vices so justly condemned in their predecessors.

Still too near to the Revolution, it is to be feared that the new Legislation may retain some of the savour of the old abuses. Nothing is more difficult to overcome than the spirit of domination. For this, circumstances will need to have turned a rich and powerful nation into a poor and subjugated one; only then will that despotic spirit, and the vices that go along with it, be extinguished, together with its gold and its power. We have not yet reached that point.

In the present situation, you cannot attempt to reform morals in the way adopted by Lycurgus, when he undertook to regenerate the Spartans. When Lycurgus was framing his Laws, as Rousseau has remarked, he only had a city to discipline; here we have a powerful nation, secure from insult by its neighbours, and with no call to defend itself or embark on conquest. Its Legislators do not have the same scope as Lycurgus, who was able to conquer and reform the vices of the Spartans and to change their habits, their affections, their prejudices and their egoism, converting these into love of country – in a word, to make them a People of heroes.

Nor is this a raw and ignorant People whom one can guide by the authority of the Gods, as Numa did so skilfully in the infancy of the Roman People, using frivolous and superstitious practices to make them into men and induce them to respect morals and the Law. No, it is a feeling and enlightened Nation, in which all superstitious ideas have been extinguished; if any vestiges of these remain, it is in certain ancient root stocks which will put out no more branches.

It is therefore in no danger from the prejudices of some or the bellicosity of others. Mature enough to know the wise maxims of Politics and to lay solid foundations, we shall (as Jean-Jacques required) see social affection as not merely the hoped-for fruit of the new regime but presiding over its very formation.

It is from respect for women that there will spring a perfect harmony between the social Virtues and the practical ones; they alone knew how to tame the savage Coriolanus and win him back for his fatherland.

What a sway will that powerful voice have over the hearts of the French who, despite their errors, have retained that precious sensibility which makes them respond to the accents of grace, gentleness, beauty and the charms of the intelligence.

A successful Legislator must know how to harness the dominant affections of a People to his legislative views.

In France, where women have strengthened their influence by their talents and by the acquisition of knowledge which they have sought for themselves, they ought, in that sphere I have assigned to them exclusively over manners and morals, to have as much authority in the Administration as a mother does in the running of her home.

I believe that to refuse them this would be both unjust and impolitic.

You may object, Monsieur, that women's morals have decayed equally with men's, making them unfit to co-operate in reforming yours. I have already answered this objection and believe I have refuted it and have justified our admission to the purely civil and disciplinary part of the administration.

If one considers the advantages to morality, which I have made clear, the value of my plan is hard to deny.

The august character acquired by women from the dignity of their functions will act on them like the lustral water sprinkled upon Roman wives, purifying them before they set foot in their husband's house.

But let us move on to the rest of your objections, Monsieur, which I mean to analyse in due order.

'To make marriages easy and happy': that is the thing, Monsieur, that seems to me most difficult of all, if Divorce is not established; for indissoluble marriage is an unnatural bond which almost always ends up a burden to those who have contracted it. I know of no rasher pledge than the vow of eternal fidelity sworn by two individuals before the altar; it can uttered only by imbeciles, by children, or by dishonest people, who submit to it merely as a formula carrying no weight.

According to Jean-Jacques in his *Social Contract*, all institutions which put the human being at odds with himself or herself are worthless. Is there an institution more diametrically opposed to the order of Nature, or more prone to defeat its own purposes, than that one which claims to fix for ever, and deprive of all mutability, the attraction which impels two individuals to seek after each other and to unite?

Of all social Laws, the most difficult to frame concerns the civil union of the two sexes. If it goes too much against Nature in the matter of constancy, tending to make it a kind of external compulsion, its precepts are bound to be ineffectual. That is why all the force, both human and divine, lavished upon Catholic marriage and in laying down the respective duties of the partners, has been, is, and always will be insufficient. All you create with these two shackled beings is two convicts, fighting each other and gnawing at their chain – a chain that one day is bound to break.

If, on the analogy of Augustus, one were to line up married people and unmarried ones in separate ranks, one would be astonished, as the Romans were, to see how many more there were in the second rank than in the first.[25] It is a gross error of moralists to regard this as the cause of the present decay of morals; the cause lies, rather, in the vices of canon Law, which has imprinted on marriage through its priests a quality of inviolability which Nature condemns.

'When there are no longer barbarian nations,' says Bacon, 'and civilization and the arts have weakened the human species, one will find mankind very little concerned to marry.'[26] He is certainly right, for civilized men, deviating from the immutable principles of Nature, will strive to subordinate her to their political schemes. If we consider man in the wild state, we see, as Jean-Jacques observes, that all women are equally good for him.[27] Follow him in his advance towards civilization, however, and we see him stray further and further from Nature and become a tyrant to himself. I search in vain the history of the first Peoples for a system of marriage like ours, neither can I find such an absurd one among Peoples who have filled the earth with the fame of their wisdom and achievements. It is a very strange thing, and one cannot too much marvel at it, that the matter nearest the heart of man's happiness, and which indeed is the very principle of it, has become through our Laws a source of bitterness poisoning life. Can there be a torture equal to being thrown for ever on the company of a person who has become incompatible with our tastes, our character and our pleasures? I see that, among all nations, divorce was thought necessary to end such a disparity; and the earliest schemes for legitimizing the union of the sexes were infinitely superior to those of later times. The Hebrews offer us an example. Marriage, among this People still close to Nature, was of a simplicity which ensured it far greater respect than all the ceremonies later invented to burden it. The father was the High Priest of the celebration; he drew up the marriage contract and wrote it and sealed it, and its articles were religiously observed. He placed his daughter's hand in her husband's and united the pair with his paternal blessing. Festivities, continuing for seven days, proclaimed the joy and harmony which rendered these unions as happy as they were decent in the manner of their forming. Rustic labour was the husband's share, household cares the wife's. It is in this simple form that marriage is, as Montaigne says, a sweet Society of usefulness, justice, honour and an infinity of good and solid services. Nature, unaided, prescribes all its duties.

Marriages of this kind were of necessity long-lasting, from the imperious obligation of parental feeling, which strengthened the bonds formed by love, and prompted parents to work together for their children's education, until such time as they could fend for themselves. In these marriages, where greed or questions of fortune and social position played no part, one would never find the monstrous alliance of old age and childhood; they were a union of two individuals as young and eager as each other. Despite this, the man, not suffering the changes undergone by women from the trouble and labour of childbearing and the accidents that can follow this, inevitably retained his vigour longer than his wife, who often would have lost her powers of procreation whilst he still possessed his in full. Acordingly, such was the happy simplicity of manners, he would acquire a second wife, without injury to the first, who would accept her as companion and friend. Thus, by wise resignation, the first wife would retain all the rights of tender friendship over her husband's heart. Her old age would be preserved from the cruel and shameful desertion suffered by wives today, when satiety, the loss of their charms, or straying affections dry up their marriage. The younger wife would be subordinate to the elder, through the deference due to the objects of their husband's affection, and the two women would combine in efforts for his happiness and the welfare of the children. What a happy time it was for husbands!

The vanity of French women would perhaps rule out such an arrangement for them. But what does their own situation bring with it? A clandestine affair on their husband's part, which they soon discover and which may ruin their fortune and even endanger their health. Their pride, which suffers more than their heart, produces a state of civil war which ends by making the husband a stranger in his own house. If, on the other hand, as tender spouses, they swallow their chagrin and try to win back their husband's heart, all they obtain is a pretended reconciliation, achieving the happiness of neither the one nor the other. Those, again, who take their husband's infidelity as a right to follow suit, suffer the full severity of the Law, which tolerates in the one what it forbids to the other. Separations, an often ignominious captivity, a meagre pension, depriving them of the comforts to which their fortune entitles them, such is their fate. Is not the modest resignation of Hebrew women incomparably preferable to our pride?

I am also aware of a form of marriage among the Greeks and the Romans which left them all the liberty which Nature demands, and which she reclaims when deprived of it. These marriages were contracted by the cohabitation of the partners for the space of a year, during which, if the wife had not spent three nights out of the house, her rights were regarded as legalized. By this means the parties assured themselves of their mutual suitability. It is true that at this period the Romans had two manners of contracting marriage. The first was the one I have just described, its sole purpose being to legitimize the children. The other, an amalgam of politics, pride and worldly interest, subordinated their women, like ours, to the Laws of continence and absolute dependence on their husband. It is to be presumed that the women who contracted it preferred the honorific privileges it brought, and the rights to their husband's estate that it gave them, to the liberty offered by the former method. Indeed, would it have befitted a Roman empress to follow the simple usages prescribed by Nature? It would have been altogether too low-bred for the majesty of the Purple. But it is to be noticed that Nature, who always resents Laws which injure her, made illustrious harlots out of these princesses, so that their husbands would end by repudiating them. One might feel surprised that the form of marriage among the Romans called *Excoemptionem*[28] should have prevailed over what was called *Matrimonium ex usu*,[29] if one did not know that the more that nations increase in power and civilization, the further they depart from Nature and the less they consult her in framing their Laws. One needs only reflect on the spirit of the ceremonies for marriage by *Excoemptionem* to realize it could only have triumphed over its rival in despotic times.[30]

I doubt whether the pride of the first Roman wives would have allowed them to bow their heads under the yoke which marriage imposed on them in the reign of the Emperors. One cannot observe without pity and contempt the spirit which the two most enlightened nations on earth revealed, by helping to perpetuate their absurd Laws on marriage.

What! Canon and civil Law only recognize as a legitimate father the person they have constituted as such, even though he himself may often not recognize it! They stretch their authority so far as to make him endow with his name and possessions, and dignify with his hereditary honours, a child produced by his wife during an absence of years, or whilst living with her in a state of absolute continence, so giving him the inward certainty that he played no part in the birth! This is to push the abuse of power to its very extreme.

It is to these plaguing abuses, rather than the decay of morals, that one must attribute men's disinclination for marriage.

The Catholic religion was the prime mover in this. Unable to dominate Peoples save by supernatural ideas, and by the celestial kingdom it offered to its proselytes, rendering them profoundly scornful of the kingdom of this world, it was easy for its apostles to detach them from their civic duties and natural affections, directing their hopes on to a future so superior to the present. Thus there was formed a crowd of cenobites of both sexes, who vowed themselves to an absolute negation so as to win a place in the heavenly vault on the right hand of the Eternal.

It was human pride which relished the delicious prospect of a place in the next world, consoling them for their abject one in this and raising them in their opinion above all the powers and principalities of the earth. Fortunately for the human species, the greater number of its members found this vision illusory.

It was not long before the clear-sighted rebelled against the tyranny of chimerical opinions, which the priestly spirit could only manage to impose upon the timid and the idle. The study of Nature arose as a rival to dogma and triumphed over it. Nature even came to occupy the leisure of cenobites who, observing it at work, noticed that it seemed indifferent to time, and that a Creation a mere four thousand years ago could not explain its products. With that observation doubt commenced, and their vocation dwindled in the course of their laboratory experiments; though the comforts of the monastic life served to prolong the devotion of some and encourage the recruitment of others. As enlightenment spread, the ministers of the Church found a new freedom. Like Gods, they descended from their seraphic throne to commune with shepherdesses. Soon they insinuated themselves into the boudoirs of our Sovereigns and of our belles, taking possession there. It is thus that the lure of an indefinite liberty, cloaked with a sacred mantle, propelled them into every kind of human enjoyment, without sacrificing the prerogatives awarded by human credulity. Under the pretext of a direct relationship with the Eternal, the successors of the humble Apostles were to be seen aspiring to temporal sovereignty and, by an extraordinary progression, becoming the dispensers of grace in this world and the next. It is to this power, created by the imagination and maintained by political astuteness, that one must attribute desertion from the standard of hymen. Holy Mother Church endowed its children and its husbands so well, it was bound to gain the preference.

To these political causes, we must add the natural causes conected with the indissolubility of our marriages. It is not within the power of man or woman to love at will, any more than to hate at will. The strongest desire, drawing two individuals together by the feeling known as 'love', has a fixed term of existence, which is almost always briefer than constancy would imagine. The commonest causes of this are the instability of physical appetites, which are easily diverted by a new and exciting object, or satiety, which extinguishes them. It is one thing to desire each other, another to possess. How much consideration, how much deference, living together requires! The least collision destroys the charm. One must fear the first quarrel above all, says La Bruyère. In countries where good morals have more force than good Laws do elsewhere, there is, so moralists tell us, no condition so happy as marriage. But this is only true up to a point: in so far, that is to say, that the only thing the marriage has to fear is the march of time, and time's power to destroy or to prolong the feeling which first prompted it.

Further, which are these countries? People no doubt have in mind Switzerland and other Protestant lands, where the idle and corrupting race of priests, abbots and monks does not proliferate, and where, despite the absence of those vermin so prone to prey upon wives, divorce is allowed (for without this latter, happiness would still be very uncertain). The chain of hymen is for these Peoples only a wreath of roses, whose thorns they remove when they begin to prick too sharply. The result is an attentive consideration on the part of spouses, a mutual regard, a responsible behaviour, such as alone can preserve a union intact. The wife's modesty prolongs the effect of her charms, and if time at last withers them, a tender friendship takes the place of love. Hence a century may pass with scarcely a single divorce. What a contrast between the effects of liberty and those of our coercive system!

What befits Peoples in closely confined communities, immediately under the eyes of the laws, is not, you will tell me, suited to large States and to great capital cities, where luxury, and all the objects of seduction it brings with it, will cause liberty of this kind to be abused.

But the abuse of this liberty can never entail the public scandal with which incompatibility between husbands and wives makes our tribunals so continually echo.

At this moment when the Rights of Man, too long ignored, are the object of a new Constitution designed to restore them, none is more important than the one claimed by Nature: the liberty to dispose of one's own person. It ought to be as possible to free oneself as it was to bind oneself, with the sole condition that a provision be made for children, it being the purpose of marriage to give them legitimacy. The Law should only intervene as the children's protector, to establish their interests and assure these by the authority of a juridical act.

It is only on this basis that one will re-establish public decency and domestic harmony. The more that manners emancipate themselves, the more flexibility the Law should have; for the passions are, and always will be, stronger than its authority, which nevertheless must not be compromised. There are no more powerful passions than hate or disgust. When they arise between two spouses, no human or divine power can overcome them, indeed can only make them worse. Only by divorce can you allay them, only by divorce can you recall mankind to the unions prompted by Nature and make marriages truly easy and happy.

It is no doubt pride, and the ambition of powerful Peoples like the Greeks and Romans, which induced them, for the greater glory of their family, to favour marriage by *Excoemptionem*, which bestowed on the children of a single union the honours and riches of a whole house. Such considerations, which are equally the basis of our own system, should be rejected as null from the moment that titles, honours and inheritances come to be divided equally between all offspring. No one has perhaps realized the true reason behind the French custom of giving the whole family inheritance to the eldest son; it is because the legitimacy of the first child seemed the least open to doubt. I find a proof of this form of reasoning in an ancient custom of Normandy, which acknowledged legitimacy only up to the fourth child. Also, the rule of primogeniture has persisted there right up today, when it has just been abrogated in France.[31]

Another aspect of the indissolubility of our matrimonial unions is physical incompatibility between the partners, rendering the wife sterile. The purpose of marriage being procreation, this is a defeat both for Law and for Nature. Only Sovereigns, in such a case, are released from their vows; but has Nature less right than politics to such a release? Every civil convention should have the same Laws. The one which makes me proprietor of a piece of land gives me the right to exchange it for another, if the soil disappoints my expectations; all the more ought I to have the right to separate from a wife who does not give me the precious harvest I expect, or allows another the tillage.

The only answer to these difficulties is to allow divorce; only this, securing the legitimacy of children, can give them an unshakeable hold on their father's heart. The Law having decreed the equal sharing of an inheritance, they will no longer have to fear the growth of weeds among their pasture. The children legitimized by a new union will never do them as much harm as ruinous Lawsuits between their guilty parents. There will at least be no stain on their birth; and, the fruitful channels of the arts, commerce, industry and places of trust being open to them, they may soon hope for independence.

Let our Legislators look at the Peoples among whom divorce is practised. They will see that the children are infinitely happier there than among us, fortunes being more equitably distributed and prosperity being more general. Such Peoples consider, however, that, the status of father continuing infinitely longer than that of child, the father's convenience should be consulted before the children's. Destined to become fathers themselves, the children have an interest in the encouraging of happy unions, where the rights of Nature are not sacrificed to an uncertain posterity. The happiness of children is a result of happiness on their fathers' part, no doubt, but they ought not to be allowed to compromise this happiness.

These considerations will, no doubt, compel our Legislators to abrogate an indissolubility which injures the Rights of Man and affects, in so many ways, the happiness of the partners to ill-assorted unions. It is the duty of education, both public and private, to work towards this liberation, which will assure the happiness of present generations and those to come. Let us see on what bases these principles should rest in order to obtain the best results.

Postscript

As I close this discourse, Monsieur, the *Mercure* for 6 February of the present year 1790 announces a work on the question of divorce and prints a criticism of its principles by M. de Marmontel.[32]

This well-reasoned work earned the esteem of its readers. I doubt if M. de Marmontel's feeble arguments will do much to change this. Here are some of them, which seem to me very unworthy of this Academician's pen.

'Fully to know what Nature requires of Man', says M. de Marmontel, 'one needs to look at man in the state of Nature. Now, in the natural state the long infancy of man evidently demands the continuity of the conjugal union. The succession of children born from the same union prolongs it and renders it indissoluble until that age when the father and mother, no longer young enough to make new ties, are going to be in need of each other and of the support of their children.'

The order of Nature is to create. It matters little to her whether all the beings fashioned by her hands are bred by the same female or the same male or are produced by the same union. The mother will always be provided by Nature with their first nourishment and, without the father's help, will be able to protect their weakness. I shall not waste time convincing M. de Marmontel of this eternal verity. It is also agreed that Nature, in her great wisdom, has made fathers very little dependent upon their children. If it had been part of her plan to make the latter necessary to them, she would have provided children with some power of protection for the weakness of age akin to that of mothers for the weakness of infancy. The sole refuge of old age is Society; it is in its bosom, its humane benevolence, that old age must look to for its protection. How many old men have seen, and see, their progeny expire and yet can do without them? Matters are different with the weakness of infancy and the need for maternal affection. But from the moment that childhood gives way to adulthood, the adult's own family becomes its prime care. Law as well as Nature excuse it from filial duty. 'Thou shalt quit thy father and thy mother', runs the divine precept, 'to follow thy husband.' If a man has to choose between saving his father or his son from some danger, his duty is clear: he flies to rescue his child and bestows a few simple tears on the father he is unable to save.

That is the natural order of things, unknown to the sophisticated M. de Marmontel. 'Temporary marriage', he says, 'would have destroyed the human species; and the grand design of Nature has been the conservation and reproduction of species.' What an absurdity! And what an abuse of words! 'The grand design of Nature' – how impressive that word 'grand' is for some readers, and how ridiculous to others! If anything could destroy the human species, it would be the fetters our matrimonial Laws impose on the union of the sexes. Before they existed, were there fewer people upon the earth? Are the States where Catholic marriage is not practised less highly populated? China and other empires prove the contrary. But high population does not suit our European governments; it is in the interest of those with power to limit abundance to their own needs, external and internal, and to the sum of their wealth. Politics acts in this respect as we do with domestic animals, when we rob them of two thirds of their offspring to prevent them losing their fatness.

Let M. de Marmontel therefore cease to find philosophical reasons for maintaining the present forms of marriage. Let him admit honestly that it is on the grounds of social conventions that he disapproves of divorce. If he does, we shall ask him if these social conventions are compatible with the needs of individuals.

He will object, no doubt, that what proves that the Law of divorce is repugnant to Nature is that the nearer man is to the state of Nature, the less he is permitted divorce.

It is an argument he may cherish if he chooses; for myself, I cannot see how he would prove it. One has the impression he has no conception of man in the state of Nature, that is to say obeying simple human Laws.

There would be no better way to instruct him than to send him on a tour among the Hurons. He would see there that the less civilized a man is, the less he is inclined to give up his liberty.

Entering, with the author of the inestimable work that he is refuting, into ill-starred households where everything bears the marks of disorder and unhappiness; from which loving confidence, innocent joy and sweet liberty have been banished; where the wife, shrewish, half-mad and unfaithful, fills her husband's heart with bitterness; where the man, perpetually dour and threatening, inflicts the tortures of hell on a virtuous wife; households where inextinguishable flames burn, without consuming executioner and victim alike. Witnessing these scenes, says M. de Marmontel, there is no one who will not cry 'Let the Law separate them', and the Law does in fact separate them. But this is not divorce; and it is divorce that is required, that is to say the freedom to form other ties.

Yes, that is the liberty that one demands, and has the right to demand, since woman, destined by Nature for the state of maternity, can only proceed to it under the authority of the Law. If the collaborator allotted to her, under the Law, is a tiger instead of a man of good will, she has the right to inform the Law of the snare she has fallen into. It is not enough for the Law to separate them, it must give her the right to re-marry, as a person still young and not having fulfilled her procreative role. To refuse is to condemn her to a sterility offensive to Nature and such as our forefathers held up to scorn.

'Let the barren fig tree be cut down and burnt', said the man-God.[33] By what perversity, then, does civil Law come to thrust itself above divine and human Law?

'It would nevertheless be fairly rare', observes M. de Marmontel, 'for the two innocent parties whom we have seen so unhappy in the bonds of a first marriage to want to expose themselves to the same regrets for a second time; and as to the guilty parties, I tremble to think of the Law giving them the terrible freedom to make further partners unhappy.'

This sentiment does more honour to M. de Marmontel's heart than to his logic. We can inform him, for his reassurance, that in the countries where divorce is permitted, it denies to the guilty spouse the freedom to enter into new marriages. In addition, when two spouses have absented themselves from each other, and give each other no proof that they are still alive, they become free to re-marry. In these countries, the absent are in the wrong in the eyes of the Law as in those of Nature.

As to the crimes which are regarded as authorizing divorce, M. de Marmontel need have no fears; they are clearly identified by the Peoples (as wise as they are enlightened) who have established this practice. One can find examples of such a judicial system near at hand, and we need do no more than copy them.

Further, we would remark to M. de Marmontel that nothing is more common than for a widow who was maltreated by her first husband to take a second, who seems to promise her consolation for her wrongs.

'Widowhood' proceeding from divorce has this advantage over widowhood resulting from death, that the visible contrast between the gentleness and Virtue of the one party and the bad character of the other brings the guilty one into public contempt and wins sympathy and esteem for the innocent one.

To prove to M. de Marmontel just how optimistic women can be, when death releases them from a wicked and vicious husband, one could do worse than remind him of the anecdote of the widow whose three husbands were hanged. The first husband of this woman, who was herself a fishmonger and an excellent character, joined a gang of brigands, the Raffiats, who terrorized Paris with their crimes, and he was hanged. The same with the second. Then there was a third, who was broken on the wheel into the bargain. She refused a fourth, so she said, for fear of his getting burnt at the stake. There are people whom misfortune makes obstinate and determined not to be beaten. M. de Marmontel would tell us that only men devoid of all shame could marry a woman so closely related to the gibbet. Well, he would be wrong there too. All her three husbands, when she married them, had a reputation as fine fellows; they became the instruments of clever villains, who led them into crime through the lure of debauchery.

Notice, I beg you, Sir, the clever trick M. de Marmontel uses to discredit our author's argument, when he writes: 'If divorce does not permit infidelity and does not render it innocent, inconstancy will soon have the art of escaping from these bonds, and it will be criminal.'

With what malign satisfaction does he skilfully use the following argument to discredit divorce: 'Must the Law be the ally of vice and authorize it, instead of stigmatizing it?'

M. de Marmontel could not genuinely have so misunderstood our author's moral argument. Here is how I interpret it myself. If divorce does not restore a person his rights, your Laws make resort to it a crime. Now, a Law which creates crime is a monstrosity in the social order.

'Shall the Law', continues M. de Marmontel, 'remove the sole remaining dam against immoral behaviour?'

Well! What is it, here again, that makes it immoral, if not that very dam, as impotent perhaps to control this kind of flood as the watery kind?

'Ah! let what is bad be bad,' concludes M. de Marmontel, 'and let shame be, if not a brake to it, at least its punishment.'

What! Am I to be ashamed of not still loving a husband who poisons my life with miseries of every kind? Am I to kiss the mouth which abuses me, the baleful eye which threatens me, the hand which batters me? Am I to cherish the faithless woman who lords it in my household, who receives rivals and corrupters in my absence, who maltreats and neglects my children, who ruins me, wrecks my days, and, as the mistress of some great man, has me imprisoned ... etc., etc.?

M. de Marmontel here speaks neither as a philosopher nor an enlightened jurist. A true philosopher needs to defend the legitimate rights of Nature; a good jurist will show what Laws will reconcile those rights with natural public order.

Retracing his tracks, M. de Marmontel says: 'No, the evil will not be the same; and the need to alleviate the worst ills of a union, given that it is indissoluble, and to accommodate oneself to it rather than exacerbate it, has often done more than might be thought to reconcile warring hearts and minds. One should never underestimate the forces of necessity.'

No, but when its fetters draw blood, we may simply succumb. The only relief for unhappy wives and sensitive husbands may be tears, followed by death or madness.

Reconcile warring hearts and minds by the Law of necessity: what barbarous logic! It is a recipe fit only for despotism, which for so long has wielded its infernal sway over poor humanity.

Moreover, no power could in fact work the miracle of which he speaks. It is not a case of 'making a Virtue of necessity'. It is plain that M. de Marmontel knows the human heart only from his study and under the influence of an amiable wife, who shelters him from any notion of the chaos of real life. Were he actually to experience the sort of unhappy plight he discusses, he would find that the worst horrors of incompatibility, and the torture they cause to husbands, and even more so to wives, arise precisely from such an accepting of the forces of necessity.

'It is above all in countries where morals still count for something', says Jean-Jacques, 'that the jealousy of lovers and the vengeance of husbands continually cause duels, murders and even worse; where the duty of eternal fidelity merely serves to produce adulteries; and where even the Laws of continence and honour seem bound to increase debauchery and multiply abortions.'[34]

The authority of that observation by Jean-Jacques, founded upon continually renewed evidence, should convince M. de Marmontel of the insufficiency of his own views.

'The Law of divorce', says its champion, 'is the greatest preservative against divorce. As soon as it becomes possible, it becomes almost unnecessary; as soon as it is permitted, it become very rare and practically dies out.'

But M. de Marmontel persists in fearing that, in countries where immorality reigns, divorce will make it worse. As fear is an emotion very hard to cure, I will not make the attempt; I will do no more than warn my weaker readers of its contagiousness.

As to the fate of mothers and children, a matter on which he seems to feel strongly, he should have confidence in the enlightened wisdom of our Legislators, who will provide for this important concern with sagacity and justice.

I do not see why the Laws dealing with inheritance should not proceed in regard to civil 'widowhood' in the same way that they do when one of the partners has died, since the spouse who is stripped of the title of spouse by divorce and is declared incapable of forming a further union is no better than a dead bough as regards his family and public order. Separated by this decree from the trunk, from which his branches grew, he becomes dead to them as if he did not exist, and under no circumstances could they be put into his charge.

A virtuous father could not but be indignant to see the Law of property-sharing extended to his children, the objects of his love, and the education of his daughters put in the hands of his guilty wife. For the same reason a tender and virtuous mother would be as indignant to see a barbarous husband and unnatural father, who has destroyed her fortune, authorized by the Law to look after her sons. But I do not, and must not, anticipate what our Legislators will decree; it will be enough if I can have proved to M. de Marmontel, and perhaps to yourself, Monsieur le President, that indissoluble marriage is as impolitic as it is against Nature; that it is a prime source of our moral corruption as of many crimes. That 'vile self-interest', so well described by Voltaire, is the only rival to it that I know of as a creator of atrocious deeds.

FINIS

Notes

1.   (Jodin's note) 'Everyone knows that the police regard prostitutes as a necessity in great cities. Is it not to tolerate them in a sense to sacrifice them to these pretended "needs"?'

2. (Jodin's note) 'M. de l'Isle de Salces, 'Epitre à Senêque, 1er Volume du *Théâtre d'un Poète de Sibérie*, page 8.' (In error for Delisle de Sales, *Théâtre d'un poète de Sybaris*.)

3. 'formed by Nature for attack' is an echo of Rousseau, *Émile* (1760), p. 322.

4. A work by the novelist, Restif de la Bretonne, published in 1769, which recommended 'Parthenions' or public establishments for prostitution, and proposed a lengthy Code of regulations for them.

5. Jodin seems to be getting slightly confused over the story of the painter Zeuxis, reputed to have combined the features of the five most beautiful women of Crotona to form his 'Helen'.

6. Lord Chesterfield, 'Women, then, are only children of a larger growth' (letter to his son, 5 July 1748).

7. See Antoine-Léonard Thomas, *Essai sur le caractère ... des femmes* (1772), pp. 142–5.

8. Jodin has taken this reference to Plato from le Moyne, *La Galerie des femmes fortes*, pp. 154–5.

9. Le Moyne, *La Galerie des femmes fortes*, p. 47.

10. (Jodin's note) 'The Countess of Guebriant' [Renée, Comtesse de Guebriant (1600–59); she undertook various diplomatic missions].

11. Juliane, Duchesse Giovane (?–1805), miscellaneous author; Madeleine Des Roches (sixteenth century), patroness of literature; Marie-Anne Barbier (1670–1745), dramatist; Marie-Catherine, Comtesse d'Aulnoy (*c.* 1650–1705), author of fairy tales; Henriette de Coligni, Comtesse de la Suze (1618–73), poet; Magdeleine de la Sablière (1536–1693), famous for her scientific interests; Anne-Thérèse, Marquise de Lambert (1647–1733), famous literary hostess; Margarita Agnesi (1718–99), mathematician; Catherine des Jardins, Mme de Villedieu (1640–83), novelist; Antoinette Ligier de la Garde (1638–94), poet; Marie de Rabutin-Chantal, Marquise de Sévigné (1626–96), the celebrated letter-writer; Félicité Ducrest de Saint-Aubin, Mme de Genlis (1746–1830), governess of the Duke d'Orléans's children and author of *Adèle et Théodore*, a celebrated education novel; Mme Beccary (fl. 1760–80), novelist. Almost all the women mentioned in Jodin's list figure in the *Dictionnaire portatif des femmes célèbres* (1788) by Jean François de La Croix, on which she is no doubt drawing.

12. In 1702 King Augustus of Poland sent the Countess of Königsmarck on a secret embassy to sue for peace with Charles XII of Sweden, but the misogynistic Charles refused to see her.

13. Blanche of Castile, mother of Saint Louis and for years his Regent.

14. (Jodin's note) 'See the *Tableau de Paris*' (of Louis-Sébastien Mercier).

15. Jean-Albert de Mandelslo (1616–44), German travel writer, author of *Voyage aux Indes* (1645).

16. (Jodin's note) 'See the learned researches of President Roland, on the prerogatives of Gaulish women.'

17. (Jodin's note) 'That of the Marshals of France.'

18. Mme de Kornmann, the young Swiss wife of the Alsatian banker Kornmann, was imprisoned by *lettre de cachet* at his instigation, on grounds of adultery. Beaumarchais, who in 1781 succeeded in getting the *lettre de cachet* revoked, was later victimised for his part in the affair.

19. Faydit de Tersac, parish priest of Saint-Sulpice, made vigorous efforts to secure the death-bed conversion of Diderot – to no effect, though Diderot held amicable discussions with him about his philanthropic work. Tersac had previously attempted to convert Voltaire, in similar circumstances.

20. Sister of Louis XVI. A pious woman, who did much work among the poor during the bitter winter of 1789. She went to the guillotine in May 1794.
21. Louise-Marie-Adelaide, Duchesse d'Orléans (1753–1821) was the wife of the Duc de Chartres, inheriting the d'Orléans title in 1787.
22. Jean-Baptiste Lynch (1749–1835), Président aux enquêtes in the Bordeaux Parlement, an ardent royalist, imprisoned during the Terror but made Pair de France in 1815. A friend of Jodin from her period in Bordeaux in 1768-69.
23. See Jean-Jacques Rousseau, *The Social Contract* (1762) trans. Maurice Cranston (London: Penguin Books, 1968), Book II, Ch. 8.
24. A Law of 22 December 1789 made the possession of some land and an obligation to pay direct taxes equivalent to a *marc d'argent* necessary qualifications for election to the National Assembly. Critics objected that this would have excluded Corneille, Rousseau, Mably and Jesus Christ.
25. Jodin has clearly taken this detail, and others, from the article 'Mariage', by the Chevalier de Jaucourt and Boucher d'Argis, in the *Encyclopédie*.
26. Quoted verbatim from the *Encyclopédie* article on 'Mariage'.
27. See Rousseau's *Second Discourse*, 'De l'Inégalité parmi les hommes', ed. J. Ehrard, (Garnier: Paris, 1975), p. 62.
28. Literally, 'marriage by purchase'.
29. That is 'marriage by use and custom'.
30. (Jodin's note) 'See the *Encyclopédie*, under the word "Mariage".'
31. A decree of the National Assembly of 24 February 1790 ordered equality in the division of inheritances.
32. Jean-François Marmontel (1723–99) was an enormously prolific writer and journalist, best known for his Moral Tales. His review of this anonymous work on divorce, Hennet's *Du Divorce* (1789), appears on pp. 18–36 of the *Mercure de France* for 6 February 1790.
33. See Luke, xiii, 6–9.
34. See Rousseau's *Second Discourse*, 'De l'Inégalité parmi les hommes', p. 63.

Poésie

'Vers à Mlle Jodin'[1]

Fière *Jodin*, accepte mon hommage,
Je ne viens point offrir des voeux à ta beauté,
Tu méprises ce ton, doucereux, affecté,
Et pour te plaire, il faut parler en sage.

Plus d'une fois la jalousie
A déjà contre toi signalé ses horreurs,
Tu fais des ennemis de tes admirateurs
Et tes succès irritent leur furie.
En serois-tu surprise? Un bourgeois hébété
Meurt, comme il a vécu, dans la tranquillité,
Mais les destins doivent être contraires
A ces esprits élevés, transcendans,
Qui se livrant toujours à leurs fougueux élans;
Se tiennent éloignés des routes ordinaires.

Rarement les mortels daignent rendre justice;
Le génie a brillé toujours à ses dépens,
Et le ciel fait fleurir la palme des talens
Sur les bords escarpées d'un affreux précipice.
Pour te soustraire à tous les maux
Que doit entrainer à sa suite
L'éclat brillant de ton mérite;
Voudrois-tu renoncer à tes nobles travaux?
Peu sensible aux attraits d'une gloire durable,
Et de tes ennemis, craignant la lâcheté,
Aux malheurs éclatans de la célébrité,
Voudrois-tu préférer le repos méprisable?
Que peut l'offrir l'obscurité?
Tu le voudras en vain. Le goût que la nature
Imprima dans ton coeur, dès les plus jeunes ans,
Plus fort que ta raison et tes conseils prudens,
Te feroit détester une existence obscure.

Si tu peux redouter les retours inconstans
D'un Parterre guidé par l'aveugle ignorance
Vole à Paris; le séjour des talens
Mérite seul d'être ta résidence.
C'est-là que tu pourras trouver

Des Spectateurs que le bon goût éclaire.
C'est-là que règne aussi la critique sévère,
Mais elle est juste, et tu dois la braver.
Clairon qui captivoit jadis tous les suffrages,
S'est dérobée à ses succès.
Et ne veut plus recevoir les hommages
Que lui prodiguoient les François
Dans le sein d'une douce yvresse
laisse couler les jours de sa beauté,
Et pour son coeur qu'énerve la mollesse
Un instant de plaisir vaut l'immortalité.
Paris enfin n'a plus d'Actrice:
O sublime *Jodin*, ce moment est propice!
Melpomène l'appelle aux honneurs de son art
Des mains de Dumesnil va prendre son poignard.

MM

1.   Mlle Jodin est une Actrice distinguée par des talens très-rares pour les rôles de Mlle Dumesnil. Elle a joué avec le plus grand succès sur différens théâtres de nos Provinces et en Pologne. Il seroit à souhaiter que, dans la détresse où se trouve le nôtre, pour cet emploi, elle voulût se prêter aux voeux de ses amis qui l'appellent à le remplir. Cette pièce où on lui donne le conseil, nous a paru dû être connu du Public. *Journal de Politique et de Littérature*, Tome 3e – à Bruxelles 1775, pp. 394–5. Becomes *Journal ou Gazette de Littérature*, 25 November 1775.

Bibliography

Manuscript Sources

Archives Départementales de Seine et Marne.

Archives Municipales de la Ville de Bordeaux: Fonds Anciens, DD-GG and 'Correspondance de Richelieu'.

Archiwumksiecia Jozefa Poniatowskiego I tersy Tyszkiewiczowej pod sygnaturami: Jodin 'Procès', Témoignage des Comédiens, 444 (karty 113–36) I 445 (karty 281–2).

Bibliothèque de l'Arsenal: Archives de la Bastille, 12, 124 (1761) ff. 160–210 – relating to Jodin's imprisonment in la Salpêtrière, 1761.

Bibliothèque Municipale de la Ville de Tonnerre: Archive du Chevalier d'Eon.

Bibliothèque Nationale: Fonds Anisson-Duperon 87, Librairie Lettres et Mémoires sous M. de Malherbes, FR 22147 (103–4).

Bibliothèque de la Pologne: Manuscrit 58, Jean Heyne, Archiwum Ks. Ksawerego Saskiego t. III, no. 222, 224.

Brotherton Library, Leeds: Special Collection, d'Eon Collection.

Landesarchiv Magdeburg: Rep. H Beetzendorff, II, II – Landeshauptarchiv Aussenstelle Wernigerode, Journal of Werner von der Schulenburg XXV.

Museum Narodwe W Krakowie: Czartorski Library, MSS. 711.

Statenskancellie for Udenlandske Affairer: State Archive Regi, Copenhagen, SKUA pa-al 49, Sachsen B, 1764–68.

Staatsarchiv Dresden: Reglement: 1768–1770, Ausgemartet ff. J. Kaster, 'Theater u Musick; Acla Schauspiele und Redouten Anno 1767–1768 vol. IV, Loc. No. 200, 908, 2713.

Printed sources

Abray, Jane, 'Feminism in the French Revolution', *American Historical Review*, 80, no. 1 (1975), pp. 43–62.

Albistur, Maïté and Armogathe, Daniel, *Historie du féminisme français* I (Paris: Des Femmes, 1977).

Aghion, Max, *Le Théâtre à Paris au XVIIIe Siècle* (Paris: Librairie de France, 1960).

Alasseur, Claude, *La Comédie Française au 18e siècle: étude économique* (Paris: Mouton et Cie, 1967).

Algemeine Deutsche Biographie, 6, ed. Elben-Fickler (Leipzig: Duncker and Humblot, 1877).

Amoia, Alba, 'Sixteen Unpublished Letters (1767–1776) of Baron Frederic-Melchior Grimm to Albrecht Ludwig, Count of Schulenburg', *Diderot*

Studies XIX, ed. Otis Fellows and Diana Guiragossian Carr (Genève: Librairie Droz,1978), pp. 15–53.

Anderson, Matthew Smith, *Europe in the Eighteenth Century 1712–1783* (London: Longman, 1961).

Andrews, Stuart, *Eighteenth-Century Europe: The 1680s to 1815* (London: Longman, 1965).

Angenot, Marc, *Les Champions des femmes* (Québec: Presses de l'Université de Québec, 1977).

Baack, Lawrence J. 'State Service in the Eighteenth Century: The Bernstorffs in Hanover and Denmark', *The International History Review*, I: 3 (1979).

Babeau, Albert, *Paris en 1789* (Paris: Firmin-Didot, 1889).

Bachaumont, *Mémoires secrets*, (1768), IV vols (London: Adamson, 1784).

Baker, George Pierce, ed. *Some Unpublished Correspondence of David Garrick* (Boston: Houghton Miflin and Co., 1907).

Baker, Keith Michael, 'French Political Thought at the Accession of Louis XVI', *Journal of Modern History* L (1978–79), pp. 279–303.

———, *Inventing the French Revolution: Essays on French Political Culture in the Eighteenth Century* (Cambridge: Cambridge University Press, 1990).

La Barre de Raillicourt, *Richelieu le Maréchal Libertin* (Paris: Tallandier, 1991).

Bell, Susan Groag and Offen, Karen M., *Women, the Family, and Freedom: the Debate in Documents*, I, 1750–1880 (Stanford California: Stanford University Press, 1983).

Berlanstein, Leonard R., 'Women and Power in Eighteenth-Century France: Actresses at the Comédie-Française', inAdams, Christine, Censer, Jack B. and Graham, Lisa Jane, eds, *Visions and Revisions of Eighteenth-Century France* (University Park: Pennsylvania State University Press, 1997).

Benabou, Erica-Marie, *La Prostitution et la police des moeurs au XVIIIe siècle* (Paris: Perrin, 1987).

Bénard, J. A. called Fleury, *Mémoires de Fleury de la Comédie Française (1757–1820)* (Paris: Dupont, 1836).

Benrekassa, Georges, 'Diderot et l'honnête femme: de Mme Necker à Eliza Draper', in *Denis Diderot 1713–1784, Colloque International*, Choillet, Anne-Marie, ed. (Paris: Aux Amateurs de Livres, 1985), pp. 87–97.

Bérenger, Laurent Pierre, *De la prostitution: Cahier et doléances d'un ami des moeurs, adressé spécialement aux députés de l'ordre du Tiers État de Paris* (Paris: au Palais Royal, 1789).

Bernacki, Ludwik, *Theatr, Drama, Muzyka za Stanislawa Augusta* (Lwow: Wydawnictwo Sakladu Norodowejo Imienia Ossolinskich, 1925).

Besterman, Theodore, ed., *Voltaire Correspondence* LXVII and LIII (Genève: Institut et Musée de Voltaire, 1961).

Billy, André, *Vie de Diderot* (Paris: Flammarion, 1932).

Blum, Carol, *Rousseau and the Republic of Virtue: the Language of Politics in the French Revolution* (Ithaca: Cornell University Press, 1986).

Bonnel, Roland and Rubinger, Catherine, eds, *Femmes savantes et femmes d'esprit: Women Intellectuals of the French Eighteenth Century* (New York: Peter Lang, 1994).

Bosher, J. F. *French Finances 1770–1795: from Business to Bureaucracy* (Cambridge: Cambridge University Press, 1970).

Bouet, François 'Le Palais-Royal de 1784 à 1831: les commencements d'un théâtre célèbre', *Les Oeuvres Libres*,153 (1934), pp. 293–338.

Boysse, Ernest, *Journal de Papillon de la Ferté (1756–1780)* (Paris: Paul Ollendorf, 1837).

Brewer, John, 'This, that and the other: Public Social and Private in the seventeenth and eighteenth centuries', in Castiglione, Dario and Sharpe, Lesley, eds, *Shifting the Boundaries: Transformations of the Languages of Public and Private in the Eighteenth Century* (Exeter: University of Exeter Press, 1995).

Brombert, Victor, *The Romantic Prison: the French Tradition* (Princeton: Princeton University Press, 1978).

Burke, Edmund, *A Philosophical Enquiry into the Origin of Our Ideas of the Sublime and the Beautiful* (1757) (London: University of Notre Dame Press, 1968).

'Cahier du Tiers État de la Ville de Paris', *Archives Parlementaires de 1787 à 1860*, Première série (1787–99) I (Paris: Paul Dupont, 1879).

Campbell Orr, Clarissa, *Wollstonecraft's Daughters: Womanhood in England and France 1780–1920* (Manchester: Manchester University Press, 1996).

Casanova, *Mémoires*, Aberached, Robert, ed. (Paris: Bibliothèque de la Pléïade, 1960).

Castries, Duc de, *La du Barry* (Paris, Albin Michel, 1986).

Chartier, Roger, Compère, Marie-Madeleine, Julia, Dominique, *L'Education en France du XVIe au XVIIIe siècle* (Paris: Société d'Edition d'Enseignement Supérieur, 1976).

Chesterfield, *Lord Chesterfield: Letters Written to his Natural Son on Manners and Morals* (Mount Vernon: Peter Pauper Press, 1936).

Chevalley, Sylvie, 'La Civilisation des comédiens', *Revue de la Société d'histoire du théâtre*, I: 161 (1989), pp. 50–56.

Clairon, *Mémoires de Mlle Clairon* (Paris: Ponthieu, 1822).

Coward, D.A. 'Eighteenth-century Attitudes to Prostitution', *Studies on Voltaire*, 189 (1980), pp. 363–409.

Cranston, Maurice, *Jean Jacques: The Early Life and Work of Jean-Jacques Rousseau* (London: Allen Lane, 1983).

———— *The Noble Savage, Jean Jacques Rousseau 1754–1762* (London: Allen Lane, 1991).

Creech, James, *Diderot: Thresholds of Representation* (Columbus, Ohio: Ohio State University Press, 1986).

Danneil, Johann Friederich, the younger, *Das Geschlecht der von der Schulenburg*, 2 vols (Salzwedel: 1847).

Davis, Tracy C., 'Private Women in the Public Realm', *Theatre Survey: The Journal of the American Society for Theatre Research*, 35: 1 (May 1994), pp. 65–72.

Devance, Louis, 'Le Féminisme pendant la révolution française', *Annales historiques de la révolution française*, 229 (July–September 1977), pp. 341–76.

Diderot, Denis, *Correspondance*, Roth, Georges, ed. (Paris: Editions de Minuit, 1959–63).

———, Denis, 'De la Poésie dramatique' (1758), in Chouillet, Jacques and Chouillet, Anne-Marie, eds, *Diderot: Le Drame bourgeois* (Paris: Herman, 1980).

———, Denis, 'Paradoxe sur le comédien', *Oeuvres Complètes*, X: Lewinter, Roger, ed. (Paris: Club français du livre, 1971), pp. 414–90.

———, Denis, 'Sur le femmes', *Oeuvres Complètes*, X: Lewinter, Roger, ed. (Paris: Club Français du Livre, 1971), pp. 28–60.

Duhet, Paule-Marie, *Les Femmes et la Révolution 1789–1794* (Paris: Julliard, 1971).

Dupleissis, Georges, *Mémoires et journal de J.-G. Wille, Graveur du Roi* (Paris: Jules Renouard, 1857).

Durand, Yves, *Finances et Mécénat: les fermiers généraux aux XVIIe siècle* (Paris: Hachette, 1976).

Edits, Déclarations et Arrests Concernans la Religion P. Réformée 1662–1751 (Paris: Librairie Fischbacher, 1885).

Estrée, Paul d', *Le Maréchal de Richelieu (1696–1788)* (Paris: Emil-Paul Frères, n.d.).

Evans, Richard J. *Tales from the German Underworld* (New Haven and London: Yale University Press, 1998).

Favart, Charles Simon, *Mémoires et correspondance littéraires, dramatiques et anecdotiques*, 3 vols (Paris: Collin, 1808).

Farge, Arlette, *La Vie fragile; violence, pouvoirs et solidarités à Paris au XVIIIe siècle* (Paris: Hachette, 1986).

Farge, Arlette and Revel, Jacques, *Logiques de la foule, l'affaire des enlèvements d'enfants, Paris 1750* (Paris, Hachette, 1988).

Flandrin, Jean Louis, *Families in Former Times*, (1976) trans. Southern, Richard (Cambridge: Cambridge University Press, 1979).

Fontenay, Elisabeth de, *Diderot ou le matérialisme enchanté* (Paris: Grasset, 1981).

Foreman, Amanda, *Georgiana, Duchess of Devonshire* (London: HarperCollins, 1998).

Fraisse, Geneviève, *Reason's Muse: Sexual Difference and the Birth of Democracy*, trans. Todd, Jane Marie (London: University of Chicago Press, 1994).

Fuchs, Max, *Lexiques des troupes de comédiens au XVIIIe siècle* (Paris: Librairie Droz, 1944).

Funck-Brentano, Frantz, *La Bastille des comédiens: le For l'Evêque* (Paris: Fontemoing, 1903).

Furbank, P. N., '"And We Are Citizens Too": Diderot and Marie-Madeleine Jodin, Actress and Feminist', unpublished MS.

———, *Diderot: A Critical Biography* (London: Secker and Warburg, 1992).

Gardener, Elizabeth J. 'The Philosophes and Women: Sensationalism and Sentiment', in Jacobs, E., Barber, W. H., Bloch, J. H., Leakey, F. W. and Le Breton, E., eds, *Women and Society in Eighteenth-Century France* (London: Athlone Press, 1979).

Gasbarrone, Lisa, 'Voices from nature: Diderot's dialogues with women', *Studies on Voltaire and the Eighteenth Century*, 292 (Oxford: Voltaire Foundation, 1991), pp. 259–91.

Gelbart, Nina Rattner, *The King's Midwife: a history and mystery of Mme de Coudray* (Berkeley: University of California Press, 1998).

Gelfand, Elissa D., *Imagination in Confinement: Women's Writings from French Prisons* (Ithaca and London: Cornell University Press, 1983).

Genlis, Mme la Comtesse de, *Adèle et Théodore: où lettres sur l'éducation* (London, 1792).

Ginisty, Paul, *Souvenirs de Mlle Duthé de l'Opéra* (Paris: Louis Michaud, 1909).

Giroud, Françoise, *Les Femmes de la révolution* (Paris: Jules Michelet, Carrère, 1988).

de Goncourt, Edmond, *Mademoiselle Clairon, d'après ses correspondances et les rapports de police du temps* (Paris: 1889).

———, Edmond and Jules, *The Woman of the Eighteenth Century*, trans. le Clercq, Jacques and Roeder, Ralph (London: Allen and Unwin, 1928).

Goodman, Dena, *The Republic of Letters: A Cultural History of the French Enlightenment* (London: Cornell University Press, 1994).

———, 'Epistolary property: Michel de Servan and the plight of letters on the eve of the French Revolution', in Brewer, John and Staves, Susan, eds, *Early Modern Conceptions of Property* (London: Routledge, 1995).

Gordon, Daniel, *Citizens without Sovereignty: Equality and Sociability in French Thought, 1670–1789* (Princeton: Princeton University Press, 1994).

Goubert, Pierre, *Les Français et l'ancien régime* (Paris: Armand Colin, 1984).

Grimm, Melchior, *Correspondance*, Maurice Tourneux, ed., VI (Paris: Garnier Frères, 1877–82).

Guerinot, J. V., *Pamphlet Attacks on Alexander Pope 1711–1744* (London Methuen, 1969).

Habermas, Jürgen, *The Structural Tansformation of the Public Sphere*, trans. Burger, Thomas and Lawrence, Frederick (Cambridge: Polity Press and Blackwell Publishers, 1992).

Hatton, Ragnhild, *George I Elector and King* (London: Thames and Hudson, 1978).

d'Holbach, Paul-Henry, *Système de la Nature* (1766) ed. Yvon Belaval (Hildesheim: Georg Olms, 1966).

————, *Système Social ou Principes Naturels de la Morale et de la Politique avec un Examen de l'Influence du Gouvernement sur les Moeurs* (London: 1773).

Holstrom, Kirsten Cram, *Monodrama, Attitudes, 'Tableaux vivants'* (Stockholm: Almqvuist and Wiksell, 1967).

Hufton, Olwen H. *Women and the Limits of Citizenship in the French Revolution* (Toronto: University of Toronto Press, 1992).

Hunt, Lynn, ed., *Eroticism and the Body Politic* (Baltimore and London: Johns Hopkins University Press, 1991).

Hunt, Lynn, *The Family Romance of the French Revolution* (London: Routledge, 1992).

Jacob, Margaret C., *The Radical Enlightenment* (London: George Allen and Unwin, 1981).

Jacobus, Mary, 'Incorruptible Milk: Breast-Feeding and the French Revolution', in Melzer, Sara E. and Rabine, Leslie W., eds, *Rebel Daughters: Women and the French Revolution* (Oxford: Oxford University Press, 1992).

Jimack, P. D. 'The Paradox of Sophie and Julie: Contemporary Response to Rousseau's Ideal Wife and Ideal Mother', in Jacobs, E., ed., *Women and Society in Eighteenth-Century France* (London: Athlone Press, 1979).

Jodin, Jean, *Les Echappemens à repos comparés aux echappemens à recul, avec un mémoire,* (Paris: Ch. A. Jombert, 1754).

Jodin, Marie Magdeleine, *Mémoire sur Déliberé pour Demoiselle Marie-Magdeleine Jodin, Actrice de Comédie Contre le Sieur Neuville, Directeur de Comédie* (Angers: J. Jahyer, 1774).

————, *Vues législatives pour les femmes: adressées à l'Assemblée Nationale* (Angers: Chez Mame, 1790).

Jones, Vivien, 'Scandalous Femininity: Prostitution and Eighteenth-Century Narrative', in Castiglione, D. and Sharpe, L., eds, *Shifting the Boundaries* (Exeter: University of Exeter Press, 1995).

Kelly, Gary, *Monsieur d'Eon is a Woman* (New York: Basic Books, 1995).

Kelly, Linda, *Women of the French Revolution* (London: Hamish Hamilton, 1987).

Kennedy, Emmet, Netter, Marie-Laurence, McGregor, James P. and Olsen, Mark V., *Theatre, Opera, and Audiences in Revolutionary Paris* (Westport, Connecticut and London: Greenwood Press, 1996).

Kirk, Linda, 'Genevan Republicanism', in Wootton, David, ed., *Republicanism, Liberty, and Commercial Society, 1649–1776* (Stanford: Stanford University Press, 1994).

Klimowicz, M., *Poczatki Theatru Stanislawaskiego (1765–1773)* (Warsaw: Panstwowy Institut, 1966).

Kotto, Jana, *Theatr Narodowy, 1765–1794* (Warsaw: Pan, 1967–68).

Lagrave, Henri, Mazouer, Charles, Regaldo, Marc, *La Vie théâtrale à Bordeaux, des origines à nos jours*, I (Paris: CNRS, 1985).

Laugier, Esprit Michel, *Tyrannie que les hommes ont exercée dans presque tous les temps et les pays contre les femmes ou inconséquence de leur conduite envers cette belle moité de l'espèce humaine* (Paris: cul-de-sac Saint-Dominique, 1788).

La Vopa, Anthony J., 'Conceiving a Public: Ideas and Society in Eighteenth-Century Europe', *Journal of Modern History*, 64:1 (March, 1992).

Lecercle, Jean-Louis, 'La Femme Selon Jean-Jacques', in Starobinski, Jean et al., eds., *Jean-Jacques Rousseau* (Neuchatel: Languages Editions, Baconnière, 1978), pp. 41–67.

Lecomte, L.-Henry, *La Montansier: Ses aventures – ses entreprises 1730–1820* (Paris: Félix Juven, n.d.).

Lewanski, Julian, 'Teatr, Dramat I Muzyka Za Stanislawa Augusta w swietle nowych zrodel' *Pamietnik Teatralny*, IX: Zeszyt I (33) (Warszawa: Instytut Sztuki PAN, 1960).

Levy, Darlene Gay, Applewhite, Harriet Branson, Johnson, Mary Durham, *Women in Revolutionary Paris* (Urbana Illinois: University of Illinois, 1979).

Lloyd, Genevieve, *The Man of Reason* (London: Methuen, 1984).

Lynch, Bernadette, *Le Comte J.-B. Lynch, Maire de Bordeaux 1809–1815* (Bordeaux: Héritiers E.-F. Mialhe, n.d.).

Lyonnet, Henry, *Dictionnaire des Comédiens Français* (Paris, E. Jouel, n.d.).

Malueg, Sara Ellen Procious, 'Women and the *Encyclopédie*', in Spencer, Samia I., ed., *French Women and the Age of Enlightenment* (Bloomington, Indiana: Indiana University Press, 1979).

Marmontel, Jean François, 'Du Divorce', *Mercure de France* (6 February 1790), pp. 18–36.

Marquard, E., *Danske Gesandter og Genandt-Statspersonale* (Copenhagen: Rigsarkivet, 1952).

Martin, Marietta, *Une Française à Varsovie en 1766: Madame Geoffrin chez le roi de Pologne Stanislas-Auguste* (Paris: Bibliothèque Polonaise, 1936).

Martin, H. J. and Chartier, R., eds, *L'Histoire de l'édition française*, II (Paris: Promodis, 1984).

Maugras, Gaston, *Les Comédiens hors la loi* (Paris: Calmann Lévy, 1887).

May, Gita, 'Rousseau's "Anti-feminism" Reconsidered', in Spencer, Samia I., ed., *French Women and the Age of Enlightenment* (Bloomington, Indiana: Indiana University Press, 1979).

Maza, Sarah, *Private Lives and Public Affairs: The Causes Célèbres of pre-Revolutionary France* (Berkeley: University of California Press, 1993).

McManners, John, *Abbés and Actresses: the Church and the Theatrical Profession in Eighteenth-Century France* (Oxford: Oxford University Press, 1986).

Meehan, Johanna, *Feminists Read Habermas: Gendering the Subject of Discourse* (London: Routledge, 1995).

Mellor, Anne K., 'English Women Writers and the French Revolution' in Melzer, Sara E. and Rabine, Leslie W., eds, *Rebel Daughters: Women and the French Revolution* (Oxford: Oxford University Press, 1992), pp. 255–72.

Mellottée, Paul, *Histoire économique de l'imprimérie: l'imprimérie sous l'ancien régime, 1439–1789* (Paris: Librairie Hachette, 1905).

Melton, Edgar, 'The Prussian Junkers, 1600–1786', in H. M. Scott, ed., *The European Nobilities in the Seventeenth and Eighteenth Centuries*, II (London: Longman, 1995).

'Mémoires de Mme de Vandeul' in Denis Diderot, *Oeuvres Complètes*, I, Roger Lewinter, ed. (Paris: le Club français du livre, 1969).

Mercier, Louis Sébastien, *Le Tableau de Paris*, 2 vols. ((London: 1781).

———, *Les entretiens au Palais Royal de Paris* (Paris: chez Buisson, 1786).

Merrick, Jeffrey W. *The Desacralisation of the French Monarchy in the Eighteenth Century* (London: Louisiana State University Press, 1990).

Michael, Wolfgang, *England under George I: the beginnings of the Hanoverian dynasty* (London: Macmillan, 1939).

Michelet, Jules, *Les Femmes de la révolution*, Françoise Giroud, ed., (Paris: Carrère, 1988).

Mittman, Barbara G. 'Women and the Theater Arts' in Spencer, Samia I., ed., *French Women and the Age of Enlightenment* (Bloomington: Indiana University Press, 1979).

Moffat, Mary Maxwell, *Rousseau et la querelle du théâtre au XVIIIe siècle* (Paris: Broccard, 1930).

Morellet, M., *Éloges de Madame Geoffrin suivis de lettres* (Paris: Nicolle, 1812).

Mours, Samuel and Robert, Daniel, *Le Protestantisme en France du XVIIIème Siècle à nos jours (1685–1970)* (Paris: Librairie Protestante, 1972).

Mouy, Charles du, ed., *Correspondance inédite du roi Stanislas-Auguste Poniatowski et de Madame Geoffrin, 1764–1777* (Paris: Plon, 1875).

Munck, Thomas, 'The Danish Reformers', in Scott, H. M., ed., *Enlightened Absolutism: Reform and Reformers in Later Eighteenth-Century Europe* (Basingstoke: Macmillan, 1990).

————, 'Absolute Monarchy in later Eighteenth-Century Denmark: Centralized Reform, Public Expectations, and the Copenhagen Press', *The Historical Journal*, I: 41 (1998), pp. 201–24.

Niklaus, Robert, 'Diderot and Women', in Jacobs, E., Barber, W. H., Bloch, J. H. and Leakey F. W., eds, *Women and Society in Eighteenth-century France* (London: Athlone Press, 1979).

Norberg, Kathryn, 'Love and Patriotism, Gender and Politics in the Life and Work of Louvet de Couvrai', in Melzer, Sara E. and Rabine, Leslie W., eds, *Rebel Daughters: Women and the French Revolution* (Oxford: Oxford University Press, 1992).

Nors, P., *The Court of Christian VII of Denmark* (London: Hurst and Blackett, 1928).

Offen, Karen, 'Reclaiming the European Enlightenment for feminism: or prologomena to any future history of eighteenth-century Europe', in Akkerman, Tjitske and Stuurman, Siep, eds, *Perspectives on Feminist Political Thought in European History* (London and New York: Routledge, 1998) pp. 85–103.

Olivier, Jean-Jacques, *Les Comédiens français dans les cours d'Allemagne au XVIIIe siècle*, Première série (Genève: Slatkine Reprints, 1971).

Outram, Dorinda, *The Enlightenment* (Cambridge: Cambridge University Press, 1995).

Parent-Duchâtelet, A.-J.-B. *De la Prostitution dans la Ville de Paris* (Paris: J.-B. Ballière, 1836).

Pateman, Carol, *The Sexual Contract* (Cambridge: Polity Press, 1988).

Phillips, Roderick, *Putting Asunder: A History of Divorce in Western Society* (Cambridge: Cambridge University Press, 1988).

Pontet, Josette, 'Morale et ordre public à Bayonne au XVIIIème siècle', *Bulletin de la Société des sciences, lettres et arts de Bayonne*, CXXXIII (1974), pp. 127–44.

Porquerol, Elisabeth, ed., *La Véritable Vie privée du Maréchal de Richelieu contenant ses amours et intrigues* (1791) (Paris: Tournon, 1954).

Poulain de la Barre, François, *De l'égalité des deux sexes: discours physique et moral où l'on voit l'importance de se défaire des préjugez* (Paris: 1673).

Py, Gilbert, *Rousseau et les éducateurs*, (Oxford: Voltaire Foundation, 1997), pp. 338–405.

Queruau Lamérie, 'Notice sur le Théâtre d'Angers', *Bulletin monumental et historique de l'Anjou* (1889), pp. 21–37.

Racz, Elizabeth, 'The Women's Rights Movement in the French Revolution', *Science and Society*, 16 (1951), pp. 151–74.

Ravel, Jeffrey S., 'Actress to Activist: Mlle Clairon in the Public Sphere of the 1760s', *Theater Survey: The Journal of the American Society for Theater Research*, 35: 1 (May 1994), pp.73–88.

————, *The Contested Parterre: Public Theater and French Political Culture 1680–1791* (Ithaca and London: Cornell University Press, 1999).

Rendall, Jane, *The Origins of Modern Feminism: Women in Britain, France and the United States, 1780–1860* (London: Macmillan, 1985).

Restif de la Bretonne, N. E., *Le Pornographe*, (1769), Didier, Beatrice, ed. (Paris: Régine Deforges, 1977).

Riccoboni, François, *L'Art du Théâtre*, (1750) (Genève: Slatkine Reprints, 1971).

Ritter, Eugène, 'Jean Jodin (1713–1761) et son frère, Pierre Jodin. Lettres de Diderot à Mlle Jodin (1765–1769)', *Mémoires et documents de la Société d'histoire et d'archéologie de Genève*, XXII: 2e série, Tome Second (1886).

Roberts, David, ed., *Lord Chesterfield: Letters* (Oxford: Oxford University Press, 1992).

Roche, Daniel, *France in the Enlightenment* (Cambridge, MA: Harvard University Press, 1998).

Roth, Georges, 'Diderot et sa Pupille Mademoiselle Jodin', *Les Lettres Nouvelles* 44 (December 1956), pp. 699–714.

Rougement, Martine de, *La Vie Théâtrale en France au XVIIe siècle* (Paris: Librairie Honoré Champion, 1988).

Rousseau, Jean-Jacques, *Lettre à Mr. D'Alembert sur les spectacles*, M. Fuch, ed. (Genève: Droz, 1948).

————, *The Confessions* (1765), trans. J.M. Cohen (London: Penguin Books, 1953).

————, *The Social Contract* (1762), trans. Maurice Cranston (London: Penguin Books, 1968).

————, *Emile* (1762), trans. Barbara Foxley (London: Dent, 1974).

————, *A Discourse on Inequality* (1755), trans. Maurice Cranston (London: Penguin Books, 1984).

————, 'Sur les femmes', Gagnebon, Bernard and Raymond, Marcel, eds, *Oeuvres Complètes* II (Paris: Pléiade, 1961), pp. 1254–5.

Sainte-Beuve, C.-A., *Portraits Littéraires* (Paris: Didier, 1852).

Sartines, *Journal des Inspecteurs de M. de Sartines*, Première série (1761–1764) (Paris: Denton, 1863).

Schama, Simon, *Citizens: a Chronicle of the French Revolution* (London: Viking, 1989).

Schazmann, Paul-Émile, 'Une correspondante genevoise de Diderot: Marie-Madeleine Jodin', *Journal de Genève* (4 April 1932).

Schiebinger, Londa, *The Mind has no Sex? Women in the Origins of Modern Science* (Cambridge, MA: Harvard University Press, 1989).

Schmidt, Georg, *Das Geschlecht von der Schulenburg* (Betzendorf, 1908).

Schwartz, Joel, *The Sexual Politics of Jean-Jacques Rousseau* (London: University of Chicago Press, 1984).

Scott, H. M. ed., *Enlightened Absolutism: Reform and Reformers in Later Eighteenth-Century Europe* (Basingstoke: Macmillan, 1990).

Scott, Joan Wallach, 'A Woman who has only Paradoxes to Offer: Olympe de Gouges claims rights for women', in Melzer, Sara E. and Rabine, Leslie W., eds, *Rebel Daughters: Women and the French Revolution* (Oxford: Oxford University Press, 1992).

Seillière, Ernest, *Diderot* (Paris, Les Éditions de France, 1944).

Soland, Aimé de, 'Le Théâtre à Angers en 1784 – Collot d'Herbois et Mlle Marie-Magdeleine Jodin', *Bulletin monumental et historique de l'Anjou* (1858), pp. 375–9.

Sonnet, Martine, *L'éducation des filles au siècle des lumières* (Paris, Éditions du Cerf, 1987).

Stern, Selma, *The Court Jew* (Philadelphia: Jewish Publishing Society of America, 1950).

Stuurmann, Siep, 'Seventeenth-Century Feminism and the Invention of Modern Equality', Paper given at the Institute of Historical Research, University of London, 2 December 1998, for the 'Feminism and the Enlightenment: 1650–1850' seminar.

Testud, Pierre, *Rétif de la Bretonne et la création littéraire* (Geneva: Librairie Droz, 1977).

Thévenot, Arsène, *Correspondance inédite du Prince François-Xavier de Saxe, Comte de Lusace* (Paris: Dumoulin, 1874).

Thomas, Antoine Léonard, 'Qu'est-ce qu'une femme ?', in *A. L. Thomas, Diderot, Madame d'Épinay: Qu'est-ce qu'une femme?*, Elisabeth Badinter, ed. (Paris: P.O.L. 1989).

Tissier, André, 'La Comédie-Française au XVIIIe siècle ou les contradictions d'un privilège', *Revue de la Société d'Historie du théâtre*, II: 32 (1980), pp. 127–41.

Tomalin, Claire, *Mrs Jordan's Profession* (Harmondsworth: Penguin Books, 1995).

Tomaselli, Sylvana, 'The Enlightenment Debate on Women', *History Workshop Journal* 20 (1985), pp. 101–24.

Traer, James F., *Marriage and the Family in Eighteenth-Century France* (Ithaca: Cornell University Press, 1980).

Trouille, Mary, 'A Bold New Vision of Woman: Staël and Wollstonecraft Respond to Rousseau', *Studies on Voltaire and the Eighteenth Century*, 292 (1991), pp. 293–336.

Vedel, Peter August Frederik Stoud, ed., *Correspondance Ministérielle du Comte J. H. E. Bernstorff, 1751–1770*, 2 vols (Copenhague: Jorgensen, 1882).

Vernière, Paul, 'Marie Madeleine Jodin, amie de Diderot et témoin des Lumières', *Studies on Voltaire* 58 (1967), pp. 1765–75.

Walpole, Horace, *The Letters of Horace Walpole-Fourth Earl of Orford*, ed. Mrs Paget Toynbee, XVI vols (Oxford: Clarendon Press, 1905).

Weiss, E., 'Europe Centrale et Orientale: les Etats Allemands', in Kopeczi, B., Soboul, A., Balzs, E. H. and Kosary, D., eds, *L'absolutisme éclairé*, (Paris: Editions du CNRS, 1985).

Whatmore, Richard, 'The Political Economy of Jean-Baptiste Say's Republicanism', *History of Political Thought*, XIX: 3 (Autumn, 1998).

Wierzbicka, Karyna, *Zrodla Do Historii Teatru Warszawskiego: od roku 1762– do roku 1833* (Wroclaw: Wydawnictwo Zakladu Narodowego Imienia Ossolinskich, 1951).

Wierzbicka-Michalska, Karyna, *Theatr Warszawski za Sasow* (Warsaw: Instytut Sztuta, Polskiej Akademie Nauk, 1964).

———, *Aktorzy Cudzoziemscy w Warszawie w. XVIII Wieku* (Warsaw: Akademii Nauk, 1975).

Williams, David, 'The Politics of Feminism in the French Enlightenment', in Hughes, Peter and Williams, David, eds, *The Varied Pattern* (Toronto: A. M. Hakbert, 1971).

Wilson, A. M., *Diderot*, 2 vols (New York: Oxford University Press, 1986).

Wisner, David A., *The Cult of the Legislator in France 1750–1830* (Oxford: Voltaire Foundation, 1997).

Wollstonecraft, Mary, *Vindication of the Rights of Woman* (1792) (Harmondsworth: Penguin Books, 1975).

Wraxall, Lascelles, *Life and Times of Her Majesty Caroline Matilda, Queen of Denmark and Norway and Sister of H. M. King George III of England*, 3 vols (London: W.H. Allen, 1864).

Wraxall, N. W., *Memoirs of the Court of Berlin, Dresden, Warsaw and Vienna in the Years 1777, 1778 and 1779*, 2 vols (London: 1798).

Zamoyski, Adam, *The Last King of Poland* (London: Jonathan Cape, 1992).

Zorawaska-Witkowska, Alina, *Muzyka na dworze I w Teatrze Stanislawa Augusta* (Warsaw: Zamek Królewski, 1995).

Index

*For Product Safety Concerns and Information please contact
our EU representative GPSR@taylorandfrancis.com Taylor & Francis
Verlag GmbH, Kaufingerstraße 24, 80331 München, Germany*

T - #0050 - 270225 - C0 - 219/153/13 [15] - CB - 9780754602248 - Gloss Lamination